AMERICAN DEFAULT

AMERICAN DEFAULT

◇◇◇◇◇

The Untold Story of FDR, the Supreme Court,

and the Battle over Gold

◇◇◇◇◇

SEBASTIAN EDWARDS

◇◇◇◇◇

Princeton University Press
Princeton and Oxford

Published by Princeton University Press,
41 William Street, Princeton, New Jersey 08540

In the United Kingdom: Princeton University Press,
6 Oxford Street, Woodstock, Oxfordshire OX20 1TR

press.princeton.edu

Jacket images: 1. Chief Justice Charles Evans Hughes with Supreme Court
Justices at the White House, Oct. 13, 1930 / Everett Collection / Alamy
Stock Photo. 2. Franklin D. Roosevelt bronze medal / U.S. Mint

Library of Congress Control Number 2017959002
ISBN 978-0-691-16188-4

British Library Cataloging-in-Publication Data is available

This book has been composed in Dante MT Pro and Kabel LT Std

Printed on acid-free paper. ∞

Printed in the United States of America

1 3 5 7 9 10 8 6 4 2

This book is for
Magdalena Figueroa Yañez

and for
Aurelia Grace Edwards

CONTENTS

◇◇◇◇◇

INTRODUCTION

⬦⬦⬦⬦⬦

This is the story of a forgotten episode in U.S. history, the story of the great debt default of 1933–1935, of the time when the White House, Congress, and the Supreme Court agreed to wipe out more than 40 percent of public and private debts. This is also the story of the nation's efforts to get out of the Great Depression, bring deflation to an end, and get people back to work. It is the story of how the three major powers of the time— the United States, the United Kingdom, and France—failed to agree on policies that would have sped up the recovery and reduced the suffering of millions of their citizens. It is the tale of how perplexed economists changed their views about the world, and discarded decades-old tenets and dogmas. Finally, it is an account of the early stages of the struggle between President Franklin Delano Roosevelt and Supreme Court Chief Justice Charles Evans Hughes, a confrontation that led to the president's attempt to pack the Supreme Court in February 1937.

There are many ways of telling this story. For instance, we could begin in October 1929, when the stock market crashed and the Great Depression was unleashed. Or we could begin on November 8, 1932, when American voters decided to turn their backs on Herbert Hoover and elected Franklin D. Roosevelt by a landslide. But possibly, the best starting point is April 5, 1933, when President Roosevelt, who had been in office for exactly one month, issued an Executive Order requiring people and businesses to sell, within three weeks, all their gold holdings to the government at the official price of $20.67 per ounce. The Order was published in every newspaper and transmitted over thousands of radio stations. Large signs were placed in post offices around the country. The posters were printed in large block letters and informed the public that everyone had "to deliver on or before May 1, 1933, all gold coin, gold bullion and gold certificates now owned by them to a Federal Reserve Bank, branch or agency."[1]

The notice stated that there were only four exceptions to the president's directive: each person could keep gold coin or certificate not exceeding $100 in value; industry and the arts could maintain enough metal as "may be required for legitimate and customary use"; financial institutions were allowed to hold gold in trust for a foreign central bank; and gold involved in "proper transactions" approved by the Treasury could be held temporarily by financial institutions. Those who didn't comply with the Executive Order faced "criminal penalties . . . [a] $10,000 fine or ten years of imprisonment, or both."

The public was shocked. Throughout the history of the nation, gold had been used as a store of value, and many families owned gold coins as part of their savings. Gold was given as wedding presents and at bar mitzvahs, and newborns often received a gift of one or two coins from their godparents. The fact that all metal had to be turned in to a relatively new institution—the Federal Reserve had been created less than twenty years earlier—made things even worse.

As the May 1 deadline approached, radio announcers reminded families of what they had to do. People could still not believe what was happening. It was true that during the previous months there had been an extraordinarily high demand for the metal and that hoarding had increased sharply, but that was exactly how the system was supposed to work: from time immemorial people resorted to gold when they faced economic uncertainty, including fears of banks' collapses.

In the early hours of March 6, when he had been barely one day in office, President Roosevelt declared a national banking holiday. Its purpose was to stop massive withdrawals of currency and gold, and to put in place an emergency plan to strengthen the nation's financial system. A week later, on March 13, banks began to reopen their doors, and people redeposited their cash and gold in massive amounts. Confidence was on the upswing after President Roosevelt delivered his first Fireside Chat on Sunday March 12. FDR assured the public that those banks that were reopened were solid and in excellent health. As the president had predicted, people were again "glad to have their money where it will be safely taken care of."[2]

So, if things were improving, why was the government forcing the public to part with their gold? Coercing people to sell their hard-earned metal was not an American thing to do. This had never happened before, not even during the Civil War, when the gold standard was suspended and the Treasury issued "greenbacks."

The secretary of the treasury, Will Woodin, a small and affable man and lifelong Republican who loved music and had composed a number of popular tunes, including "Raggedy Ann's Sunny Songs," tried to explain the policy by saying that "gold in private hoards serves no useful purpose under current circumstances. When added to the stock of the Federal Reserve Banks it serves as a basis for currency and credit. This further strengthening of the banking structure adds to its power of service toward recovery."[3]

The weeks that followed changed America forever. On March 5, after President Roosevelt convened Congress into an Extraordinary Session, the legendary "Hundred Days" began. Between March and June, 1933, Congress passed legislation that would fundamentally alter the way the economy functioned, and set the bases for the welfare state. Some of this legislation was later challenged in the courts system, and some was eventually declared unconstitutional by the Supreme Court. There is little doubt, however, that these feverish weeks of continuous debate and lawmaking planted the seeds of a new America, a country where the federal government would take an active role in economic and social affairs, a nation that would create an intricate safety net for the poor, the unemployed, and the disadvantaged.

While the foundations of the American economy were being profoundly changed by one act of Congress after another, the gold saga initiated with the April 5 Executive Order continued to unfold. On April 19, during the thirteenth press conference of his young presidency, President Roosevelt stated unequivocally that the country was now off the gold standard. He explained that the fundamental goal of abandoning the monetary system that had prevailed since Independence was to help the agricultural sector, which had been struggling for over a decade.[4] He declared: "The whole problem before us is to raise commodity prices."[5]

The next step in this drama came on May 12 when Congress passed the Agricultural Adjustment Act (AAA). Title III of this legislation included the "Thomas Amendment," which authorized the president to increase the official price of gold to up to $41.34 an ounce.[6] A devaluation of the dollar, many thought, would rapidly result in "controlled inflation" and would help farmers by raising commodity prices and by lightening their debts when expressed in relation to their incomes. A number of experts noted that Great Britain had devalued the pound in September 1931, and had slowly begun to recover.

Things, however, were not as easy as they seemed. In the United States, most debt contracts—both private and public—included a "gold clause," stating that the debtor committed himself to paying back in "gold coin."

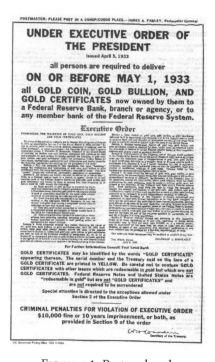

FIGURE I.1. Poster placed
in post offices around the
country explaining Executive
Order No. 6102.
(*Source*: US Government Printing
Office)

These clauses were introduced into contracts during the Civil War, a time
when two currencies circulated side by side—a currency backed by bullion and one unbacked, the so-called greenbacks issued by the Union's
Treasury. Debts that included the gold clause were considered to be more
secure, since the amount to be received in payment at some future date was
anchored to the price of gold and, thus, not affected by possible changes
in the purchasing power of paper money.[7] After the end of the Civil War
there had been no need to invoke them, but with time gold clauses
came to be considered a "normal" component of debt contracts; it became
customary to include them in corporate and utilities bonds, and in many
mortgage contracts. In 1933, however, it became evident that these
clauses were a problem. If the currency was devalued with respect to
gold, the dollar value of debts subject to the clauses would automatically

increase by the amount of the devaluation. This would result in massive bankruptcies and in a huge increase in the public debt. For all practical purposes, then, when FDR was inaugurated as president the "gold clauses" stood in the way of a devaluation of the dollar.

Three months after Roosevelt had become president, on June 5, Congress passed Joint Resolution No. 10, annulling all gold clauses from future and past contracts. This opened the door for a possible devaluation. Republicans were dismayed and argued that the nation's reputation was at risk. The government, on the other hand, claimed that the Joint Resolution didn't imply "a repudiation of contracts." The secretary of the treasury stated that since gold payments had been suspended in April, all Congress had done was clarify that "the holder of an obligation cannot specify in what type of currency [gold or paper money] the contract is payable." He was quick to state that the annulment of the gold clause "from all contracts and obligations, public and private, should have no depreciating effect on their value."[8]

On January 31, 1934, the other shoe dropped when President Roosevelt officially devalued the dollar by fixing the new price of gold at $35 an ounce, an increase of 69 percent relative to its century-old price of $20.67 an ounce. Conservatives deplored the decision, and argued that it would inevitably lead to a steep decline in America's power. Others, including the farm lobby, were disappointed by what they considered an insufficient adjustment in the value of the dollar. In explaining the decision, FDR said that the devaluation was necessary, since the nation had been "adversely affected by virtue of the depreciation in the value of currencies to other Governments in relation to the present standard of value."[9] Many considered this to be a direct reference to the devaluation of Sterling.

Not surprisingly, those who had purchased securities protected by the gold clause claimed that the Joint Resolution of June 1933 was unconstitutional. Various lawsuits were filed and made their way through the courts system. Four of them got to the Supreme Court, and were heard between January 8 and January 10, 1935. Two had to do with private debts, and two with public obligations. The most salient case involved a government bond in the series of the Fourth Liberty Loan issued on October 15, 1918. The obligation for this *"4¼% Gold Bond"* expressly stipulated that "the principal and interest hereof are payable in United States gold coin of the present standard of value" (*Perry v. United States*). The question before the Court was whether Congress had the constitutional power to alter contracts retroactively. Could Congress annul private and public debt promises and, in the process, affect the wealth of debtors and creditors? And if, in the opinion of the Court, Congress had exceeded its power, what were the damages?

On February 18, 1935, the Supreme Court announced its decision. In all cases the Court voted 5 to 4 in favor of the government position. The majority's opinions were written by Chief Justice Charles Evans Hughes, a distinguished jurist who had been governor of New York, secretary of state, and presidential candidate for the Republican Party in 1916.

There was a single dissent signed by the four conservative members of the Court, known as the "Four Horsemen." When the time came to deliver the minority opinion, Justice James Clark McReynolds, a southern lawyer who favored bow ties and had served as attorney general during Woodrow Wilson's first administration, decided to depart from protocol: instead of reading the prepared text he gave a short speech. He opened his remarks in a low tone. Slowly, he raised his voice and his southern tones quivered with anger.[10] A minute into the speech he paused; it was a classical pregnant silence. He then said: "The Constitution as many of us understood it, the instrument that has meant so much to us, is gone." He then talked about the sanctity of contracts, government obligations, and repudiation under the guise of law. It was clear, he stated, that Congress had the power "to adopt a monetary system. But because Congress may adopt a system, it doesn't follow that this may be enforced in violation of existing contracts." He ended his speech with strong words: "Shame and humiliation are upon us now. Moral and financial chaos may be confidently expected."[11]

COLLECTIVE AMNESIA

I became interested in the abrogation of the gold clauses some fifteen years ago when I received a phone call from a partner of a well-known New York law firm. He wanted to discuss Argentina's devaluation and debt default of 2002. He had read some of my work on balance of payments crises, and he thought that I could help him with a case he was working on. During the years that followed, I wrote a number of expert reports on the Argentine crisis, and I collaborated with teams from several law firms in their efforts to get compensation for clients impacted by the Argentine devaluation and debt restructuring. The vast majority of these lawsuits involved the breaching of long-term contracts; Argentina unilaterally annulled contracts in dollars and rewrote them, retroactively, in pesos. We prevailed in every one of these cases; arbitration tribunals ruled, repeatedly, that Argentina had some responsibility in the unleashing of the crisis and, thus, had to compensate claimants—mostly large international companies—for damages.

In 1991, and as a way of ending a bout of hyperinflation, the Argentine government adopted a fixed exchange rate regime that pegged the value of the peso to the dollar at parity: one peso was equal to one dollar. In addition, it prohibited the central bank from issuing pesos without foreign exchange backing. This system was supposed to work in a way similar to the traditional gold standard, and its main purpose was to eliminate currency uncertainty and risk. As a way to add credibility to the new regime, a law forbade contracts from including clauses that indexed prices, wages, and other payments to past domestic inflation. Instead, most long-term contracts—and in particular contracts involving massive investments in infrastructure—were denominated in U.S. dollars. These measures were part of an ambitious program to stabilize the Argentine economy, attract foreign investors, and reignite growth after more than a decade of stagnation, high inflation, and instability. However, the plan—known as the "Convertibility Plan"—ran into serious problems, and barely lasted a decade. In late 2001, Argentina defaulted on its debt—it ended up paying twenty-three cents on the dollar—and in early 2002 the fixed exchange rate regime ended.

In a matter of weeks, the exchange rate jumped from one peso per dollar to over three pesos per dollar. After the devaluation, the government decided to alter contracts retroactively, and to "pesify" them: instead of dollars, contracts were unilaterally rewritten in pesos at the original one-to-one parity. This resulted in huge losses to investors and savers. International public utilities, construction companies, and financial institutions that had made large long-term investments in Argentina were seriously affected.

From early on, a particular aspect of Argentina's legal argument attracted my attention. According to Argentine lawyers, the annulment of contracts that followed the devaluation of the peso in 2002 had a historical precedent in the United States in the 1930s. Argentina's legal team noted that in June 1933, and in preparation for the devaluation of the dollar that eventually took place in January 1934, the Roosevelt administration unilaterally and retroactively changed the currency of denomination of public and private debt contracts. The Argentine lawyers noted that in 1935 the U.S. Supreme Court had sided with the government.[12]

Argentina's legal point was simple: if the United States' abrogation of the "gold clauses" in 1933 was legal, so was Argentina's own rescinding of the "dollar clauses" in 2002.

I was vaguely aware of Congress's 1933 Joint Resolution that changed the currency of denomination of contracts, but I did not know the details surrounding the episode, nor did I know the reasons given by the Supreme Court when it supported the government's position. I decided to ask some colleagues whose field was macroeconomics about what had actually happened. To my surprise, almost no one knew details; in fact, some prominent scholars were not even aware that this had occurred. I then turned to Milton Friedman and Anna Schwartz's encyclopedic *A Monetary History of the United States, 1867–1960* and discovered that in spite of their detailed analysis of the Great Depression they mentioned the nullification of gold contracts only in passing. Consultation of Allan Meltzer's magnificent *A History of the Federal Reserve* yielded a similar result. This 800-page oeuvre covered the episode only briefly.

I found this situation fascinating: only seventy years before Argentina devalued its currency and rewrote contracts retroactively—an action denounced by U.S. politicians and editorialists as openly populist and illegal—the United States had gone through a similar process. Yet, almost no one remembered this important chapter in U.S. financial history. It seemed to me that the nation had gone through a process of collective amnesia, and had decided to forget an episode that did not live up to the vision that Americans have of their country: in the United States we respect the law, contracts are sacred, and we have never defaulted or restructured the federal debt.[13]

As I dug more deeply, I discovered two things: The Supreme Court ruling was extremely controversial during its time. In 1935, some analysts even asserted that it meant the end of the rule of law. In many ways, the ruling presaged the clash between the Court and President Roosevelt that was to take place during the next two years, and that led FDR to attempt stacking the Court in February 1937. I also discovered that although there was no in-depth study of the episode, a small number of economic

historians were well aware of it, and had strong views about its signifi-
cance and consequences. Many of them—the vast majority, I would
say—thought that annulling gold-denominated contracts retroactively
had contributed to the end of the Great Depression. According to these
experts, this action had facilitated the abandonment of the gold standard
and the devaluation of the dollar, and in this way had helped generate
large inflows of gold between 1934 and early 1937. According to the dominant view on the Great Depression—a view supported by scholars such
as Milton Friedman, Ben Bernanke, and Christina Romer, among others—
this inflow of gold allowed the Fed to increase the supply of money and
credit, and thus contributed to the increase in output and the decline in
unemployment after 1933. It appeared to me that most of these scholars
would have sided with Argentina during the legal proceedings that followed the 2002 default and devaluation.

In the years that followed, and as I worked my way through the litera-
ture and several archives, I became convinced that the abrogation could
not be addressed in isolation. It was necessary to tell the complete and
complex story on how the United States decided to abandon the gold
standard and devalue the dollar. With the passage of time, the popular version of the episode has been simplified and sanitized, and many people—
including many academic economists—believe that the decision was
clean and straightforward.

Nothing was further from the truth.

The path to devaluation was tortuous and long—full of impediments,
intellectual battles, uncertainties, and unknowns. In 1933, economists did
not quite understand what going was on, and many of their theories were
unable to explain some of the basic developments of the period. The politics of the devaluation were extremely complex, and the personalities
of some of the main players made the episode perilous and at times
explosive.

In trying to reconstruct the intricate paths that led to the abrogation of
the gold clauses, I found myself, again and again, delving into the historical details of that era; some of these details are related to politics and international relations, and others to economic reform, including changes in
monetary policy. Hopefully, the reader will find out that what may appear
to be only side discussions are actually necessary to provide adequate
background on what really happened during that intense year of 1933.

Here are some of the many questions that sprung into my mind as I plowed into the archives and analyzed the historical data:

- Was the abrogation a partial default on the government debt, or could it be described in any other way?
- Did it create a serious confidence crisis, as Supreme Court Justice James Clark McReynolds wrote in his minority opinion?
- How did investors, both domestic and international, react to this event?
- Was this a necessary step prior to abandoning the gold standard?
- What were the roles of academic economists, politicians, and the president himself during this episode?
- Was it true that, as argued by Friedman and Schwartz, "the nationalization of gold, [and] the abrogation of the gold clauses . . . had the opposite effects [from the devaluation of the dollar] by discouraging business investment"?[14] Could it happen again in the United States or in other nations?

ACKNOWLEDGMENTS

During this book's long gestation, I had the good fortune to discuss the gold standard and the issues surrounding the abrogation of the gold clauses with a number of extraordinary individuals. Slowly, they educated me and opened my eyes to the fascinating world of the Great Depression. During 2004 and 2005, I had several conversations with Milton Friedman on monetary policy during the 1930s, one of the subjects that made him famous and that was cited by the committee that awarded him the *Prize in Economic Science in Memory of Alfred Nobel*. At the time, we were both members of California governor Arnold Schwarzenegger's Council of Economic Advisers. The Council met regularly in Sacramento, and during coffee breaks I would ask Milton questions, listen to his answers, and take detailed notes. We talked about the Fed, silver, the velocity of money, and open market operations. He told me some anecdotes about the discussions that surrounded the gold-clause debates in the 1930s, and directed me to what to read. Throughout those conversations Milton stood by what he had written forty years earlier: in his view the retroactive nullification of private and public contracts had introduced uncertainty, and had been detrimental for the nation. I also had the fortune of talking about these issues with Anna Schwartz. We would meet at the National Bureau of Economic Research Summer Institute, and Anna would illuminate me by telling me what she thought about the subject. She was generous enough as to send me copies of some of her own notes on the abrogation, including a memorandum she had prepared for a law firm in the 1980s. Allan Meltzer helped me clarify my thinking on the role of the Federal Reserve during long conversations in different places. The instance I remember most vividly was a long hike in Jackson Hole. Otmar Issing was with us, and he provided many deep thoughts from a German and European perspective. When we came back to the lodge, I rushed to put down in my notebook everything I had heard.

The economic history fraternity has been generous, and has been willing to accept an outsider into their ranks. In particular, I have benefitted from long discussions with Michael Bordo. As always, my conversations with Ed Leamer—often while driving to UCLA football games at the Rose Bowl—have been illuminating; he asked difficult questions, ventured explanations to some of the puzzles that kept me awake, and raised important methodological issues. Doug Irwin read an almost complete draft of the manuscript, and made extremely useful suggestions. Daniel Artana made helpful comments to an earlier draft. Conversations with George Tavlas helped me clarify the role of the Chicago School during the policy debates of 1933–1935. The late Craufurd Goodwin forced me to think deeply about the role played by the members of the advisory group known as the "Brains Trust" during the events discussed in this book. Throughout the years I befitted from conversations and exchanges with a number of colleagues. Although many of them may not have been aware of it at the time, they provided invaluable insights into my understanding of the topic of this book. In particular, I enjoyed talking to Randy Kroszner, Tom Davis, Jerry Jordan, Adam Posen, José de Gregorio, Barry Eichengreen, Charles Calomiris, Andy Atkeson, Guillermo Calvo, Gene White, Alan Taylor, Al Harberger, Harald Beyer, Angel Soto, Pablo Guidotti, Dora Costa, Alejandra Cox, David Romer, Jerry Nickelsburg, Liaquat Ahmed, Eric Rauchway, Carmen Reinhart, Scott Sumner, and Chris Meissner. I thank my co-authors Francis Longstaff and Alvaro García Marín. I thank Jill Harris and Jay Boggis for their help during the editing process. The book is much better because of them. I am grateful to the Center for Global Management, at UCLA's Anderson Graduate School of Management, for financial support. I thank Michael Poyker, Alvaro Garcia, and María Carolina Arteaga for their efficient and thorough research assistance throughout the years. I am also grateful to seminar participants at Duke, Berkeley, UC Davis, the Economic Society of Chile, and the BIS-HKMA conference for helpful discussions. I am particularly indebted to two magnificent editors at Princeton University Press: Seth Ditchik (now at Yale University Press), who many years ago convinced me that this was a worthwhile topic of research, and to Joe Jackson, who saw the project through to completion. Without their encouragement the final product would have been much poorer. Finally, I thank my daughter Victoria with whom I discussed many of the legal issues surrounding the abrogation of the gold clauses, the abandonment of the gold standard, and the devaluation of the dollar.

TIMELINE

The Road to the Official Devaluation of the Dollar and to the Supreme Court Decisions on the Gold-Clause Cases

1933

March 4	FDR Inauguration.
March 5	The president calls Congress into an Extraordinary Session. Proclamation No. 2038.
March 6	Bank holiday is declared through Presidential Proclamation No. 2039.
March 8	Federal Reserve announces that will publish a list of "gold hoarders" that have not redeposited their gold in a bank by March 13.
March 9	Emergency Banking Act enacted by Congress and signed into Law by FDR. It calls for a temporary gold embargo.
March 10	Executive Order No. 6073, "Relative to the Reopening of Banks." Maintained restrictions on gold exports.
March 12	First Fireside Chat. The president explains process to be followed in the reopening of banks.
March 13	Most banks reopen.
March 16	FDR sends message to Congress urging it to pass the Agricultural Adjustment Act (AAA). Message is officially titled "New Means to Rescue Agriculture."
March 20	Government Economy Act is passed. Its goal is to balance the budget. This had been a campaign promise.

March 22	Beer-Wine Revenue Act.
March 27	Executive Order No. 6084 consolidating Federal Farm Credit Agencies. Henry Morgenthau Jr. appointed governor of the Federal Credit Administration.
March 31	Civilian Conservation Corps is created through Executive Order No. 6101.
April 5	Executive Order No. 6102: All gold holdings have to be sold to Federal Reserve.
April 6	FDR extends an invitation to British prime minister to visit Washington, DC, to discuss the world economic situation and the upcoming World Economic Conference in London.
April 12	U.S. dollar declines below gold points in international markets. This means that it is profitable to ship gold out of the United States.
April 13	First license for exporting gold granted.
April 15	Three additional gold export licenses are approved by the Treasury.
April 17	Thomas Amendment is introduced to Senate. Gives the president authority to undertake three specific policies to end deflation: reduce the gold content of the dollar by up to 50 percent; issue up to $3 billion in greenbacks; remonetize silver at a ratio of 16 to 1 with respect to gold.
April 18	USD drops in global currency markets. (April 13 through 17 markets closed due to Easter holidays). FDR decides to support Thomas Amendment.
April 19	President Roosevelt gives thirteenth press conference of his administration. Towards the end he announces that the United States is definitely off gold. Metal exports are forbidden.
April 20	Executive Order No. 6111: All exports of gold are suspended indefinitely. The United States is effectively off the gold standard.
April 23	Secretary Woodin announced that half a billion notes in 2.875 percent Treasury notes would be issued. Many analysts noted that it was ironic that this issue still carried the gold clause, even though it was illegal to hold, sell, buy, or export bullion.

April 24 / June 3   Representatives from nations from around the world converge to Washington, DC, to discuss the upcoming London World Economic Conference.

April 27   In view of imminent vote on the Thomas Amendment, the German government announces that it will not make payments on its dollar-denominated debts on gold bases.

April 28   Thomas Amendment passed by Senate 55–35. Several Democrats, including Senator Glass vote against it.

May 1   Coupons for a number of private U.S. bonds with gold clause are due. They are paid in currency, triggering legal procedures. Coupon payments of Panama Canal government bonds are also made in currency, not in gold.

May 7   Second Fireside Chat. The president argued that the gold standard was abandoned because there was not enough gold in the world to honor all contracts written in "gold coin."

May 12   Agricultural Adjustment Act (AAA) is signed into law. It includes the Thomas Amendment. Newspapers refer to it as "relief-inflation legislation." Federal Farm Emergency Relief Act is passed.

May 18   Tennessee Valley Authority Act.

May 22   First legal plea involving the gold clause is presented in court. The Irving Trust Company, which was the trustee for a group of mortgage holders, asked the New York State Supreme Court whether it should consent to payment in paper dollars, and "not insist on gold."

May 24   New York State Supreme Court Justice Phoenix Ingraham rules that payments on gold clause debts may be made (and received) in paper dollars.

May 26   The government announced that there is a need to have a uniform legal standing with respect to the gold clause. The administration asks Congress to officially void, through a Joint Resolution, the gold clause both for past and future contracts.

May 27   Securities Act is signed. It establishes that the government will cease to issue debt denominated in "gold coin."

May 28   British economists point out that since all gold clauses on all securities and debts would be repealed, the UK would

	save millions of pounds in war debt payments to the United States.
May 29	The House approves resolution abrogating gold clauses.
May 31	The French government announced that it was paying its 7½ and 7 percent bonds issued in the United States in 1921 and 1924 according to the gold value of the dollar.
June 1	Treasury omits gold clause on new bills to be auctioned on June 7. This is done as Congress discusses the abrogation of the gold clauses.
June 3	Gold clause repeal passed by the Senate by the overwhelming margin of 48 to 20.
June 5	Joint Declaration of Congress abrogating gold clauses is passed and signed into law.
June 11	The Swiss government announces that in spite of the abrogation of the gold clause in the United States, it will pay in gold its sovereign dollar-denominated debt.
June 12	Monetary and Economic Conference opens in London.
June 13	Home Owners Loan Act.
June 16	Glass-Steagall Banking Act.
June 16	National Industrial Recovery Act.
June 16	Emergency Railroad Transportation Act.
June 16	Farm Credit Act.
June 16	Congress's Special Session adjourns. The "Hundred Days" come to an end.
July 3	FDR's "bombshell." In brief communiqué announces that the United States will not participate in the global effort to stabilize exchange rates.
July 8	Harold L. Ickes is appointed Administrator of Public Works, and becomes one of the most powerful men in the Administration.
July 9	First NRA. First code is approved for the cotton textile industry.
July 21	The House of Commons approved overwhelmingly (131 to 22) a provision that cancelled payment in gold on the World War I debts.
July 27	The London Monetary and Economic Conference comes to an end without achieving any of the objectives discussed by world leaders during their early discussions.

August 25   New York Group (advisory group to the president on monetary policy) issues first report criticizing the idea that a higher price of gold will result in higher commodity prices.

August 28   Executive Order No. 6260 replaces Orders Nos. 6102 and 6111. It outlaws the holding and exportation of gold, and lists four exceptions.

August 29   Executive Order No. 6261 authorizes the Reconstruction Finance Corporation to buy newly minted gold at "the best price obtainable in the free market of the world."

October 11   The Treasury retires 30 percent of the Fourth Liberty Loan (originally issued with the now defunct gold clause) and replaces them with twelve-year bonds with a 1 percent coupon. The new offer was greatly oversubscribed.

October 11   The "Advisory and Protective Committee for American Investments" is formed in London. Its purpose is to take part in negotiations and legal actions that will protect British investors from the "default in gold payment and gold-clause situation."

October 22   Fourth Fireside Chat. The president explains a new policy on gold purchases. Prices will be set by the secretary of the treasury and the president, and may deviate from world prices. In addition to buying newly minted gold in the United States, the RFC will buy and sell gold in the world markets, if needed.

November 17   National Emergency Council to coordinate different agencies involved in the recovery is created through Executive Order No. 6433A.

November 28   Japan and Brazil cancel gold clause on their corporate and sovereign debts. The justification is that the United States has annulled its own gold clause.

November 28   The Italian government announces that it will make payments on its 1925 Morgan loan in depreciated paper dollars, in spite of the fact that the contract contained a gold clause.

December 4   Executive Order No. 6474 creates the Federal Alcohol Control Administration.

December 5   Prohibition comes to an end. The president proclaims the repeal of the Eighteenth Amendment. Presidential Proclamation No. 2065.

December 18   The House of Lords rules that a Belgian Utility (*Société Intercommunale Belge d'Electricité*) has to make debt payments on its 1928 bonds in gold sterling bases to debt holders in the UK Although the decision has no effect on dollar-denominated debts, it may serve as a precedent in the gold-clause cases in the United States.

December 21   Proclamation No. 2067 authorizes the U.S. mint to buy silver at above market prices and to mint silver dollars.

December 28   All gold in excess of $100 in hands of private parties now has to be sold to the Treasury, which will pay the official price of $20.67 per ounce. This resolution replaced the requirement to sell gold to a Federal Reserve Bank.

December 30   Proclamation N0. 2070 restores nonmember banks to the jurisdiction of their own state banking regulating authority.

December 31   John Maynard Keynes publishes an "open letter" to the president in the *New York Times* where he criticizes the Administration policy mix, including the "gold-buying" program.

1934

January 15   FDR announces plan for stabilizing value of the dollar, and asks for authority to change value of USD within parameters of Thomas Amendment.

January 30   The Gold Act of 1933 is signed into law.

January 31   The president sets the new official price of gold at $35 an ounce. The Treasury announces that it is willing to buy and sell any amount of metal at that price, internationally. U.S. residents are not allowed to hold gold.

June 5   Britain defaults on its World War I debt to the United States. At the end, of the seventeen countries that borrowed from the United States during the Great War, only Finland repaid its debts in full.

June 20   A federal court in St. Louis rules that the Joint Resolution abrogating the gold clause is constitutional. This is the *Bankers Trust* case.

July 3   A district court in New York rules in the *Baltimore and Ohio* case that the abrogation is constitutional. The lawyer for the plaintiff declares that he is willing to take the case all the way to the Supreme Court.

November 15   The administration announced that it was asking the Supreme Court to consolidate a number of cases related to the abrogation of the gold clause and to hear them together.

November 18   The solicitor general asked the Supreme Court to hear four gold-clause cases on January 8; two on private debts and two on public debts.

1935

January 8–10   Four gold-clause cases are argued in front of the Supreme Court. Attorney General Homer Cummings personally argues one of the cases. The press reports that the government legal team did rather poorly. Administration lawyers had trouble answering many of the Justices' questions.

January 13   The *New York Times* pointed out that due to "the speculative fever for 'gold'" the price of Liberty Bonds had reached their highest since their issuance in 1917.

January 14 / February 17   The government's lukewarm performance at the Court makes the markets very nervous. The Securities and Exchange Commission said that it would ask the president for authority to close the nation's exchanges at the time of the ruling, if needed.

February 18   The Supreme Court rules on the gold-clause cases. It confirms the constitutionality of the Joint Resolution for private contracts by a 5 to 4 vote. It rules by a vote of 8 to 1 that the abrogation of the gold clause in public contracts is unconstitutional. However, it also rules, by a 5 to 4 vote, that there are no damages involved. Thus, plaintiffs have no right to be compensated.

DRAMATIS PERSONAE

◇◇◇◇◇

The story told in this book is centered on 1933, possibly the most eventful year in American history during times of peace. But in spite of covering a short period of time, it involves numerous, complex characters. Men— yes, the overwhelming majority of them were white males—who shaped the American economy for decades to come. Here are some of the most important and recurrent personages of this saga.

THE PRESIDENT AND HIS ADVISERS

Franklin Delano Roosevelt The thirty-second president of the United States, elected by a landslide in November 1932. He had been governor of New York, and assistant secretary of the navy. During the presidential campaign he promised to help the "forgotten man," to raise commodity prices, and bring deflation to an end.

Raymond Moley A professor at Columbia University. During 1932 he was the head of the advisory group known as the Brains Trust. During most of 1933 he was the closest adviser to FDR. He saw the president almost daily, when he was having breakfast in bed. After the inauguration, he was appointed assistant secretary of state.

Rexford G. Tugwell Professor of economics at Columbia, and member of the Brains Trust. During the campaign he stressed the importance of economic planning, and developed the "concert of interests" idea. In March 1933, he was named assistant secretary of agriculture.

Adolf Berle Professor of law at Columbia, and the third member of the Brains Trust. Believed that large conglomerates and trusts had to be controlled and regulated. He did not join the Administration in 1933.

Will Woodin   Industrialist and life-long Republican. He was FDR's first secretary of the treasury. A composer and avid collector of rare coins, he was extremely loyal to the president. He resigned his post in late 1933 when he became seriously ill.

Henry Morgenthau Jr.   A neighbor of FDR in Dutchess County, New York. In early 1933 he was appointed governor of the Farm Credit Administration. In November 1933, he became undersecretary of the treasury, and in January 1934 he replaced Will Woodin as secretary of the treasury.

Homer Cummings   A lawyer who had chaired the Democratic National Committee. Appointed attorney general in March 1933. As such he had to opine on the constitutionality of many of the New Deal initiatives. He argued the gold-clause cases in front of the Supreme Court in January 1935.

Cordell Hull   Former senator from Tennessee. He was appointed secretary of state in 1933. A convinced free trader, he led the American delegation to the London Monetary and Economic Conference of 1933. He intensely disliked Raymond Moley.

James P. Warburg   Wall Street banker and son of the legendary Paul Warburg. An adviser to FDR on international finance issues during the first few months of 1933. He opposed the devaluation of the dollar.

Dean Acheson   A graduate of Harvard Law, appointed undersecretary of the treasury in 1933. Asked to resign in November of that year, after he resisted, for legal reasons, implementing the Administration's "gold-buying program." He became secretary of state during the Truman Administration.

Lewis Douglass   Former congressman from Arizona, and FDR's first director of the budget. He held extremely orthodox views on economics, and opposed the abandonment of the gold standard and the devaluation of the dollar.

THE SENATORS

Elmer Thomas   Senator from Oklahoma. A progressive democrat and a keen defender of farmers. He believed that devaluing the dollar would rapidly result in higher agricultural prices. The author of the Thomas Amendment of May 1933, that gave FDR the power to devalue the dollar.

Burton Wheeler   Senator from Montana. He was a "radical democrat" and an isolationist. He championed silver, and introduced an amendment to remonetize the white metal. One of the leaders of the "devaluationist bloc" in the Senate.

Carter Glass   Senator from Virginia. Expert on banking issues and one of the founders of the Federal Reserve System. He was asked to join the administration as secretary of the treasury in February 1933. He declined after President-Elect Roosevelt refused to assure him that the dollar would not be devalued.

THE ECONOMISTS

Irving Fisher   Professor of economics at Yale, and one of the nation's better known public intellectuals. He was a strong critic of the gold standard, and advocated the adoption of a "compensated dollar," or dollar linked to a basket of commodities. His reputation was tarnished after he assured, in 1929, that the stock market would continue to climb.

George F. Warren   Professor of agricultural economics at Cornell, and fierce critic of the gold standard. According to him, a devaluation of the dollar would immediately result in higher agricultural prices. In his view, there was a strict one-to-one relation between the price of gold and the price of commodities. He was the intellectual father of the controversial "gold-buying" program of late 1933.

J. Harvey Rogers   Professor of economics at Yale. He was a critic of the gold standard, and advocated an economic program based on a devaluation of the dollar and a significant increase in "public works."

Oliver O. A. Sprague Former professor of economics at Harvard, where FDR was one of his students. A strong defender of the gold standard, and presidential adviser during the first few months of the Roosevelt administration.

John Maynard Keynes A don at Cambridge University in the United Kingdom, and the world's most famous economist in 1933. A critic of the gold standard, and a prolific commentator of the economic situation in the United States.

Hebert Feis An economic adviser to the Secretary of State Cordell Hull, and the only professional economists who participated in the complete process that led to the abandonment of the gold standard, the abrogation of the gold clauses, and the official devaluation of the dollar.

THE NEWSPAPERMEN

Walter Lippmann Influential columnist for the *New York Herald*. He often wrote on economic and international issues. Close to Raymond Moley and John Maynard Keynes.

Ernest Lindley Commentator and columnist. Author of a 1932 biography of FDR, and of an early account of the administration's first year.

THE SUPREME COURT JUSTICES

Charles Evans Hughes chief justice, former governor of New York and former secretary of state. A highly respected moderate Republican, who frequently provided the deciding vote in a deeply divided Supreme Court.

James Clark McReynolds A conservative lawyer from Kentucky. A "gold democrat," he had served as attorney general during the early years of the first Woodrow Wilson administration. He was the leader of the conservative bloc at the Court. The group was known as "the Four Horsemen."

Louis Brandeis   Liberal lawyer, very close to FDR. He strongly believed that large conglomerates and trusts were a threat to democracy. He was extremely influential among the liberal Justices.

Harlan Fiske Stone   A liberal lawyer, and former dean at Columbia's School of Law. He tended to side with Justice Brandeis, but wrote his own concurring opinions. In 1941, he became chief justice.

Benjamin Cardozo   Highly respected liberal jurist. Before joining the Supreme Court, he served for almost two decades as an appellate judge in New York. Considered to be one of the most elegant legal writers of his generation.

Owen Roberts   A moderate lawyer. He often provided a swing vote in the court.

Pierce Butler   A conservative Democrat and former railroad lawyer. A member of the "Four Horsemen."

George Sutherland   A Republican and former senator from Utah. A defender of private property and the sanctity of contracts. A member of the "Four Horsemen."

Wills Van Devanter   Appointed to the Court by President Theodore Roosevelt. A former chief justice of the State of Wyoming. Very close to Justice McReynolds. A member of the "Four Horsemen."

AMERICAN DEFAULT

CHAPTER 1

◇◇◇◇◇

Gold and the Professors

March 1–August 1, 1932

From today's perspective, it is difficult to imagine the depth of the Great Depression, and the desperation and deprivation it created among people from all walks of life and social conditions. Complete industries disappeared, the ranks of the unemployed swelled to unthinkable levels, families lost their life savings and had no one to turn to. Homes and farms were repossessed by the thousands. Soup kitchens could not serve enough meals to those going hungry, banks collapsed in rapid succession, farmers lynched judges performing foreclosure auctions, and children stopped going to school. Complete families thought about emigrating, only to find out that the Depression was a worldwide phenomenon and that relatives who had stayed behind in the old world were suffering as much as they were. Not only that: uncles and cousins who had gone to faraway places, such as Argentina or Australia, were in even worse conditions. There were no jobs, no relief, and nowhere to go.

Between 1929 and 1932, gross domestic product (GDP) measured in current dollars—that is, unadjusted by inflation—dropped by almost 60 percent, production of durable goods, including automobiles, declined by 81 percent, and the value of agricultural production was down by 63 percent. During the same period, employment declined by almost 50 percent—one out of every two people who in July 1929 had a job had lost it by March 1932—and the number of unemployed surpassed 15 million people. Those who still had jobs were earning much less than during 1929: according to the Federal Reserve, average wages had declined by

67 percent, and cash income in the rural sector had gone down by more than 70 percent.[1]

The United States had had recessions and financial panics before, but nothing resembled what the nation was going through in the early 1930s. The most recent slump had happened in 1921–1923, but in every single category that downturn had been milder, and the recovery had been much faster.[2] The panics of 1907 and 1873 had been serious and had wrecked many businesses and banks, but they were rather small disturbances in comparison to what President Herbert Hoover called the Great Depression.[3] The 1929–1933 collapse was several times deeper and more devastating than anything America had seen in the past. It was also much more profound than any downturn the country would experience in the years to come, including the 2008–2009 Great Recession.

The generalized collapse in prices was one of the most destructive aspects of the crisis. Between mid-1929 and mid-1932, the index of wholesale prices went down by approximately 70 percent; during the same period the cost of living for the typical household dropped by 40 percent. But behind these figures there were individual stories. In some industries, prices fell by significantly more than the average, driving small and medium companies into bankruptcy.[4] Things were particularly bad in the agricultural sector, where the prices of some crops were so low that it was not worth it to harvest them. In 1932, New York governor Franklin D. Roosevelt decided that his campaign for the presidency would be run around the issue of raising commodity prices and providing relief to the unemployed. In speech after speech, in interviews and radio broadcasts, he promised that when he was elected president his most important goal would be to end the deflation and help little people to find work once again.

One of the most devastating effects of this drop in prices was that debt burdens, when measured relative to the price of goods produced, increased very significantly. Consider the case of cotton, the commodity that Roosevelt would monitor throughout his first presidency. Its price declined from 12 cents per pound in 1926, to 6.52 cents in 1932—a reduction of 48 percent. This meant that in 1926 a mortgage of $10,000 was equivalent to 83 thousand pounds of cotton; by 1932 a debt of the exact same monetary value was equivalent to 154 thousand pounds of cotton, an increase of almost 84 percent. With collapsed prices, farmers could not pay their debts and were rapidly losing their land to banks and mortgage companies.

THE PROFESSORS

By March 1932, Roosevelt's campaign had gathered considerable force, and it looked as if he would get the two-thirds of the votes required to win the Democratic nomination. Voters liked the governor and appeared to trust him. The press, however, had a different view. Most reporters thought that he was a good speaker, but they questioned his substance and the seriousness of his thinking. During the earlier months of the primary campaign, Roosevelt had assailed the Republican administration for letting the economic situation deteriorate markedly and for allowing unemployment to grow to 15 million people. What he hadn't done, however, was make many specific policy proposals on how to get the country out of the Depression; most of his statements were considered to be general and without much forward-looking content. Now that he had the largest number of delegates the press was scrutinizing every one of his statements. Reporters were looking for inconsistencies, platitudes, and knowledge gaps.

Ernest Lindley, an influential journalist who followed the campaign closely, and who had written an early biography of Roosevelt, thought that the candidate "ought to say more than he had been saying about what has to be done."[5] Walter Lippmann wrote that FDR was "a pleasant man who, without any important qualifications for the office, would very much like to be President."[6] And a *New York Times* editorial compared President Hoover's specific plans for getting out of the crisis with what the editorialist considered to be the governor's collection of generalities: "The contrast between the two leaps to the eye of every reader. Mr. Hoover is precise, concrete, positive. Governor Roosevelt is indefinite, abstract, irresolute."[7]

In view of these criticisms, Governor Roosevelt asked Sam Rosenman and Basil "Doc" O'Connor, two of his long-time associates, to put together a small group of advisers to assist him gather information for speeches and press conferences, and to draft policy proposals. He suggested that they look among university people, among academics interested in public policy, among individuals who had thought about policies that could take the country out of the crisis.

The first member recruited for the advisory group—which would soon be known as the "Brains Trust"—was Raymond Moley, a forty-six-year-old law professor at Columbia University. Trained as a political scientist,

Moley was an expert in the administration of criminal justice. He had advised Roosevelt on New York state judicial issues and had been director of the New York State Commission on the Administration of Justice. His interests, however, went well beyond criminal law, and although he was not an economist he knew enough about the subject to carry out an informed conversation with experts in the field. He had an elongated face, penetrating dark eyes, thinning grey hair, large ears, and very thick eyebrows. He wore crumpled dark suits, and more often than not had a pipe in his hand, which he seldom lit. He was born in Berea, Ohio, in an Irish-Catholic middle class family, and was proud of the fact that before turning twenty-five he had been elected mayor of Olmsted Falls, Ohio.

Raymond Moley was a gifted writer and had a remarkable capacity for synthesizing complex issues into a few memorable phrases. One of his first assignments was to draft the "Forgotten Man" speech, in which Roosevelt argued that in 1932 the situation in the United States was as grave as in 1917, when the nation entered World War I. The most famous passage said:[8]

> These unhappy times call for the building of plans that rest upon the forgotten, the unorganized but indispensable units of economic power, for plans like those of 1917 that build from the bottom up and not from the top down, that put their faith once more in the forgotten man at the bottom of the economic pyramid.

Another of Moley's many contributions to the campaign was coming up with the term "New Deal." At first FDR did not pay much attention to the expression, but with time he started using it in informal discussions with advisers and close friends. On July 2, in his acceptance speech at the Democratic National Convention in Chicago—a speech drafted by Moley—the governor said, "I pledge you, I pledge myself, to a new deal for the American people." The term struck a chord with the public, and in no time FDR's approach towards solving the nation's economic problems was universally known as the New Deal. To some it meant hope and salvation, the opportunity of getting a job and having a future, the possibility of not losing the family farm to foreclosure; to others it meant government intrusion and grab, the end of the American way, and a dangerous step towards socialism and perdition. Ray Moley was also the principal writer of FDR's famous inaugural speech, the speech with one of the most memorable lines in American politics: "The only thing we have to fear is fear itself."[9]

But Moley's role went well beyond that of a speechwriter. During the campaign he would constantly be at the governor's side; he would carry bags and briefcases, write memoranda and letters, look for answers to the most difficult questions, and talk incessantly with Roosevelt about ways of ending the Depression. In many of those conversations, they pondered whether some of the policies promoted by Roosevelt as governor of New York would be appropriate for the nation. During the interregnum, as the long transition between the general election and the inauguration was then known, Moley accompanied the president-elect to two meetings with President Herbert Hoover. He also helped the president-elect assemble the cabinet. He interviewed prospective candidates, conveyed messages from FDR, and unabashedly gave his opinion. In his view, the cabinet should be formed by individuals who favored solving domestic problems over international ones. As Moley would later declare, those conversations stayed away from issues related to gold or the exchange rate. This was not because these where forbidden topics, but rather because they were not at the center of the governor's concerns, nor were there central to the political discussions of the campaign.[10]

As a speechwriter and presidential adviser, Moley witnessed some of the most dramatic and significant political events of 1932 and 1933. He eventually wrote two memoirs that have provided historians and analysts with invaluable insights on FDR's personality and on the inner workings of the administration's famous Hundred Days. Moley's archives, held at the Hoover Institution, contain an incredibly valuable trove of information and details about the developments in 1932–1933.

The second member of the Brains Trust was Rexford Guy Tugwell, a forty-one-year-old economics professor at Columbia, and Moley's neighbor in Morningside Heights, in New York City. Tall and very handsome, with wavy auburn hair and a quick smile, he had the looks of a matinee idol. Rex Tugwell got his Ph.D. from the University of Pennsylvania, and was convinced that modern management techniques could bring generalized prosperity. He believed that if left on its own, modern industry would fall into the traps of "overproduction." This danger could only be

FIGURE 1.1. Raymond Moley, the head of the Brains Trust, and President Franklin Delano Roosevelt in February 1933. (With permission from Getty Images)

avoided by careful planning through a national economic council run by the private sector and coordinated by the government. After visiting the Soviet Union in the late 1920s, he became an even stronger believer in the merits of economic planning. Although he was a tenured professor at Columbia, he was not a member of the Graduate School, and his teaching was confined to undergraduates. Years later he would write that talking about economics with Roosevelt was like teaching the rudiments of the discipline to college freshmen.[11]

Tugwell was born in upstate New York, and while his father was in commerce, his ancestors had been farmers in Chautauqua County. This gave him endless topics of conversation with Roosevelt, who considered himself a gentleman farmer and was proud of his various farming undertakings in Dutchess County, New York, and in Pine Mountain, Georgia. Tugwell's interests in farming also helped him to be on good terms with FDR's wife, Eleanor, not a minor accomplishment during the campaign. Rex Tugwell was responsible for introducing the "concert of interests" notion into FDR's speeches, the idea that the policies of the new administration should favor every group in America, and not only large banks and corporations, as he claimed Hoover had done during his presidency.

Tugwell was a prolific and forceful author. He developed Columbia's famous year-long course on Contemporary Civilization, and in 1925 he published, with two colleagues, a 633-page textbook to be used in that course.[12] In 1934, after ten years of work, Tugwell published a new version of the textbook, this time aimed at high school students. The new edition included a long chapter on how to improve farm production, and an extensive discussion on the possibilities for "economic planning in the United States," an issue that he had already tackled in some of his scholarly writings, and that would become the intellectual bases for both the Agricultural Adjustment Act (AAA) and the National Recovery Act (NRA) of 1933, two key and controversial components of the New Deal structural reform policies.[13]

In spite of his vast interests and versatility, Tugwell knew little about monetary theory, the gold standard, and currency values. The following entry in his diary is telling: "I told [FDR] what I knew and thought [about the gold standard] which was little enough, except that I was prepared with a satisfactory precis, having written an elementary economic text whose relevant passages I could display."[14] In later writings, Tugwell came back to the fact that neither he nor the other members of the Brains Trust knew much about gold or exchanges. Given their very limited knowledge, he thought that it was surprising that FDR would not ask for true experts' advice on monetary issues and questions related to gold and the devaluation of the dollar. Tugwell wrote in his diary: "We were not monetary theorists, and we said so repeatedly . . . I had told him [FDR] frankly that my own knowledge of monetary theories came only from dealing with them as a part of the courses I taught, and since the others were not more expert, I wondered why he discussed . . . [monetary policy] with us."[15]

Rex Tugwell was a keen observer of people. He quickly captured their personalities, temperament, depth, and modus operandi. He wrote this about the first time he met FDR in Albany: "It occurred to me that, during the now eleven years struggle to get back the use of his legs, the rest of his body had really become overdeveloped. I wondered what his jacket

FIGURE 1.2. Rexford G. Tugwell, the only economist in the Brains Trust. (*Source*: Farm Security Administration—Office of War Information Photograph Collection, Library of Congress Prints and Photographs Division)

size must be."[16] In his memoirs, he commented on Roosevelt's custom of greeting his advisers early in the morning, while still in bed. During those meetings FDR would smoke the first cigarette of the day. Tugwell was always impressed with the vigor with which Roosevelt put the match out, and thought that it had to do with Roosevelt's handicap: "[B]eing trapped [in case of a fire] is something no one likes to contemplate. For a man without legs it becomes something to guard against as a special risk. The rest of us can make some easy and quick adjustment to circumstances, but a cripple that is otherwise vigorous has not only to see that his escape way is open but also to do so furtively."[17]

The third member of the Brains Trust was Adolf Berle, also a professor of law at Columbia. His father was a Congregationalist minister whose sermons focused on social issues and on the obligation of fortunate people towards the poor and the disadvantaged. This Social Gospel perspective had a deep effect on Adolf's approach to life, politics, and academic work. A Harvard College graduate, Berle was considered to be somewhat of a boy wonder. In his final year as an undergraduate, he completed the requirements for his master's degree. His thesis dealt with Alexander Hamilton's Assumption Act, or assumption by the federal government of the state debts.[18] Since that time Berle was convinced that the government's creditworthiness was sacred, and that the public sector debt should provide an unshakable basis for the pyramid of credit in the nation. He graduated from Harvard Law School at age twenty-one, and briefly worked at Louis D. Brandeis's law firm in Boston. It was from Brandeis that Berle got his dislike for large banks and financiers. In 1919, at age twenty-four, he was appointed acting chief of the Russian Section of the American Delegation in Versailles.

Until 1928, Berle had been a registered Republican. But this did not deter Raymond Moley from recruiting him for the Brains Trust. What he and Governor Roosevelt were after was Berle's technical capacity, his deep understanding of corporate structures and of credit. The important question that Berle was asked to tackle was why banks were not lending and companies were not borrowing any longer. In 1932 he co-authored a book on the modern corporation that showed, for the first time, how rapidly economic power had become concentrated in America. The book—which is still in print at the time of this writing—pioneered the idea that in the modern corporation there was a major conflict between the interest of the thousands of dispersed owners, on the one hand, and the interests of managers, on the other. With time the problem came to be known as the "principal-agent problem" and has been at the center of major modern controversies, including the benefits of granting valuable options to senior executives. The book also put on the table the idea that the separation of ownership and control had created new management problems and challenges, and that the United States needed to implement a major reform in corporate governance.[19]

As the presidential campaign unfolded during 1932, new members joined the advisory group as somewhat informal Brains Trust "associates": Robert K. Straus, a graduate of Harvard's Business School; General Hugh Johnson, a lawyer who for many years had worked for the financier and

FIGURE 1.3. Adolf Berle, Jr., lawyer and member of the Brains Trust. Photographed in 1965. (*Source: New York World-Telegram & Sun Newspaper* Photograph Collection, Library of Congress Prints and Photographs Division)

FDR supporter Bernard M. Baruch; and Charles W. Taussig, a successful businessman who in 1932 was president of the American Molasses Company and the Sucrest Corporation (he was a nephew of the respected Harvard professor and trade expert Frank Taussig). With time other professionals wrote memoranda and gathered information for the Brains Trust. Although they were not full members of the mythical group, they made important contributions to the campaign. The list included Joseph McGoldrick, James W. Angell, Schuyler Wallace, and Howard Lee McBain. Of these, only Angell was a professional economist. Not one of these advisers was paid for his services.

HIGH-GRADE RESEARCH ASSISTANTS?

What made the Brains Trust unique was that until that time no presidential candidate had conveyed a group of academics to provide technical advice on campaign and policy issues. The closest to the Brains Trust was Woodrow Wilson's study group *The Inquiry*, set up in 1917 to advise him on how to handle the forthcoming peace process. *The Inquiry*, however, was much larger, and it mostly worked in secret. Many of its members were, as in the case of the Brains Trust, associated to Columbia University.

As soon as the Brains Trust was put together, Raymond Moley and his associates attracted attention (and criticism) from the press. They were followed, and "reporters besieged [them] . . . for a word"; at times they were treated with respect, while at others they were ridiculed.[20] FDR referred to them as "my privy council," and on more than one occasion the press called them, rather derisively, "the professors."[21]

When recruiting the Brains Trust, FDR was not interested in theoreticians or great thinkers. He wanted smart people able to analyze and summarize vast amounts of data and put them in historical perspective. He also wanted individuals with a literary bent who would help him find the right turn of phrase and coin catchy terms for his speeches and public addresses. At some level, then, it may be argued that the members of the Brains Trust came on board as "high-grade research assistants."[22] It didn't take too much time, however, for the trio to prove its value and to gain significant influence over the candidate. Even before the Democratic Convention in June 1932, they had helped FDR define key aspects of his program, including the agricultural allotment system that was to become the core of the AAA. As Arthur M. Schlesinger Jr. points out, it was soon clear to FDR that Berle and Tugwell were "continuously fertile in ideas, and neither was constrained by the past or intimidated by the future." H.G. Wells made the following remarks after meeting Berle: "He began to unfold a view of the world to me that seemed to contain all I had ever learned and thought, but better arranged and closer to reality."[23]

From early on, the meetings between the Brains Trust and FDR were productive and helped him clarify concepts and draft policies. Schlesinger described the gatherings in Albany as follows: "Moley urbanely steering the discussion, Tugwell and Berle flashing ahead with their ideas . . . and always Roosevelt, listening, interrupting, joking, needling, and cross-examining, absorbing the ideas and turning them over in his mind."[24] According to Ernest Lindley when the Brains Trust met with the governor "the conversation roamed over the whole field of economics: the causes of the depression, the methods [and policies] of relieving it, the main points of attack."[25] After a few weeks in the job, it was clear to anyone that saw them in action—including the members of the press that followed the candidate anywhere he went—that the members of the Brains Trust were not mere assistants; they were real—and very influential—advisers to the governor of New York and Democratic frontrunner.

The Brains Trust sphere of influence, however, was strictly confined to ideas and policy advice; they played no role in the purely political aspects of the campaign. Lindley recounts that one day after the convention FDR made things clear to his inner circle: Jim Farley was appointed national chairman and was in charge of getting him elected; Ray Moley was put in charge of policies, issues, and speeches. Responsibilities were kept separate. Farley put things succinctly to Moley: "Issues aren't my business. They are yours and his [FDR's]. You keep out of mine, and I keep out of yours."[26]

What neither Moley or his fellow Brains Trusters imagined when they embarked on this adventure was that they would be called to give their opinions about very specific questions related to monetary theory and the gold standard, the stabilization of the exchanges, the gold points, the Federal Reserve's cover ratio, the possible devaluation of the dollar, and the gold clause in private and public debt contracts. Those were issues well beyond their expertise, and yet their opinions would become crucial in the events that unfolded during 1933 and that helped change America forever.

CHAPTER 2

◇◇◇◇◇

A Tragic Disaster

August 1, 1932–February 10, 1933

During the earlier part of 1932 the gold standard was not a major campaign issue; it was barely debated in the press; and no alternatives to it were seriously discussed by the candidates. To be sure, there were individuals who wanted the United States to follow Britain and devalue the dollar—Irving Fisher, the famous Yale professor, was the best known critic of the gold standard—but for most people this was a question of secondary importance, a possibility that after some thought was considered impractical, and discarded. In a 1932 lecture, Jacob Viner, the respected University of Chicago professor who in 1934 would join the Treasury as an adviser, captured the dominant view when he declared that although the gold standard had problems, it was still the best monetary regime available for the nation. He asserted that abandoning it would not end the Depression, and would create a great deal of uncertainty and wreckage. In Viner's view with "minor changes in our gold reserves requirements we can go sufficiently far in experimenting with the possibilities of stabilization without imperiling our continuous adherence to the gold standard."[1] Those who sided with Viner argued that at the time the United States had the largest stock of gold in the world, and that the "cover ratio," or percentage of the monetary liabilities covered by gold holdings at the Federal Reserve, amply exceeded the statutory requirement of 40 percent.

Between January 1 and election day (November 8, 1932), *the New York Times* published eighty-nine articles that included the words "gold standard" and "Roosevelt." Of these, just six appeared in the January–March period, and only one of them dealt with the possible connection between a devaluation of the currency and "controlled inflation," the term generally used to indicate a gradual increase in prices that would take them back to their mid-1920s level. During the next three months the *Times* published another fifteen articles that contained those three words, but most of them were of a historical nature and did not delve into the possibility of the United States getting off gold any time soon. In late September, however, things changed when President Hoover decided to campaign vigorously and to go on the offensive. His campaign strategy was partially based on denouncing his Democratic opponent for wanting to get the country off gold and devaluing the dollar.[2] On October 31, President Hoover said in New York that "fiat money is proposed by the Democratic party as a potent measure for relief from the depression." But this path, he warned, would produce "one of the most tragic disasters to . . . the independence of man."[3]

AN EXPERIMENTER

FDR was not an "inflationist" in the sense of William Jennings Bryan, nor was he a fan of devaluations. In his 379-page biography of Roosevelt, published in 1931, Ernest Lindley does not mention "inflation" or "gold" as policy issues or concerns. Neither of these words is in the index. This is particularly telling, since the purpose of that book was to explain to the American public the views and policy inclinations of the governor of New York, a politician in the ascendant who was likely to play a prominent role on the national scene. More than anything, Roosevelt was an "experimenter." He liked to consider—and sometimes try—different methods and tools, and see if they would produce the desired outcome. According to Rexford G. Tugwell, the only economist in the Brains Trust, FDR did not quite know what to do about the dollar, or the gold standard. Tugwell added that Roosevelt "liked to elaborate possibilities, play with alternatives, and suggest operating improvements."[4] This desire to experiment came out clearly in the Oglethorpe Speech, where FDR said: "The country needs and, unless I mistake its temper, the country demands bold, persistent *experimentation*. It is common sense to take a method and try it: If it fails, admit it frankly and try another. But above all, try something."[5]

FDR's desire to experiment extended to monetary issues. In February 1933, Raymond Moley was acting as an intermediary in negotiations between the president-elect and Senator Carter Glass, to whom Roosevelt had offered the post of secretary of the treasury. Moley writes in his 1939 memoirs: "I didn't know the exact nature of the President-elect's monetary plans. But I knew his *experimental*, tentative, and unorthodox temperament."[6]

The Democratic Party platform, drafted by A. Mitchell Palmer, who had been attorney general during the Wilson administration, stated that there was a need to maintain a policy of "sound money." For most observers, this meant that the Democratic Party candidate would not tinker with the value of the dollar, and would maintain the gold standard. Walter Lippmann commented that the platform had Wilsonian values, and noted that it "starts with a declaration for drastic economy and a sound currency. It does not contemplate a currency inflation in the spirit of Bryanism or an expansion of governmental activity to create a new social order."[7] On several occasions, FDR reaffirmed the party's official views on money and the dollar. For instance, in a radio address delivered on July 30, 1932, he said: "A sound currency [is] to be preserved at all hazards, and an international monetary conference called, on the invitation of our government, to consider the rehabilitation of silver and related questions."[8]

In late 1932, as the banking crisis deepened, sentiments regarding exchange rates and gold began to change. People who only a few months earlier had completely ruled out devaluation began to think that the issue should be analyzed in detail and even considered seriously. At the same time, The Committee for the Nation, a private group financed by William Randolph Hearst and Henry Ford, among others, stepped up its lobbying for the abandonment of gold. More and more people began to talk about Irving Fisher's "compensated dollar" proposal, a plan to unlink the dollar from gold, and pegging it to a broad basket of commodities. In a number of publications Fisher had claimed that this reform would put an end to instability and deflation.[9]

Raymond Moley characterized the situation in the weeks following the election as follows:

a source of trouble . . . was the growing talk in Congress, in the press and in semi-private talk that the gold value of the dollar would be reduced. For the first time in history, talk of a cheaper dollar was not the monopoly of populistic farmers. . . . This time it came from urban politicians, college professors and even some of the more prominent businessmen.

In the middle of this upheaval the president-elect still did not appear to have a strong view on the matter of gold, nor had he made a decision on how to handle the massive withdrawals of currency and bullion from the nation's banks. According Raymond Moley, the man who saw Roosevelt for several hours every day, "in the midst of all the talk of 'reflation' by dollar manipulation, no one knew where the President-elect stood."[10]

A SOLEMN COVENANT WITH THE AMERICAN PEOPLE

Herbert Hoover barely campaigned during the first nine months of 1932. He believed that his post was at the White House, dealing with the nation's many problems. He also believed that voters would understand that the Depression was the result of external forces and that he had done everything possible to ameliorate its effects.

In August, after the Democratic convention, Roosevelt redoubled his attacks on the administration. In speech after speech, he argued that Hoover had not done enough, that his policies were not sufficiently bold, and that they only scratched the surface of the problem. On August 20, the governor delivered a long campaign speech in St. Louis where he unleashed his criticism of the Hoover administration with all his force. The climax came when he said that the administration had followed policies that devastated the nation:[11]

So I sum up the history of the present Administration in four sentences: First, it encouraged speculation and overproduction, through its false economic policies. Second, it attempted to minimize the crash and misled the people as of its gravity. Third, it erroneously charged the cause to other Nations of the world. And finally, it refused to recognize and correct the evils at home which had brought it forth; it delayed relief; it forgot reform.

These four attack points became a staple of the Roosevelt campaign, and were repeated again and again in speeches throughout the nation. On October 25, the Democratic candidate's rhetoric became even more strident when he referred to his four-part criticism as "the Four Horsemen of the present Republican leadership: The Horsemen of Destruction, Delay, Deceit, Despair."[12] It didn't escape perceptive analysts that the four conservative members of the Supreme Court, the institution with which President Roosevelt would clash a few years later, were called by the media "the Four Horsemen."[13]

In his memoirs published in 1952, Herbert Hoover devotes page after page to debunking the attacks launched by FDR twenty years earlier. It is a moving and sad document; it is clear that the former president spent years consumed by the need to set the record straight, to convince the American public that he cared, that he was a hands-on leader, that he didn't stand on the sidelines while destruction, deflation, and destitution ravaged the country. Even the title of the second volume of the memoirs—*The Great Depression, 1929–1941*—is aimed at exculpating himself. The dates suggest that the New Deal was a failure and that the contraction lasted until 1941, the time the United States entered World War II. And yet, in spite of the carefully constructed arguments, the detailed timelines, the abundant data, the multitude of quotes and testimonials, this was a futile exercise. As it became clear during the 2008–2010 financial crisis, Hoover's name is still a synonymous of lack of empathy, of laissez-faire at its worst, and, to put it starkly, of a "do-nothing" president. Analysts such as Nobel Laureate and *New York Times* columnist Paul Krugman repeatedly referred to Hoover as an example of a failed president who had not faced the crisis head on, and had blindly followed the dictates of the laissez-faire doctrine. It may be unfair, but this is the way it is.

In October 1932, and after it seemed that things were getting better and that recovery was finally around the corner, there was a new wave of bank failures, and commodity prices fell once again. Reelection did not look so clear after all, and President Hoover decided to go on the attack. He denounced Governor Roosevelt as an irresponsible "inflationist," as someone who would tinker with the unshakable value of the dollar, one of the most sacred aspects of the American economic system.

In his memoirs Hoover wrote: "Secretary Mills and I determined to smoke out in the campaign the whole devaluation-managed currency and fiat money issue." On October 4, in what he considered to be his "campaign launch," the president gave a speech in Des Moines, in which he explained the importance of the gold standard, stated how close the nation had been to a terminal crisis, and remarked with vehemence that if Roosevelt was elected the country would move towards a chaotic future. Hoover said: "Going off the gold standard is no academic matter [presumably a reference to 'the professors' of the Brains Trust]."

The president then referred to the importance of the gold clause in contracts, and said "our people have long insisted upon writing a large part of their long-run debtor documents as payable in gold." The president then shocked everyone by stating that in February 1932, the nation had been two weeks away from being unable to "hold to the gold standard . . . [and] to meet the demand of foreigners and our own citizens for gold." He then said that his "administration kept a cool head and rejected every counsel of weakness and cowardice. . . . We determined that we would stand up like men, and render the credit of the United States government impregnable."[14]

A few days later Hoover was back on the offensive, and in Indianapolis he asserted that "the Democratic candidate has yet to disavow the [idea] . . . to issue greenback currency." And on October 31 he said in New York that "fiat money is proposed by the Democratic party as a potent measure for relief from the depression." But this path, he warned, would produce "one of the most tragic disasters to . . . the independence of man."[15]

In view of these attacks, the Roosevelt campaign decided to follow a two-part strategy. First, Senator Carter Glass, a venerable figure who was known for his orthodoxy in monetary affairs, was recruited to give a radio speech on the subject of gold and money. Second, it was decided that the candidate himself would respond directly to Hoover's attacks a few days before the elections.

Glass's speech was a masterful piece of oratory. It opened with references to Hans Christian Andersen, Karl Grimm, and Aesop. The old senator then moved to the history of monetary policy in the United States, and to what he called Hoover's "ingratitude" towards him and other members of Congress who had stood by the president during the crisis. He argued that the Democratic Party had always supported stability, gold, and low inflation. He then criticized Secretary of the Treasury Ogden Mills for allowing thousands of banks to fail. He closed with a reference to his party's platform, and he assured his listeners that the Roosevelt administration would pursue the policies of sound money.[16]

Immediately after Hoover's first attack, FDR's advisers began to think of how the candidate could best respond to the accusations that he was going to lead the country to inflation, devaluation, and perdition. Brains Trust member Adolf Berle described in his diary the strategy to be followed. He also stated that even at that late date—a few days before the election—FDR was unsure on how to handle the whole gold standard and dollar issue:[17]

> [We were drafting] a speech answering Hoover at Des Moines. We decided to eliminate the gold standard part, because the financial district already made that argument; also because the Governor said. 'I do not want to commit to the gold standard. I haven't the faintest idea whether we will be on the gold standard on March 4th or not; nobody can foresee where we shall be.' *I gather that the Governor would rather stay on the gold standard than not. But he is not undertaking to say now what the policy will be.*

On November 4, 1932, at the Brooklyn Academy of Music, Roosevelt replied to Hoover's claim that he was a "devaluationist." He opened his speech by praising Senator Carter Glass for his "magnificent philippic." He then forcefully denied that he would tinker with the value of gold. He said "the President is seeing 'rubber dollars.' But that is only part of his campaign of fear." The most important part of FDR's speech was reaffirming a point made by Senator Glass in his radio address. Roosevelt reiterated that since 1917 there had been a covenant between each U.S. government and the American people.[18] He then reminded his listeners that the Democratic platform declared that sound currency had to be preserved at all costs, and repeated what he had said on June 30: "Sound money is an international necessity; not a consideration for one nation alone. That is, I want to see sound money in all the world. . . . Sound money should be maintained at all regards."[19]

To some, this speech is the ultimate example of a cunning politician's doublespeak; he pledged support to sound money and not to the gold standard. Further, when referring to the covenant implicit in the gold clauses, he said it in a way that could be interpreted as being a statement by

Senator Glass, and not by him. This, indeed, was Hoover's interpretation. But there is another reading. The Covenant Speech was sincere, and the decision to avoid a pledge to maintain the gold standard was not because of the Governor's maliciousness, but it reflected, as Adolf Berle pointed out in his diary, FDR's genuine doubts and hesitations. He plainly didn't know what to do. Be it as it may, it is interesting to note that five years later, when the first volumes of FDR speeches and public papers were published, the Covenant Speech was not included. Indeed, today it is difficult to find a complete version of what the candidate said on the verge of the elections, a promise that according to many, Roosevelt would renege on less than a year later when in June of 1933 the gold clause was repealed for all contracts, past and future.

As March 4, Inauguration Day, approached, there was no concrete or definitive plan for taking the United States off gold and devaluing the dollar. Worse yet, as recognized years later by Raymond Moley and Rexford Tugwell, the incoming administration had no plan of its own for saving the banking system, which was about to collapse. It seemed that in many ways FDR was taking the ideas of experimenting and improvising a bit too far.

CHAPTER 3

◇◇◇◇◇

The Quest for Money

February 10, 1933–March 3, 1933

On February 15, Franklin D. Roosevelt ended an eleven-day fishing vacation on board Vincent Astor's yacht *Nourmahal*. A *New York Times* reporter wrote that on his way to the train station, and "because of requests from many Miami residents the President-elect will probably ride through the streets of the city during his short stay here." The article went on to say that there was concern among many politicians regarding the new administration. Less than three weeks before Inauguration Day, "details of the Roosevelt [economic] program are not known. . . . In fact, it is not completed in the form in which it will have to be presented [to Congress], and Mr. Roosevelt adviser Professor Raymond Moley . . . [has] been working on it during the President-elect's absence."

The reporter then made a list of the topics the new president's program was likely to include: balancing the budget, farm relief, improving the farm credit situation, revising the international tariff from the high levels introduced by the Smoot-Hawley Act, and negotiating the war debts owed by U.S. allies. Not a word was said about the possibility of devaluing the dollar, annulling the gold clauses, or adopting a more flexible exchange rate regime, such as Irving Fisher's "compensated dollar." During the second week of February, only twenty days from inauguration, policies related to gold were considered by the press to be off the table.[1]

When the *Nourmahal* got to port, a large crowd was waiting. Everyone wanted to see the man who had pledged to work for the "forgotten man," and had promised a new deal. After delivering a short speech in

Bay Front Park, the president-elect got into an open car and headed to the railway station. Secret Service men stood on the car's running boards and Mayor Anton J. Cermak from Chicago, who during the primary had supported Al Smith and had traveled to Florida to ingratiate himself with FDR, sat at the president-elect's side. The streets were lined with supporters and well-wishers. The car moved slowly, so the people could get a glimpse at the president-elect. He waved at the adoring crowd, smiled broadly, and when the car stopped briefly he would stand up and salute with both hands.

At 9:35 a loud thud was heard; it was followed, in rapid succession, by four additional bangs that sounded like controlled explosions. Some though that they were fire crackers in celebration of the nation's next chief executive. But they weren't. Giuseppe Zangara, an unemployed bricklayer from New Jersey, had shot at FDR. Thanks to an alert woman who at the last second jerked his hand, he missed the president-elect. However, he critically wounded Mayor Cermak, who died a few days later. After the fifth shot, and after Zangara was seized by Miami's police, "a cheer of relief arose from the crowd in the park as Mr. Roosevelt . . . raised his hand in the air in reassurance. 'I am alright,' he shouted and summoned a smile. The crowd cheered again. With two Secret Service men on each running board the automobile bearing Mr. Roosevelt threaded its way out of the park and with a police motorcycle escort proceeded to the hospital."[2]

Although in the aftermath of the attempt FDR appeared calmed and collected, the episode was a major distraction. During the days that followed, neither he nor his closest advisers focused on the financial storm that was gathering considerable force. In state after state, banks faced long lines of depositors who wanted to get their money back; some wanted cash, while others demanded gold certificates. The situation was so difficult that on February 16, one day after Zangara took aim at the president-elect, none other than Vincent Astor, FDR's friend and host in the fishing vacation, sent a cable to Raymond Moley urging FDR to meet with Winthrop Aldrich, the chairman of the Chase Bank, to discuss the ramifications of the crisis, and the consequences of the rapid decline in bank deposits.[3]

On the night of February 18, while attending a news media dinner in New York City, the president-elect received a handwritten letter from Herbert Hoover, who had misspelled his last name as "Roosvelt." He read it quickly, while still at the table, and passed it on to Ray Moley, whose role and influence had grown significantly and who "was now functioning more than ever as his [FDR's] alter ego—a whole cabinet rolled into one, trying to herd all major issues of both domestic and foreign policy."[4]

Hoover's note went straight to the point: the financial crisis, he wrote, had surpassed the state sphere, and had become national. Something needed to be done. What was at stake was the future of the nation's banking system. In Hoover's view, the generalized bank run was largely the result of a confidence crisis. It would only abate if the president-elect would make a statement where he committed himself to maintaining the gold standard and not devalue the dollar. Unless people heard from him, the bank run would not stop. For one reason or another—there are still conflicting stories and explanations—Roosevelt took some time to reply. And when he did, on February 23, he curtly said that he would not make such statement. Until inauguration day, Herbert Hoover was the president, and what he decided to do was his own responsibility.

According to Moley, one of the main reasons for not replying to Hoover's note promptly was that FDR had not chosen his secretary of the treasury yet. His negotiations with Senator Carter Glass had stalled, and he had decided to look for a new candidate for the post. Any practical discussion on what to do about the banks—if anything—had to be conducted by the outgoing and incoming Treasury chiefs.

HENRY FORD LETS HIS BANK GO

On February 14—only a few hours before Joe Zangara aimed at the president-elect—Governor William A. Comstock of Michigan issued a proclamation declaring an eight-day banking holiday in his state. The next day a front-page article in the *New York Times* said that the Governor's announcement had come without any warning: "Few persons had ready cash, following a two-day holiday, and as a consequence business throughout the State showed a marked decrease. . . . Many Detroiters crossed the river to Windsor, Ont. On their quest for money to meet obligations or to continue in business."[5]

This was the final banking crisis of the Great Depression, the crisis that would eventually lead to the gold embargo, the abrogation of the gold clause, and the devaluation of the dollar. Problems had begun in early February 1933, when the Guardian National Bank of Detroit, one of the largest banks in the city, ran into serious trouble. The Guardian Group, which was controlled by the Ford Family, had been losing deposits for a long time. In January 1933, the pace of withdrawals accelerated to almost $2 million a week.[6] During the first week of February, Guardian executives asked the Refinance Finance Corporation (RFC) for a large loan. The bank had already received government assistance, but more was needed. Without additional financing, the bank would have to be liquidated, bringing havoc to Detroit and its surroundings. After examining the Guardian books and those of its holding companies and affiliates, RFC executives concluded that they could only increase the Corporation's exposure to the Group if the Ford companies would agree to subordinate $7.5 million of deposits to the new loan. That is, the controlling family had to agree that the RFC loan would have seniority over the Ford deposits.

When the RFC plan was presented to the Guardian Group board, Henry Ford flatly refused to subordinate his deposits. He said that his family had already contributed significant funds to the bank, and that he would not provide additional monies in any form. This generated a serious problem for the authorities: without subordination of the Ford deposits there would be no loan, and without fresh money the bank would have to close its doors in less than a week. This was not a small rural bank; it was a major institution in one of the nation's industrial hubs. Without any doubt its failure would send ripple effects throughout the nation; panic and large withdrawals of deposits and gold would surely follow.

When President Hoover learned about Henry Ford's position, he became so concerned that he decided to send a high level team to talk things over with the industrialist. On February 13 at 10 A.M. an extraordinary group met in downtown Detroit. Since it was a banking holiday—Lincoln's Birthday—the conferees had a few hours to talk things over and to come to an agreement before the bank reopened its doors to the public. Henry Ford, Edsel Ford and E. G. Liebold represented the bank's side; the government negotiators were Ray Chapin, secretary of commerce, and Arthur A. Ballantine a respected lawyer who at the time was undersecretary of the treasury.

Ballantine explained to the Fords that their bank had already received a large secured RFC financing ($15 million), and that there was not enough collateral for a new large loan. The RFC could only step in and lead the rescue package if the family would indeed agree that its $7.5 million would have a junior status relative to the new funds. Before Ford could reply, the undersecretary added that that was not all: in order for things to work out the Ford family would also have to provide between $2 and $4 million in fresh cash.

Henry Ford, who was seventy years old and looked very fit, reiterated that he would not agree to subordination. He then went into a long tirade where he talked about the state of the world, the economic policies of the Hoover Administration, and the effects of the Depression on productivity and attitude towards work. He asserted that there was a conspiracy against him and his companies, that labor unrest in one of his plants—the Briggs plant—had been incited by his competitors, and that the run on his bank was the result of a vindictive plot. If the bank had to go, it would go. If he was ruined, so be it. He felt young, and he would start a new business, and once again he would succeed.

Secretary Chapin and Undersecretary Ballantine explained that the situation was so grave that its consequences would go beyond the Ford companies and the state of Michigan. What was at stake was the future of the United States. Ford replied that of course he understood the ramifications of his bank's failure. He then stated that if the RFC didn't assist the Guardian Group, the next day he would withdraw his deposits ($25 million) from the First National Bank of Detroit—the other major institution in the city. Ballantine was shocked. That meant that the First National would also fail, and that contagion would be unstoppable. Everyone could visualize what would happen: thousands and thousands of people demanding their money, taking out loads of currency and gold, destroying what was left of the U.S. banking system.

At that point the conferees took a break and Secretary Chapin called Washington, where a group of regulators and policy makers were assembled in the RFC conference room. Those in attendance included, among others, Eugene Meyer, chairman of the Federal Reserve Board, Jesse Jones, who was to become chairman of the RFC, George Harrison, president of the Federal Reserve Bank of New York, and Francis G. Awalt, the acting comptroller of the Currency. The two United States senators from Michigan were later called into the meeting. The discussion was on what to do next.

It was decided that neither the Guardian Bank nor the First National would be allowed to open for business the following day. But, beyond that, the course of action was unclear and full of dangers. Should the governor issue a proclamation declaring a bank holiday in the state? And if so, for how long? Or should Michigan move to a system based on clearing house certificates, or scrip, such as the one used during the panic of 1907? Francis G. Awalt, who ended up playing a key role in the process that eventually saved America's banking sector from destruction, had this to say about the Detroit situation:[7]

> I was at the time against a banking holiday in Michigan. I felt sure that it could not be localized and that it would spread to other states. I knew we had a situation entirely different from the panic of 1907, which was a money panic, when the certificates were used generally for clearance between the banks themselves. In the situation we were facing [in 1933], the question of soundness of assets was present, and clearing house certificates could not be issued in the same way as in 1907. Moreover, many places where it would have been necessary to issue the certificates had no clearing house.

During the hours that followed desperate efforts were made to convince Henry Ford to cooperate and to find a solution to the crisis. Senator James Couzens, who had been an early large stockholder in the Ford companies, called the industrialist several times, and so did Undersecretary Ballantine.[8] But it was to no avail. The Fords maintained their position, and so did the regulators.

NOT THE TIME FOR TEA AND BISCUITS

In early January 1933, as the president-elect was assembling his cabinet, a House resolution was passed requiring the RFC to publish all loans made prior to July 21, 1932. This action had two consequences that greatly added to uncertainty and fear: banks that had received RFC assistant became "suspect" in the eyes of the public, and had to withstand new waves of withdrawals. In addition, banks that had considered asking for RFC help decided not to do so, as the sole act of requesting a government loan would make them suspect. The publication of the names of those who received loans had been first proposed by Speaker of the House John N. Garner. Apparently, he wanted to embarrass the prominent Republican politician Charles G. Dawes, whose Central Republic National Bank and

Trust of Chicago, had received a very large ($90 million) loan from the government.

In retrospect, many observers, including Herbert Hoover and Raymond Moley, believed that the Garner resolution was a catalyst for the banking panic and massive gold withdrawals that ensued in early 1933. In a 1948 article, Arthur A. Ballantine, Hoover's undersecretary of the treasury and the negotiator during Ford bank's crisis in Michigan, described the situation as follows: "During January and strikingly in February [of 1933], came gold withdrawals. . . . Earlier the trouble had been with the panic desire to turn bank deposits into cash; at this time the idea was the most disastrous one of turning cash into gold, in the belief that more gold could be obtained for the dollar then than later."[9]

President Herbert Hoover did not want to stand idle; conditions had deteriorated significantly, and the danger of a complete collapse of the banking sector was real. But more important, inaction would cement the notion that he was a "do nothing" president, an accusation that he had fought hard during the campaign, and that would haunt him for the rest of his life. By the end of February, some of Hoover's advisers considered declaring a national banking holiday to cool things down. Another group thought that the president could use the authority of the Trading with the Enemy Act of 1917 to issue an executive order "stopping payments from the banks to depositors except for necessities, and stop foreign exchange [i.e., gold] so as to stop the flight of capital or speculation."[10]

There was a problem, however. Hoover's Attorney General did not think that such a legal authority existed; after all the country was not at war, and without any doubt the Executive Order would be challenged in court. This is how Hoover remembered the episode in his 1952 memoirs:[11]

I then developed the idea of me issuing an executive order under this power [the Trading with the Enemy Act], provided Roosevelt would approve. My legal advisors agreed that, if approved, it could be done because he could secure ratification in a few days from his overwhelming majority in the incoming Congress . . . [Secretary] Mills pressed the idea on Mr. Woodin [incoming secretary of the treasury], that reported to us that Roosevelt declined all our suggestions.

As conditions worsened, Hoover tried a two-pronged approach. On the one hand he conferred with senators from both political parties and asked them to talk to the president-elect about issuing a statement committing him to a noninflationary course of action. His letters to members of Congress had a dramatic tone. For example, in a February 21 note to Senator Simeon D. Fess, from Ohio, President Hoover wrote: "We are in the verge of financial panic and chaos. Fear for the policies of the new administration has gripped the country. People do not await events, they act. Hoarding of currency, and of gold, has risen to a point never before known."[12]

Hoover's second line of attack involved the Federal Reserve. On March 1—barely three days before the transfer of power to Roosevelt—he wrote to the Board and asked for advice on two possible measures that, in his opinion, would help calm the markets: "Some form of Federal guarantee on banking deposits," and establishing a "clearing house system [i.e., issuing scrip] in the affected areas." The Board's reply came promptly on March 2, advising the president not to move in either direction. Worse yet, the Board didn't want to get implicated in the conversations between Hoover and Roosevelt. And thus, as crews of carpenters put the finishing touches to the stands for the inauguration parade, the run on the nation's banks continued to gather force.[13]

March 3, 1933, was the day of the big gold rush. That day the Federal Reserve Bank of New York lost $250 million in gold and $150 million in currency.[14] At the close of business, it was $250 million short of the gold reserves required to cover its currency liabilities—the required cover ratio at the time was 40 percent. The normal way to deal with such a situation was to get a transfer of metal from another Federal Reserve Bank. The logical candidate was the Chicago Fed, the second-largest in the nation. But on March 3 Chicago was also in trouble, having lost approximately $100 million in bullion. Things had deteriorated so much that just a few hours before a new president took the oath of office, the largest democracy in the world had no banking system to speak of. It appeared that both New York state and Illinois would have to declare banking holidays to stem the outflow of metal.

On the afternoon of March 3, as banks in New York and Chicago tried to fend off the latest speculative attacks, the outgoing and incoming presidents met at the White House. This was a meeting called by protocol, and no business was supposed to be discussed; it was time for tea and biscuits, civilized conversation and pleasantries. President Hoover, however, decided to break with tradition and during his opening remarks he brought up the banking crisis. He said that the situation had reached a very difficult point, and that a simple declaration would not be enough. It was necessary to issue a proclamation restricting the withdrawal and exportation of gold. He then came to the crux of his argument: he would only issue such proclamation if the president-elect would support him publicly. That would give him assurance that Congress would not disavow his actions. FDR was polite in his answer. He said that he understood the gravity of the circumstances. His own advisers—including Homer Cummings, whom he had drafted at the last minute to be his attorney general—believed that the 1917 Trading with the Enemy Act provided the required authority for Hoover to move forward. But the president-elect didn't go further than that. On the issue of a joint statement he was clear: until the next day at noon, Herbert Hoover was the president, and he had to proceed on his own.

CHAPTER 4

◇◇◇◇◇

A National Calamity

March 4, 1933–March 18, 1933

William Woodin was not President Roosevelt's first choice for secretary of the treasury. The president-elect wanted someone with ample political experience, someone who knew the ins and outs of congressional politics and who could help him pass the legislation required to fight the Depression. His first choice was Senator Carter Glass, the courteous southerner and seasoned member of Congress who was highly respected by bankers, business leaders, and his colleagues on Capitol Hill. The senator thought long and hard about the offer and finally decided against it. He had asked FDR for assurance that the new administration would not pursue, in any way, inflationary policies. This, Roosevelt was unwilling to do; after all, he was convinced that all options had to be available to him. He was not an inflationist, but, as noted, he was not afraid of controlled inflation, if that would help the nation to get out of the Depression.

In mid-February, twenty days before inauguration and as the banking crisis deepened, FDR still had not chosen his secretary of the treasury. Then, someone thought of William Hartman Woodin, a long-time Republican industrialist and music lover, who had supported Roosevelt from early on. At the time of his appointment, Woodin was the CEO of the American Car and Foundry Company, a Philadelphia firm founded by his grandfather, which had successfully turned to the production of railroad equipment. The fact that he understood the business world, but was not aligned with Wall Street was considered a big plus by the president-elect and his close advisers. Woodin, a small and frail man with a permanent smile in his face, accepted the post without making any demands. When his name was announced, "[t]here were those that shook their heads. They had heard that the new Secretary was a composer, a collector of prints, of postage stamps and objects of art. Would such a man do in such a national calamity?"[1]

Woodin would prove to be a dependable and loyal member of the Cabinet. He stood by FDR and supported his policies, even if some of them were contrary to what he had espoused throughout his life. He worked hard, analyzed alternatives, negotiated with members of Congress, and never tried to get the limelight. In July 1933, he became very ill with what his doctors thought was a throat infection; as it turned out, it was cancer. He resigned his post later that year, even before the gold saga got to an end. He was replaced in the post of secretary of the treasury by Henry Morgenthau Jr. Will Woodin died on May 3, 1934, at age sixty-five.

A NATIONAL BANKING HOLIDAY?

On the night of March 3, Will Woodin, the frail-looking man that FDR had tapped for the most difficult job in the new administration, found himself in an almost impossible situation. The next day he would become secretary of the treasury, and the country had no banks to speak of. Worse yet, the president advisers had no plan on what to do next. He talked to Ray Moley and Adolf Berle, he conferred with the senior members of Congress, including Senator Glass, he quizzed bankers and noted reporters, and he questioned officials from the Federal Reserve. But he obtained no concrete answers; all he got were platitudes, generalities, and some whining. He decided to turn to a group of men who had been thinking about the banking problem for a long time: the members of Herbert Hoover's Treasury team.

Early in the morning of March 4—Inauguration Day—government officials from both administrations met at the Treasury to discuss what to do about the banks. The group included Secretary of the Treasury Ogden Mills, incoming Secretary Will Woodin, Acting Comptroller of the Currency Francis Awalt, Undersecretary Arthur Ballantine, Federal Reserve officials, and several lawyers.

Ray Moley, who was about to become assistant secretary of state, and who continued to be FDR's most trusted adviser, came in and out of the meeting; he listened intently, but didn't say much. The other participants assumed that he was relaying the proceedings to FDR; they were right; that was exactly what he was doing. The discussion focused on what to do once the new president took the oath of office in a few hours. Should he declare a national banking holiday? And if so, under what legal authority? And for how long? Another question that kept coming up was how to stop, and even reverse, the hoarding of currency and gold. At the practical level, the conversation dealt with several key issues: After the holiday, which banks to open? When to open them? How to make sure that they would stay open? And, what to do about gold? No one wanted to mention the fact that implicit in these questions was the idea that many banks would not be reopened at all; indeed, a very large number of them would have to be liquidated, and their depositors would lose their savings.

That afternoon, the group reconvened without Woodin, who attended the inauguration ceremony. Little by little, a plan began to emerge. Three groups of banks were defined: Class A banks were healthy enough as to be reopened immediately; Class B banks needed some assistance and recapitalization, in order to open for business; Class C banks were those that would not open again and would have to be liquidated. Francis G. Awalt, the man who knew the most about the state of the banking sector, estimated that out of 5,938 national banks, about 2,200 were liquid enough as to be classified as Class A. The number was too small to reestablish a seminormal payments system; consequently, finding ways to open quickly a large number of Class B banks was essential. Federal authorities knew very little about the approximately 14,000 state banks, and in order to classify those into the three categories A, B, and C, they requested information from the regional Federal Reserve Banks.

A few minutes after 1 P.M. President Roosevelt delivered his famous Inaugural Address asking the nation to be hopeful, not to fall in the grips of fear, and to "convert retreat into advance." He added that there was a need for "a strict supervision of banking and credit and investments, so that there will be an end to speculation with other people's money." However, he did not mention the fact that in most states in the country the banks were closed and that people's fears were intimately linked to the banking crisis and to the fact that they had no access to their own monies

FIGURE 4.1. Secretary of the Treasury William H. Woodin. (*Source*:
George Grantham Bain Collection, Library of Congress)

and savings.[2] Five years later, in 1938, FDR had this to say about the state
of banks and the economy on March 4, 1933:[3]

By Inauguration Day, 1933, the banks of the United States were all
closed, financial transactions had ceased, business and industry had

sunk to their lowest levels. The widespread unemployment that accompanied the collapse had created a general feeling of utter helplessness. I sought principally in the foregoing Inaugural Address to banish, so far as possible, the fear of the present and of the future.

Roosevelt's Inauguration Address had a brief and oblique reference to the gold standard and the dollar. He said that "there must be a provision for an adequate but sound currency." Investors, analysts, and bankers at home and abroad tried to understand what this meant exactly. Clearly, by "sound currency" the new president meant that his administration would not pursue reckless inflationary policies, as some of his enemies had insinuated again and again. But what did he mean by "adequate currency"? Wasn't the value of the dollar already adequate? Was he thinking about a onetime devaluation, followed by a new fixed value of gold? Something along those lines had been done in 1834, when the price of gold had been raised from $19.50 an ounce, to $20.67 per ounce. That, however, had been a very small change (only 6 percent), aimed at aligning the relative prices of gold and silver. Also, in 1834 contracts were not linked to gold, and debts did not escalate automatically in value with the currency adjustment.

In September 1931, when England went off gold, the pound sterling had been devalued by a hefty 30 percent. Did the president have something along those lines in mind? No one knew the answer to this question, not even FDR. What actually happened in the months that followed, including the abrogation of the gold clauses, was the result of experimentation and improvisation; it was the result of the administration's reaction to speculative forces and unforeseen events; it was the product of FDR's deep desire to increase agricultural prices, and in particular the prices of cotton and wheat. As will be seen in the chapters that follow, it was also the president's way of dealing with an increasingly powerful and vocal agricultural lobby.

As the afternoon of March 4 advanced, the Treasury group began to put in writing what seemed to be a reasonable plan. Ogden "Oggie" Mills, who had been the secretary of the treasury until a few hours earlier, dictated a memorandum addressed to the new secretary, Will Woodin. He timidly titled the document "Tentative outline of a possible line of approach to the solution of our banking problem." The paper stressed the need to issue a presidential proclamation closing all banks in the nation for a week or so. The next step was to define a specific schedule for re-opening those banks that were in financial conditions to carry on with business. This could be done in a staggered way, following the tree-type of banks plan discussed that morning. Class A banks in large cities would reopen first, followed by the rest of the Class A banks; then Class B institutions could be reopened. In most cases, this required injecting fresh capital, either through the sale of newly issued shares to private investors, or the sale of preferred stock to the RFC. It was essential to provide enough cash to those banks that were to be reopened; the worst that could possibly happen was that a bank that was certified to be in good shape would run out of cash. Once it was printed, the document was delivered to the Carlton Hotel, where Woodin had a set of rooms. At approximately 7 P.M. Ogden Mills, the former secretary of the treasury, retired to his Georgetown home for the evening.

ALL BANKING TRANSACTIONS SHALL BE SUSPENDED

Early in the morning of March 5—a Sunday—the group reassembled at the Treasury. Not much had changed since the previous day, except that Will Woodin now sat at the secretary's desk and Ogden Mills occupied an armchair across from him. The discussion revolved around the "tentative outline" prepared under Mills's direction the previous day. The memorandum stated from the outset that since the banking problem affected every state in the Union, any solution would have to be national in nature. Unequivocally, it said that the "first and immediate step that should be taken would be to put all banks on the same closed bases by means of a national proclamation."[4]

As Sunday came to an end, only one thing was clear: there had to be a national banking holiday, and the president had to issue a proclamation to that effect. A draft prepared during the Hoover administration was used as a basis for the legal document. A few minutes passed midnight, and after it had been approved by Attorney General Homer Cummings, the proclamation was signed by the president. The dates of the holiday were March 6 through March 9, both days included. In its key part it stated that stopping the outflow of gold was a fundamental goal of the banking holiday. The legal authority used to issue the proclamation was, as Herbert Hoover had suggested to no avail, the Trading with the Enemy Act of 1917. The fact that the country was not at war, and that there was "enemy" to speak of, was generally overlooked. In its operative part the proclamation said:[5]

> Whereas there have been heavy and unwarranted withdrawals of gold and currency from our banking institutions for the purpose of hoarding . . . by virtue of the authority vested in me by said Act [the Trading with the Enemy Act of October 6, 1917] and in order to prevent the export, hoarding, or earmarking of gold . . . [I] hereby proclaim, order, direct and declare that from Monday, the Sixth day of March, to Thursday, the Ninth day of March. . . . There shall be maintained and observed by all banking institutions and all the branches thereof located in the United States of America, including the territories and insular possessions a bank holiday. . . . During such holiday . . . no such banking institution or branch shall pay out, export, earmark, or permit the withdrawal or transferred in any manner or by any device whatsoever, of any gold or silver coin or bullion or currency.

The banking holiday had an instantaneous effect at home and abroad. A luxury hotel in Pasadena issued scrip to stranded millionaires, including Princess Erik of Denmark and Mrs. C. Vanderbilt Barton of New York City. Sales in big department stores declined by as much as 70 percent, as people held on to currency. A milk shortage developed as farmers rebelled against the idea of delivering it without receiving payment. Banks in Cuba and Puerto Rico were closed for three days, and the Tokyo stock exchange did not open for business. American tourists in Montreal discovered all of the sudden, that their traveler's checks were worthless; tourists in Cairo found out that they could get only seventeen piastras per dollar, while the previous day a dollar got no less than twenty-eight piastras.[6]

On March 6, the first day of the banking holiday, Secretary Woodin told the *New York Times* that it was "ridiculous and misleading to say that we are off the gold standard. . . . We are definitely on the gold standard. Gold merely cannot be obtained for several days."

The next morning the front page of the *Times* illustrated the gravity of the situation. An eight-column headline announced the bank holiday. Some of main stories' titles were "Roosevelt puts embargo on gold," "Prison for gold hoarder," and "Scrip to be ready today or tomorrow to replace currency." Buried among this news, on the leftmost column, there was a story from Germany titled "Hitler bloc wins a Reich majority."

The real effort to develop a specific program to reopen banks began early in the morning on March 6. The previous night Secretary Will Woodin had promised the president that by Thursday he would have a proposal for banking legislation that could be submitted to Congress. The proposal, added Woodin, would specify how to reopen the banks in an orderly way, as well as the required steps to bring the financial system back to health. Based on that promise, President Roosevelt had called Congress into an Extraordinary Session on Thursday March 9, at 12 noon. The session was to last until June 10. This extraordinary period would come to be known as the "Hundred Days."

Most of Monday, March 6, was spent discussing generalities. At some point during the early afternoon it became clear that having so many people in the meetings was counterproductive. Bankers—most of whom had been whining, and had offered no concrete solutions—were dismissed, and legislators were politely asked to go back to Capitol Hill. By the early morning of March 7, the plan was beginning to acquire a concrete form. Throughout that day, information was sought from the regional Federal Reserve Banks about the health of the nation's almost 20,000 banks. Under the direction of Francis Awalt, every bank in the Union was classified as Class A, B, or C. Early in the morning of March 8, barely thirty hours before Congress was to convene to discuss what to do about the crisis, legislation begun to be drafted.

THE EMERGENCY BANKING ACT AND THE GOLD EMBARGO

The Emergency Banking Act of 1933 was approved by Congress on March 9 in record time and with barely any debate. The legislation was based, with very few variations, on a plan that Herbert Hoover's team, led by Secretary Ogden Mills, had put together several months earlier. What was in some way ironic was that Mills and Roosevelt disliked each other intensely. They had been classmates at Harvard and were neighbors on the Hudson River. Ogden Mills, who joined the Hoover Administration as undersecretary of the treasury in 1928, and replaced Andrew W. Mellon as secretary in 1932, was among those who believed that FDR was an ambitious lightweight without any credentials for high office, let alone to be president of the United States. And yet, Mills was fiercely loyal to the country, and even after stepping down as secretary he worked until the early hours of the morning helping the new administration solve the nation's financial crisis.[7]

The Emergency Banking Act had three key provisions. The first allowed the Federal Reserve System to issue "bank notes" to meet deposit withdrawals from those banks opened after the banking holiday. The difference between these "bank notes" and "Federal Reserve notes" was that the former were not backed by gold holdings, while the latter had bullion as collateral. According to the plan, and in order not to frighten people, the new bank notes would look exactly like the old ones, except for small print specifying the (lack of) metal backing; it would be almost impossible to distinguish them. Will Woodin noted that the beauty of the plan was that the new notes would be money that looked like money.[8] This, he told Ray Moley, made them very different from the infamous Civil War–era Treasury greenbacks, which had a distinctive look that clearly informed the public that they were a special—and less valuable— kind of money.

The second provision of the legislation was the appointment of Conservators to help reorganize Class B and Class C banks. This idea, which was captured in Title II of the Act, had been developed fully during the latter months of the Hoover administration. It was essential to move forward with the reorganization of the banking sector, even if some creditors or shareholders opposed restructuring. The third key aspect of the Emergency Banking Act was the issuing of preferred stock by national and state banks, which would be purchased by the Reconstruction Finance Corporation. This would recapitalize the banks and allow them to reopen their doors to the public.

A fundamental issue discussed during March 8 by the small team drafting the banking plan, was the geographical location of those institutions that were to be reopened. The consensus among those working in Washington, DC, was that every region—and in particular, every large city— needed to have enough operating banks. A large map of the country issued by the Post Office was used to mark the site of banks to be opened during the first few days. Color pins were used to show their exact location. When FDR was shown the map, he asked a barrage of questions regarding banks accessibility in the rural area. A controversy arose regarding the Bank of

America. The Federal Reserve Bank of San Francisco believed that this was a Class B bank, and couldn't be opened right away. Woodin and Awalt realized that postponing its opening would create a huge problem, as the bank had hundreds of thousands of depositors who would not be able to access their funds. This would create hardship—and even panic—in California. After long and difficult negotiations, it was finally agreed at 2 A.M. on March 9—less than twelve hours before Congress went into session—that the bank would be allowed to reopen. The RFC provided a $30 million loan, using preferred stock as collateral. Four months later, when confidence on the banking system had returned, the bank paid the loan back in full. In his diary Raymond Moley recalls the intensity this particular debate during late hours at night; in several places he refers to the Bank of America by its old name, "Bank of Italy."

The House approved the Emergency Banking Act by show of hands, even before the members had had a chance to read what it was all about. The Senate, being a more deliberate institution, spent two hours debating the issues. The acting comptroller of the currency, Francis Awalt was the only witness that testified in front of the Banking Committee. After a brief debate that pitted Senator Carter Glass against Louisiana's populist Huey Long, the bill cleared the Senate at 7:52 P.M. by a vote of 73 in favor to 7 against. This show of force by the new administration would prove invaluable during the rest of the Hundred Days, when one piece of legislation after another was passed by Congress.

Title I of this legislation amended the Trading with the Enemy Act of 1917 and provided clear authority to the president for closing the banks. This section included a key provision regarding gold that gave the government the authority to decree a gold embargo, of any length. It said that[9]

> the Secretary of the Treasury, in his discretion, may require any or all individuals, partnerships, associations and corporations to pay and deliver to the Treasurer any or all gold coin, gold bullion, or gold certificates. . . . Upon receipt of such gold . . . the Secretary of the Treasury shall pay therefor an equivalent amount of any other form of coin or currency under the laws of the United States.

Once the Emergency Act was passed by Congress on the evening of March 9, FDR extended the bank holiday "until further proclamation by the President."[10] Two days later he stated that "technical difficulties" had been overcome and that banks would be opened slowly, under a "progressive plan." He was quick to clarify that no one should "draw the inference that the banks opening on Monday are in any different condition as to soundness from the banks licensed to open on Tuesday or Wednesday or any subsequent day."[11]

Sunday March 12 marked an important turning point in the path towards recovery. That evening, at 10 P.M., the president delivered his first Fireside Chat, in which he explained the reach of the Emergency Banking Act and reassured people that those banks that were opening were sound. He spoke slowly, with friendly intonations; he eschewed technical terms and addressed the nation's concerns in a clear pedagogical way. To the estimated 60 million Americans who listened over the radio, his words were reassuring, as if they came from a trusted family doctor. Even today, more than eighty years later, it is comforting to listen to his slightly nasal voice coming through the wireless static. A few days later, after people had brought back their currency and gold to the opening banks, it became clear that the most important passage in his speech came when he said: "People will again be glad to have their money where it will be safely taken care of, and where they can use it conveniently at any time. I can assure you that it is safer to keep your money in a reopened bank than under the mattress."[12]

The crisis had been averted. As Raymond Moley put it in his 1939 memoirs, "capitalism had been saved in eight days."[13]

WHERE IS THAT GOLD?

In most respects the Emergency Banking Act was a success. It showed that FDR could get major legislation through Congress at a very fast pace. The Act was also an economic success: it saved the banking sector by bringing back confidence, injecting new capital into those institutions that needed it, and closing many small banks with inadequate capital and few performing assets.

In the days that followed the reopening of the banks, and to President Roosevelt's delight, many commodity prices began to go up. On March 30, the price of corn was 31 cents a bushel, up from 23 cents the day before inauguration. The price of rye climbed from 35 to 41 cents a bushel, and that of wheat from 50 to 54 cents a bushel. Only the price of cotton, the commodity closest to FDR's heart, had not increased during those four weeks; on March 31 it was 6.3 cents a pound, the same price it had commanded in early March. In figure 4.2 I present daily prices for these four commodities between January 1 and March 30, 1933; a vertical line has been drawn to signal Inauguration Day. During the next twelve months, the president would obsessively follow these prices, as well as those of other agricultural commodities; their movements often guided public policy. When commodity prices went up, the president felt confident; however, when prices faltered, the president would become very upset, and his tendency to experiment and try new policies would rise to the surface.

By March 29, 11,878 banks had reopened, out of 17,349 in operation before the holiday; deposits in the reopened banks were estimated to add to more than 90 percent of total deposits. Of the banks that had been licensed to resume operations, 5,387 belonged to the Federal Reserve System. More important, after the Act was passed the demand for cash, and thus hoarding, declined precipitously. By April 5, almost $1.3 billion dollars in currency had returned to the banking system.[14] What was particularly important was that the Federal Reserve had acted as a lender of last resort, by agreeing to issue its own (unbacked) notes and to make them available to all licensed banks—including those that were not members of the System—with any-high quality asset as collateral.

Markets reacted to the passing of the Emergency Banking Act—and to the president's Fireside Chat, for that matter—very positively. The New York Stock Exchange reopened on Wednesday March 15 to brisk business. More than three million shares changed hands, and prices increased by an astonishing 15.7 percent relative to March 3, the last day of trading before the bank holiday. The reaction abroad was also very optimistic, with the dollar strengthening considerably with respect to the pound sterling, a currency that was off gold and whose value responded to market forces; the dollar appreciated by 7 percent relative to its March 3 value.

A week later, and in spite of the apprehension of some government officials, a new $800 million issue of Treasury bills with coupons ranging from 4 percent to 4.5 percent was oversubscribed by a ratio of 2.3 to 1, and easily sold. Ironically, and in spite of the fact that banks were not allowed to make payments in gold, these new securities included the gold clause, and were to be paid in "gold coin." The fact that throughout the first three months of the Roosevelt administration the Treasury continued to issue debt denominated in gold coin, or subject to the gold clause, was to become a key issue in future legal (and policy) discussions on the abrogation of the gold clause and the annulment of private and public debt contracts.

The fact that the Trading with the Enemy Act of 1917 was used as the legal authority to declare a national banking holiday, led many observers to believe that the gold embargo would be temporary. After a few weeks, once things were fully under control, gold purchases and shipments would once again be allowed. On March 7, respected reporter Walter Lippmann wrote a column titled "A good crisis," in which he asserted that gold payments had only been "suspended" and that at some point in the future they would resume.[15]

But things did not turn out to be that way. In spite of the Emergency Banking Act's overall success, there was one area were progress was more sluggish than anticipated: the amount of gold redeposited into the banking system was lower than expected. On March 29, three weeks after the new Administration had taken over, the stock of monetary gold stood $188 million below its February 21 level. Even the prospects of having lists of "gold hoarders" published by the press did not result in gold returning to banks at the rate anticipated by the Federal Reserve. According to informed sources, after the banks had reopened on March 13 one billion dollars of bullion and gold certificates continued to be hoarded.

The government decided to deal with this problem by issuing, on April 5, an Executive Order that forbade "the hoarding of gold coin, gold bullion and gold certificates." As noted in the Introduction to this book, "individuals, partnerships, associations and corporations" were required to sell all their gold holdings to the Federal Reserve at the official price of $20.67 an ounce. Those who failed to deliver their metal by the May 1 deadline were subject to a fine of not more than $10,000 and a prison term of "not more than 10 years." This Executive Order also authorized the secretary of state to issue licenses for the exportation of gold under certain circumstances; what this circumstances exactly were, was not specified, a situation that created considerable confusion among market participants.[16]

As soon as the banking collapse was averted, FDR turned to other matters. He was under no illusion that the success of the Emergency Act

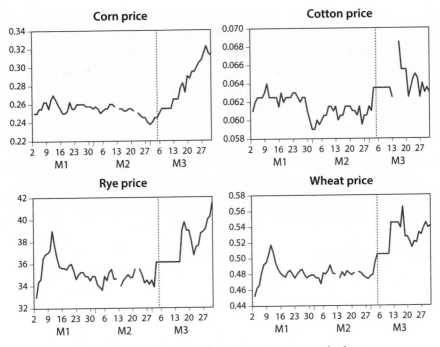

FIGURE 4.2. Daily price of corn, cotton, rye, and wheat,
January 2 1933–March 31 1933.

would suffice; new initiatives had to be put in place to get out of the Depression. But where to start? What to do first and what to do next?

Two things were clear to his closest advisers, including the members of the Brains Trust: First, the economic situation continued to be critical. In particular, unemployment, the fiscal deficit, and depressed prices were pressing and persistent problems. Second, getting the national economy going was a priority that superseded any international consideration or policy objective. That is, it was more important to raise domestic prices than to stabilize international exchanges or to forge a new international order that would allow (or entice) the UK to return to the gold standard and a fixed parity. It was true that the London Monetary and Economic Conference, an international gathering of over sixty nations, was looming in the horizon, but any issue related to the international economy that conflicted with domestic goals was to be postponed. Besides these broad principles, FDR and his team were largely in the dark. This is the way Raymond Moley put it in his second volume of memoirs: [17]

While there were plenty of campaign promises to keep, there was lack of specifics. There was no over-all plan. There were only pieces of a program and ideas that still lacked formulation. . . . On March 18 we were at a much greater disadvantage than we had been when facing the bank crisis. For then we had blueprints from [Undersecretary Arthur] Ballantine and other Hoover holdovers. . . . Now, so far as a legislative program went, we had only a few prefabricated specifics.

CHAPTER 5

◇◇◇◇◇

Moderate Inflation Is Necessary and Desirable

March 18, 1933–April 17, 1933

Senator Burton K. Wheeler from Montana was a "Radical Democrat," a progressive who for a long time had championed the rights of unions and farmers, and who believed that inflation would solve the country's ills in little time. The high point of his political career was not his effort to generate inflation, nor that he parted ways with FDR after the president's attempt to pack the Supreme Court in 1937, but the fact that almost twenty-five years after his death he became a fictional U.S. vice president in Philip Roth's novel *The Plot against America*. In that story, Charles Lindbergh has been elected president in 1940 instead of FDR, and the famed aviator has chosen Wheeler, who was an ardent isolationist, as his running mate. In the Lindbergh-Wheeler administration America decides not to enter World War II, and maintains a friendly attitude towards the Axis. An assimilation program is put in place, and young Jews are forced to move to the countryside and work on farms, where according to the fictional Wheeler they would become imbued with America's pioneer spirit, would learn to raise pigs, and would end up loving bacon.

In January 1933, during Congress's lame duck session, Senator Wheeler introduced a bill to remonetize silver. His rhetoric was similar to that of William Jennings Bryan in 1896. He attacked the gold standard and celebrated bimetallism; he praised the men in the prairies and declared that America's values were best represented by the agricultural states. The amendment was easily defeated by a 56 to 18 vote.[1] But Senator Wheeler did not give up easily, and in early April 1933, he reintroduced his bill. There was a new Congress with many new Democratic members from the silver and agricultural states, and a new president who during the campaign had vaguely said that he would "do something for silver." Wheeler's bill, which was entered as an amendment to the Agricultural Adjustment Act, was simple: the Treasury would be allowed to purchase silver in massive amounts, in order to move the price ratio of gold relative to silver to 16, a ratio that had prevailed during most of the bimetallism period—until 1873 when silver was demonetized. That meant raising the price of silver from approximately 40 cents to $1.29 an ounce. The very popular priest Father Coughlin supported the amendment in many of his speeches. His radio programs had a decisive Bryanian flavor, and when listening to him older people remembered the fiery words delivered by Bryan himself: "You shall not crucify mankind upon a cross of gold."

Secretary of the Treasury Will Woodin opposed Wheeler's silver coinage amendment strongly, as he believed that it would result in the reopening of scores of abandoned silver mines, in an enormous injection of liquidity, in massive outflows of gold, and in very high inflation. FDR also rejected the amendment. If it passed, he would be forced into a single course of action to fight the Depression. As noted, the president liked to experiment, and that meant having multiple options on the table. He wanted to consider all the alternatives, choosing one and then the other, until one of them worked.

A RURAL EMERGENCY

The president and his advisers knew that the political situation was volatile. On April 3, 1933, four weeks after the passing of the Emergency Banking Act, Rex Tugwell, who had taken the post of assistant secretary of agriculture, wrote in his diary: "It is hard to foresee for how long the general public's approval we have had so far will last. Not very long, I think."[2]

This feeling of fragility was shared by others, including by many key Democratic members of Congress. The public had great expectations about the new administration, and at the same time very little patience. It was true that the total collapse of the banking system had been averted, that a number of legislative initiatives had been launched, and that the first steps towards repealing Prohibition had been taken, but people expected much more. There was no indication that unemployment would abate any time soon, or that meaningful relief was coming. In spite of the Emergency Banking Act, many banks in small cities and towns still hadn't reopened their doors to the public. Frustration was particularly deep in the rural states where the pace of farm foreclosures had picked up since Inauguration. In many communities, unrest was so profound that political leaders feared that there would be generalized riots, and that mobs of angry farmers would lynch officials in charge of foreclosure auctions. Indeed, that was what happened in Lemars, Iowa, where more than 500 irate debtors tried to hang Judge Charles Bradley.[3] The National Guard was called in to patrol the roads of Plymouth County, and fifteen farmers were arrested and court-martialed, as civil tribunals had been suspended. This made things even worse, and the community rioted once again, demanding that the accused be tried before a jury of their peers.[4] In early May, FDR received an urgent call from Governor Floyd B. Olsen of Minnesota who told him that "unless something was done soon, he was afraid that . . . they might have a repetition of what happened in the State of Iowa: namely a demonstration by the farmers against the courts."[5]

At the center of this deep discontent was the fact that agricultural prices continued to be depressed; they had climbed up immediately after Inauguration, only to slide back once again. For some crops, such as cotton, prices were even lower than what they had been just before the presidential election. For others, including wheat, corn, rye, and barley, prices were barely higher than what they were in the final days of the Hoover Administration.

During the presidential campaign Roosevelt promised, again and again, to aid farmers and to help the little people who lived in the rural sector. He proposed mortgage relief, conservation programs, and improved rural infrastructure—power, roads, and waterways. But the most important way of helping farmers, he said repeatedly, was to end the deflation and to make sure that, one way or another, agricultural prices would increase. In his famous "Forgotten Man" speech of April 7, 1932, candidate Roosevelt had said:[6]

> approximately one-half of our whole population, fifty or sixty million people, earn their living by farming. . . . They are receiving for

farm products less than the cost to them of growing these farm products. . . . I cannot escape the conclusion that one of the essential parts of a national program of restoration must be to restore purchasing power to the farming half of the country.

Between 1919 and 1932, the average price of an acre of land for farming declined by almost 60 percent; the average price of cattle dropped by 63 percent, and that of hogs by almost 80 percent. The price of a dozen eggs went from 41.3 cents in 1919 to only 14.2 cents in 1933—a decline of 66 percent. A bushel of wheat that in 1919 had commanded 1.53 dollars was sold at 13.5 cents in 1932. And the price of cotton, the commodity that Roosevelt would monitor throughout his presidency, experienced a decline from 35.34 cents per pound in 1919, to 6.52 cents in 1932—a reduction of 82 percent. As soon as he was sworn in as president, FDR pointed out that he wanted to see a price of cotton above 10 cents a pound by the end of 1933. In May, however, he became more ambitious and announced that the goal of his economic policy was to return agricultural prices to their 1926 level. For wheat that was 1.22 dollars per bushel, while for cotton it meant 12.5 cents per pound, almost double what it had been during 1932.[7] Some analysts noted that using 1919 as the base year for comparison was misleading, as commodity prices where abnormally high as a result of the Great War. This, however, was not an argument favored by farmers. Many of them had incurred debts around that time, and the real value of their mortgage payments had increased significantly relative to their income. In the months to come, FDR would repeatedly use 1926 as the point of reference for discussing commodity prices. Again and again he pointed out that the goal of his Administration was to return prices of agricultural goods to the level they had had in that particular year.

Throughout 1919–1932 prices of manufactured goods and of inputs used in the agricultural sector—including tractors and fertilizers—also declined, but by much less than those of agricultural commodities. Throughout the campaign, the members of the Brains Trust were insistent on the need for "relative prices" to be realigned. Deflation had moved many prices out of line with each other, and planning of some sort—probably along the lines of the future National Recovery Act (NRA)—could bring prices in different sectors back into equilibrium.

Before the presidential election, Rex Tugwell told the governor that the "real trouble was lack of correspondence, of fair relationship among prices, and a general lifting would not cure that."[8] In August 1932, Tugwell came back to relative prices and their misalignment, when he told FDR, "It is not the collapse of prices but the collapse of some prices and the rigidity of others which has resulted in the present untenable predicament."[9] Roosevelt addressed the relative prices issue when he wrote that "the prices which the farmer paid for things he bought did not decline as rapidly [as farm products' prices]. In contrast with the 55 percent decline in farm prices from 1929 to 1933, the prices of things he [the farmer] bought fell by only 30 percent."[10]

On March 9, the day the Emergency Banking Act was signed into law by the president, a group of eight farm organizations, including the National Grange and the National Association of Milk Producers, issued a statement urging the government to put in place a program "of monetary reform to definitely raise price levels, increase employment, protect the values, and to preserve equities and bank assets."[11] Implicit in this statement was the idea that the dollar should be unhinged from gold, and devalued.

Rex Tugwell and his new boss, Secretary of Agriculture Henry A. Wallace, realized that there was no time to waste; farm relief legislation was urgent. Tugwell wrote in his diary: "On the first Sunday after Inauguration, it occurred to us that something like the broad powers assumed for banking might also be used for farming. . . . We had hoped to get the thing through before lobbyists . . . could descend on Washington."[12]

After holding a conference with farm leaders from throughout the country, it was decided to push forward with a series of emergency initiatives aimed at providing farm relief. On March 16, the president sent to Congress a message titled "New Means to Rescue Agriculture," where he presented the general ideas in his plan. Time was of essence, the message said, because "the spring crops will soon be planted and if we wait another month or six weeks the effect on the prices of this year's crops will be wholly lost."[13] On April 3, Tugwell confided to his diary that "the administration of this farm bill, we are perfectly aware, can make or break this whole Democratic venture."[14]

The government's proposal was based on four key principles: First, there was a need to restrict supply. This was to be done by paying farmers for not planting all of their land. This meant that in some regions crops had to be ploughed under, a policy resisted by many farm leaders and social commentators, who argued that in a world where so many people went hungry it was immoral to destroy crops. Second, mortgage relief was to be provided directly by the government. Third, funds to pay farmers for restricting the acreage planted were to come from taxes levied on food-processing companies and manufacturers of farm equipment. It was this provision of the law that the Supreme Court objected to in early 1936, when it ruled that the Agricultural Adjustment Act (AAA) was unconstitutional. And fourth, the government would work to open foreign markets. This required broad international negotiations aimed at lowering import tariffs and encouraging international trade, a subject of great interest to Secretary of State Cordell Hull, and a topic that he expected would be at the center of the forthcoming London Monetary and Economic Conference.

The agricultural lobby reacted in a divided way to the president's message. Food processors and equipment manufacturers were up in arms, and rapidly became organized to oppose the legislation. Naturally, they were not happy that their sales would be taxed to subsidize farmers for not planting their land. Small farmers, on the other hand, were happy with the notion of mortgage relief, but what they really desired were higher incomes, and that meant higher prices for their crops and products. Tugwell wrote that "for real radicals such as Wheeler . . . [the proposed legislation] is not enough; for conservatives it is too much; for Jefferson democrats it is a new control which they distrust."[15]

What everyone within the agricultural bloc agreed on was that the bill would not increase commodity prices fast enough. They had waited for a long time—at least since the early 1920s—and they now demanded quick results. That meant that the bill had to include measures that, in their view, would very rapidly impact prices. For many, including for the members of William Randolph Hearst's Committee for the Nation, the only way to raise prices rapidly was to give up the gold standard and devalue the dollar. Walter Lippmann was broadly in agreement with the need to generate some form of inflation. But he also saw dangers. On March 8, he published a column stating that it was very important to keep in mind that there was a "difference between a moderate inflation, which is now necessary and desirable, and an immediate and uncontrolled inflation, which would be disastrous."[16]

INFLATION BY STATUTE

After Inauguration, sentiment in Congress changed markedly. In April, the new inflationary amendment proposed by Senator Wheeler gathered considerable force among members from both political parties. So much so that senators friendly to the administration feared that it would pass. Ray Moley noted in his 1939 memoirs that this forced FDR to formulate a new strategy. The White House promised some senators that if they changed positions and opposed Wheeler's plan, the administration would go along with a different amendment that would give the president several options for generating "controlled inflation." After much negotiating and cajoling, and after a number of senators switched sides, on April 17 the Wheeler amendment was defeated by 43 to 33. However, no one failed to notice that in barely ninety days the votes for silver had almost doubled.

According to Raymond Moley, "Roosevelt had conclusive evidence on April 17 that the Senate contained a majority in favor of inflation."[17] Walter Lippmann agreed, and on April 18 wrote: "The vote in Congress shows that resort to a definite plan of controlled inflation cannot be delayed much longer. Either the Administration acting through the Treasury and the Federal Reserve System will take charge of the inflation and manage it, or Congress will produce the inflation by statute."[18] Herbert Feis, an adviser to the State Department and the only professional economist who participated actively in the whole process leading to the abrogation of the gold clause and, eventually, to the official devaluation of the dollar in January 1934, wrote in his memoirs: "By the spring of 1933 diverse organizations and groups were crying aloud for some kind of monetary inflation or devaluation, or both."[19]

Senator Elmer Thomas from Oklahoma was not as well-known as his colleague Burt Wheeler, but he was a respected progressive who had always defended the interest of farmers and of Native Americans. He had been in the Senate since 1927, and from the first day he had supported an expansive monetary policy. He was tall and silver-haired, dressed smartly, and spoke slowly and in long and elaborate sentences. He was such a severe critic of the Federal Reserve that on January 15, 1934, he was featured on the cover of *Time Magazine* with Father Coughlin; the article referred to them as the two most prominent leaders of the "inflationist" movement.

FIGURE 5.1. Senator Elmer Thomas from Oklahoma.
His amendment to the AAA forced FDR to consider seriously
the devaluation option. (*Source*: Harris & Ewing Collection,
Library of Congress)

As soon as the Wheeler amendment was voted down by the Senate,
Elmer Thomas was ready to offer his own amendment to the Farm
Relief Act. It called for the issuing of greenbacks, the free coining of silver,
and a devaluation of the dollar with respect to gold. According to Ray
Moley, "here were all three of the dreaded proposals for inflation bound
up together in a way calculated to enlist all the inflationary support in
Congress."[20]

On the morning of April 18 an urgent meeting was called by the White House to discuss this new amendment. After counting votes and talking to some loyal senators, including James F. Byrnes from South Dakota, it was resolved that "Roosevelt would accept the Thomas Amendment provided Thomas agreed to a thorough rewriting of it."[21] In particular, the president wanted him to strip a sentence that stated that currency could be created to meet government current expenses. This run against FDR's belief in a balanced budget and against the Economy Act of March 20, which was aimed at reducing the deficit by cutting expenses, including civil servants' salaries. After intense negotiations with Ray Moley, Senator Thomas did revise his resolution, and later during the day the president decided to back his proposal.

The *New York Times* pointed out in a front-page article that the main goal of the Thomas Amendment was the expansion of credit, not of currency.[22] There were four key components of the proposed legislation. The first provision authorized the president to negotiate with the Federal Reserve banks to get them to perform open market operations using government securities as eligible paper, a policy similar to what in the 2009, during the so-called Great Recession, became known as monetary "quantitative easing."[23] The amount of these operations was not to exceed $3 billion dollars. To put things in perspective, the monetary base was, at the time, $8.1 billion. The second provision authorized the Treasury to issue up to $3 billion in unbacked currency, or "greenbacks." These notes were to be used to retire federal debt. The third provision was the most important one, and gave authority to the president to reduce the gold content of the dollar by up to 50 percent, by proclamation. It also allowed him to determine the price ratio between gold and silver. And the fourth provision, which was included as a way of placating legislators from silver-producing states, including Senator Key Pittman from Nevada, allowed the president to accept up to $100 million in silver as payment for war debts.

According to the *Times* the "Democratic leaders in the Senate considered passage of the inflation bill a certainty." Republicans, however, were not willing to surrender easily, and decided to fight it with as much force as possible. Senator David A. Reed, from Pennsylvania, was to lead the opposition. According to him "if the American people knew what actually was contemplated by the bill they would be opposed to it."[24]

CONFUSION IN THE CURRENCY MARKETS

During the second half of March, and in spite of the gold embargo, the dollar had been stable in global currency markets. On April 10, only a week before the Wheeler amendment was voted on the Senate's floor, Alexander D. Noyes, the *New York Times* financial editor, wrote that many market participants were surprised by the fact that "the dollar is not depreciated in terms of other gold standard currencies; it continues to exchange at normal valuations."[25]

In figure 5.2 I present the daily evolution of the franc-dollar and sterling-dollar exchange rates between January 1, 1932, and June 30, 1933. The first four months of the Roosevelt administration are presented by a shaded area. Several things are apparent from this graph: Until April 1933 the dollar-franc moved very little, since both nations were on the gold standard. It is also apparent that the dollar-pound rate fluctuated even before April 1933, reflecting the fact that sterling had gone off gold in September 1931 and that its price was influenced by market forces. But the most salient aspect of this diagram is that the dollar remained stable in international currency markets even after the gold embargo was declared on March 6. As may be seen, the dollar only depreciated significantly against the franc during the second week of April.

On April 11, the dollar lost significant value relative to the franc, and came very close to the "gold point," or level at which it was profitable to export gold. The *New York Times* pointed out that "according to a recent executive order of President Roosevelt, the Secretary of the Treasury is authorized to license legitimate exports of gold. The banking community does not know whether shipments of gold designed to equalize exchange quotations will be included under the heading of legitimate transactions."[26] This mystery was clarified a day later when the dollar was subjected to a speculative attack and sank to record lows relative to the so-called gold-bloc currencies, and a number of banks applied for gold export licenses.

After demurring during most of the day, in the late afternoon of April 13 the Federal Reserve reported that the Treasury had licensed a shipment of gold to Holland. Once this news was known, a number of large banks applied for licenses for exporting bullion to France.[27] On April 15, three shipments were licensed. However, neither the Federal Reserve nor the Treasury disclosed the amounts of the consignments. In spite of these

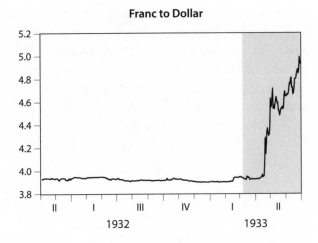

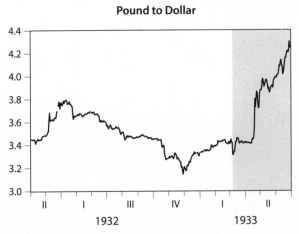

FIGURE 5.2. Daily franc-dollar and sterling-dollar
exchange rates, January 1932–June 1933.

authorizations, market participants found it difficult to understand why
"some officials of the Federal Reserve or the Treasury had not privately
suggested gold exports [as a way of stabilizing the exchanges], if these
were allowed under the regulations."[28] More than three decades later,
Herbert Feis, the senior adviser to Secretary of State Cordell Hull, wrote
in his memoirs that in mid-April "the foreign exchanges were in confusion as a result of the uncertainty that still surrounded the United States
Treasury with respect to gold exports."[29]

Two days before the Thomas Amendment entered the Senate, Alexander F. Noyes wrote in his popular financial column in the *New York Times* that gold holdings in the Federal Reserve stood at $3.32 billion, only a little shy of their highest level ever.[30] Why, then, was the dollar losing value in international markets? Noyes pointed out that policy makers in France wondered aloud whether the weakening of the dollar was a deliberate move by FDR to gain an upper hand in the negotiations to be held at the London Monetary and Economic Conference in June of that year.

CHAPTER 6

◇◇◇◇◇

A Transfer of Wealth to the Debtor Class

April 18, 1933–April 30, 1933

On the night of April 18, the president met with his close advisers to discuss issues related to the impending visit of British Prime Minister Ramsay MacDonald, who was on his way to Washington for preparatory meetings on the London Economic Conference. The group that assembled in the Red Room was small and included the Secretary of State Cordell Hull, the Secretary of the Treasury Will Woodin, advisers James Warburg, William Bullitt, and Herbert Feis, Budget Director Lewis Douglas, Senator Key Pittman from Nevada—an ardent supporter of silver—and the ever-present Raymond Moley, who in spite of being officially an assistant secretary of state continued to work directly with the president. Only Moley knew that Roosevelt had been negotiating a new initiative for "controlled inflation" with a group of key senators, including Elmer Thomas from Oklahoma. When FDR told them, with a chuckle, that the next day he would announce his support for the Thomas Amendment, Feis, Douglas, and Warburg became livid; they couldn't believe what they were hearing and interrupted each other in their efforts to convince the president that this was a mistake of historical proportions.[1] In 1934 Warburg wrote that as late as April 18, those who were in daily contact with the FDR had no "idea that he was seriously considering such a move."[2] Throughout the evening the president continued to smile and seemed to be enjoying himself. He teased the secretary of state and with "unruffled good nature" explained that getting off gold was his final decision.[3] After leaving the White House late that night, Lew Douglas told the rest of the group that without any doubt this was "the end of Western civilization."[4]

The next day, on April 19, President Roosevelt gave the thirteenth press conference of his young presidency. Reporters were particularly interested in understanding the implications of the April 5 Executive Order banning gold holdings: Were coins of numismatic value excluded from the embargo? Could gold be exported? Was the nation really off the gold standard? Throughout the conference, the president was in great spirits; he answered questions sharply, smoked several cigarettes, and joked with some of the reporters. Towards the end of the meeting he told the press corps that he was coming down with a cold. He then added:[5]

> If I were to write a story, I would write it along the lines of a decision that was actually taken last Saturday, but which really goes into effect today, by which *the Government will not allow the exportation of gold*, except earmarked gold for foreign Governments, of course, and balances in commercial exchange.

There it was: the president himself had clarified that gold could not be exported and, thus, that the nation had abandoned the gold standard. Then he explained that the main goal of this policy was to help the agricultural sector, which, as he had repeated so many times, had been struggling for over a decade. He declared:

> The whole problem before us is to raise commodity prices. For the last year, the dollar has been shooting up [this was a reference to the depreciating pound sterling] and we decided to quit competition. The general effect probably will be an increase in commodity prices. It might well be called the next step in the general program.

The official announcement came the next day through Executive Order No. 6111, which stated that "until further order . . . the export of gold coin, gold bullion or gold certificates from the United States . . . are hereby prohibited."

The reaction of global currency markets was instantaneous. In one day the dollar lost 10 percent of its value relative to the pound sterling, and 8 percent relative to the French franc. But, of course, not everyone was unhappy. A number of prominent businessmen—including James H. Rand Jr., William Randolph Hearst, and Henry Ford—who had organized themselves around the Committee for the Nation, were delighted. A few weeks later the Committee published a pamphlet whose first lines read as follows: "We should celebrate April 19 [the day the United States went "off gold"] as a Second Independence Day because it is one of the few important dates in our history."[6]

Commodity markets also reacted with force, reflecting the dominant sentiment among market participants and the general public that getting off gold, and implementing some (or all) of the policies in the Thomas Amendment, would help raise prices and bring deflation to an end. Between April 18 and April 24, the price of cotton increased by 12 percent, from 6.85 cents to 7.65 cents per pound. The price of corn jumped by almost 14 percent during those six days; the price of rye by 11 percent, and that of barley by 10.8 percent. During the rest of 1933 agricultural prices would fluctuate, and on some days they would even experience significant declines, but throughout most of the period their levels remained above what they had been on April 18, the day before the Thomas Amendment was introduced to the Senate.

In his 1934 book *On Our Way*, President Roosevelt told the story of what happened on the morning of the April 19, the day he announced that the nation was off the gold standard and that all exports of bullion were prohibited. The anecdote reflects how he felt about supporting the Thomas Amendment, and bringing a century-old monetary system to an end:[7]

> The next morning the Secretary [of the Treasury] came in to see me. I think that he and I felt very happy because we had cut the Gordian knot. His face was wreathed in smiles, but I looked at him and said "Mr. Secretary, I have some very bad news for you. I have to announce to you the serious fact that the United States has gone off the gold standard." Mr. Woodin is a good sport. He threw up both hands, opened his eyes wide open and exclaimed: "My heavens! What, again?"

Astute observers, however, noticed that there was a major contradiction. In spite of the significant changes that had taken place in the course of two weeks, there was a fundamental inconsistency: while it was illegal for Americans to hold gold, and it was prohibited to make gold payments to foreigners, the official price of the metal continued to be $20.67 per ounce.

SENATOR GLASS REGRETS TO DISAGREE

In Congress, the debate on the "inflation amendment," as the press labeled Senator Thomas's proposal, was intense and at times dramatic. Senators switched sides and alliances, and gave fiery speeches. On April 24, Senator Thomas gave a three-hour peroration in the floor of the Senate, where he said: "No issue placed before the Parliaments of the world in 6,000 [years] of history was equal to the one we face today."[8] When asked by Senator Reed if the motive of his amendment was to transfer wealth to the debtor class, Thomas replied, "No. My purpose is to add another plan to raise the commodity prices of the farmers and the producers of raw materials so they can live."[9]

Democratic senator Carter Glass, the man who only days before the presidential election had assured the American public that FDR would not devalue the dollar, or abandon the gold standard, gave a moving speech opposing the amendment. "With a low but intense, firm voice, and with tears in his eyes," he told the Senate that with his own hands he had written the "sound money" plank in the Democratic Party's platform, a promise that now was being betrayed. In his view, the Thomas amendment meant ruin for the country's credit and reputation. He ended his speech in a low voice, almost in a whisper: "I regret to disagree with my colleagues. . . . But whether it be a common-place, or whether it be sensational, I am one Democrat who is going to vote against this inflation amendment if every one of the ninety-five other senators vote for it."[10]

On April 28, 1933, and even though ten Democratic senators joined Senator Carter Glass in opposing it, the Thomas Amendment was passed by the Senate by a vote of 55 to 35, opening the way for the official devaluation of the dollar. However, eight months would pass before that step was taken. It was not until January 31, 1934, when FDR raised the official price of gold from $20.67 an ounce to $35 an ounce, a price that prevailed until August 1971, when Richard Nixon closed the Treasury's "gold window" and foreign central banks were unable to freely exchange their dollars for the yellow metal.

While the Senate debated the Farm Relief Act, including its inflationary component, the president continued to worry about the evolution of commodity prices. One of the first things he did every morning was read the financial press. He canvassed the prices of wheat and cotton, of rye and corn, of milk and eggs. He also analyzed the evolution of exchange rates between the dollar and the pound, and the dollar and the French franc. He would always do this before getting up. Sometimes he would do it alone, but more often than not he would do it with a small and selected group of visitors who gathered around his bed. The entries in the White House usher's logbook show that the bedroom invitees tended to repeat themselves morning after morning. Between March and June 1933 the president was usually joined at 9 A.M. by Ray Moley, Budget Director Lewis Douglas, and Secretary Will Woodin. When the visitors walked into the bedroom, the newspapers were scattered all over the place, and the president was finishing his breakfast. He would greet them, and then he had the first cigarette of the day. He took a Camel out of a shiny silver case and tapped both ends to make sure that the tobacco was firm. He then placed it in his ivory cigarette holder and lit a match. After taking a deep drag, he carefully put the match out and placed it on a large crystal ashtray.[11]

Being summoned to Roosevelt's bedroom was a badge of honor, an unequivocal sign of having made it into the inner circle, into that small group that got a glimpse of the big man in his private surroundings. And yet, as participants in these meetings observed many years later, it was awkward. To be sure, there was an intimate element to the reunions, but at the same time there was a clear sense that he was exercising his power over those that came to him. He had a quick sense of humor and could crack a joke or two, but he wasn't particularly kind. Indeed, at times he could be outright nasty or condescending to his advisers as well as to his valet Irvin McDuffie.[12] Dean Acheson, who was undersecretary of the treasury until November 1933, said that although these morning meetings were often "gay and informal . . . they nevertheless carried something of the relationship implied in a seventeenth-century *levée* at Versailles." He added that he often felt as if FDR saw him as a "promising stable boy." This sensation was echoed by many of his close advisers, including Raymond Moley and Rex Tugwell, who in his memoirs said: "Certainly I was not made to feel that I was an equal." [13]

THE "INFLATION LAW"

On April 28, the day the Senate passed the Thomas Amendment, the price of cotton closed at 7.5 cents a pound, still way off FDR's goal of 12 cents a pound. In fact, during the last few days, prices of most commodities had moved down. For instance, the price of rye had retreated to 44.5 cents a bushel, from almost 50 cents a bushel on April 24. Money markets also showed movements against FDR's plans, with the dollar strengthening against most currencies. On April 28 Sterling fetched 3.79 dollars in London, down from 3.90 just a few days earlier. The House adopted the amendment on May 3, and the AAA, including the Thomas Amendment, was signed into law by the president on May 12.

While the Thomas Amendment was being debated in both houses of Congress, a short story was buried in the inside pages of the *Chicago Daily Tribune*. On April 23, Secretary Woodin announced that the Treasury was about to issue half a billion in notes carrying a 2.875 percent coupon. The securities, to be floated on May 2, would be sold mostly to small investors.[14] A day later several newspaper stories noticed that, surprisingly, and in spite of the Executive Order banning gold exports, this new bonds carried the gold clause. According to the *New York Times*, many investors made much of "the fact that the terms of the new issue specify that it will be 'payable in United States gold coin at the present standard of value.'"[15] More than a year later, during the Supreme Court hearings, Justice James Clark McReynolds emphasized the fact that although the administration had already decided not to pay in bullion, it had included the gold clause in the May issue. To McReynolds, this was duplicity of the worst kind. Walter Lippmann also made that point when he discussed the morality of annulling the clause. He said that the "fundamental moral question . . . [is] whether a solemn contract may be altered when in the judgement of the representatives of the people their welfare requires it."[16]

On May 13, the *New York Times* published a front-page article titled "President signs farm bill, making inflation the law." The piece noted that the act gave the president unprecedented control over agricultural production and marketing, and power to generate inflation through money creation and a possible devaluation of the currency through the reduction of the gold content of the dollar of up to 50 percent. The article pointed out that there was no "indication to how much, if any, of this sweeping authorization will be utilized by Mr. Roosevelt, except that in a recent radio speech he reaffirmed his promise to maintain a sound money system."[17] After signing the bill, the president read a prepared statement, emphasizing the importance of mortgage relief for farmers around the nation. Not a word was mentioned about the value of the dollar, or the inflationary component of the act.

With the passage of the Thomas Amendment, President Roosevelt finally had the legal authority to officially devalue the dollar. A number of people had assured him that a weaker dollar with respect to gold would result in a rapid increase in agricultural prices. This was what the president was after: higher prices that would increase farmers' incomes and would reduce the burden of their debts in real terms. There was, however, one last difficulty for actually devaluing the dollar: the existence of the gold clause in most debt contracts. If this clause was valid, and debts had to be discharged in gold or gold-equivalent, a devaluation of the currency would result in an automatic ballooning of debts, and in generalized bankruptcies. Under these circumstances, devaluing the currency would be self-defeating. This problem, of course, was well known by analysts and financial experts. In fact, for a long time detractors of the gold standard had argued that the extensive use of gold clauses represented one of the most serious obstacles to any policy that sought to devalue the dollar and through this channel generate some "controlled inflation." Barely a month after the election, on December 16, 1932, Yale's Irving Fisher wrote to Ray Moley: "Personally, I would like to cut loose from the gold standard, but it is not an easy matter both because of the absolute necessity of gradually changing the price of gold and of the complications of the gold clause contracts." At approximately the same time, Professor George F. Warren of Cornell, the man who would play a key role in monetary and dollar policy during the second half of 1933, delivered a paper at the meeting of the American Farm Bureau Federation where he addressed the problem head on.[18] He recognized that a large number of bonds had clauses that called for payment in gold, and pointed out that this was a real problem. He then added that that was not the case for many farm mortgages or life insurance contracts. He explained that the Federal Land Bank and the Joint Stock Land Banks "agree to pay their creditors in lawful money and are therefore protected if they collect lawful money from their debtors." He then argued that if Congress devalued the dollar it could also invalidate the gold clause. He acknowledged that this act could be found unconstitutional, but argued that if that was the case, the profits obtained by creditors because of the gold clause could be taxed away. He ended by stating that "the gold clause is probably of little value to any creditor and even if it is enforced it is a minor matter when considering the innumerable effects of deflation. Ten million unemployed is far more serious matter than the gold clause."[19]

CHAPTER 7

◇◇◇◇◇

The Gold Clause Is Gone

May 1, 1933–June 16, 1933

During the second half of April, even before the Thomas Amendment was passed, lawyers began to discuss whether Executive Order No. 6111, which banned gold exports, implied an immediate and automatic invalidation of the gold clauses in debt contracts.[1] This question became particularly pressing on May 1, when coupons on a number of bonds were due, including on a United States Government Panama Canal issue. The contract explicitly stated that payment on these bonds was to be made in "United Sates gold coin of the present standard of weight and fineness." Clearing houses, which were in charge of collecting coupon payments, were not sure of how to proceed. The main problem was that even though gold holdings were prohibited, it was possible that some investors would demand payment in bullion for those bonds that included the gold clause. If that was the case, what was the clearing house to do? After several rounds of meetings with some of Wall Street most prominent lawyers, the New York Clearing House Association decided to make payments in paper dollars, unless the holder of the bond insisted in getting gold. In that case a certificate with the following statement was issued: "Demand for payment in gold refused." The owner could then use this document in legal proceedings against the issuer of the security, or against the government.[2]

On May 7, a *New York Times* editorial stated what everyone knew: eventually the validity of the gold clause would be decided by the courts. The editorialist noted that the Court's decision would have a major and lasting effect on America's financial and business world. The *Times* asked rhetorically: [3]

> What will the Supreme Court say about the fulfillment of a contract which is "payable in principal and interest in United State gold coin of present standard of value"? On the answer to this question will depend the policy of the Treasury and the whole American financial community in their approach of making good on approximately $100,000,000,000 in gold-clause contracts.

A day later, Turner Catledge, a prominent journalist who was to become the *New York Times* managing editor, wrote, "Will the Supreme Court hold that . . . any other dollar can be called a gold dollar in redeeming an obligation payable under its own terms, in actual gold coin?"[4]

THE SECOND FIRESIDE CHAT

Nine weeks after Inauguration, on May 7, the president gave his second Fireside Chat, where he explained in great detail the goals of his administration and the accomplishments of its first thirty days. He began by saying that when he moved into the White House the economy was on the brink of collapse, and that the "country was dying by inches." He argued that "deflation" was at the heart of the problem, and he proceeded to list the problems faced by industry, farmers, banks, and railroads. He declared that "all of this has been caused in large part by a complete lack *of planning*," an idea that had been planted in his mind by Rex Tugwell during the campaign. The president then addressed the question of whether recent actions—including the barrage of Executive Orders—meant that the government was taking over the economy. He said, "It is wholly wrong to call the measures that we have taken government control. . . . It is rather . . . a partnership in planning, and a partnership to see that the plans are carried out." [5]

And then, towards the end of his chat, FDR went into what everyone was expecting to hear, a long and detailed explanation of his gold and dollar policies, and of what the government was planning to do regarding contracts that included the gold clause. He started by saying that the nation had only one currency, and that although both the government and

FIGURE 7.1. President Franklin D. Roosevelt delivering a Fireside Chat in 1933. (*Source*: Harris & Ewing Collection, Library of Congress)

the private sector had issued large amounts of debt—approximately $120 billion—subject to the gold clause, they had done it knowing "full well that all the gold in the United States amounted to only between three and four billions and that all of the gold of the world amounted to only about eleven billion." In the eventuality that everyone wanted gold, he declared, only one twenty-fifth of claimants would get it, and the rest, "who did not happen to be at the top of the line, would be told politely that there was no more gold left."[6]

His administration, he added, had decided to place "everyone on the same basis in order that the general good may be preserved." This meant that every creditor, no matter how important or humble he was, would be paid in paper legal currency; this would be the case both for public and private contracts. He did not mention, however, how the government was planning to deal with the challenges to its policies in the courts—not a word on the looming lawsuits or on what he expected the Supreme Court to do once the issue reached it. The president finished the chat by restating that the main goal of these policies was to generate significant price increases: "The Administration has the definite objective of *raising commodity prices* to such an extent that those who have borrowed money will, on the average, be able to repay that money in the same kind of dollar which they borrowed."[7]

Two days after the Fireside Chat, Henry Morgenthau Jr., the governor of the Farm Credit Administration, and an old friend and neighbor of the president in upstate New York, told FDR that he thought that the speech was even better than the one delivered during the first Fireside Chat, on March 12, just before the banks were reopen. The president agreed, and said that he was eager to see the Thomas Amendment approved by congress. He said, "As soon as I have the authority from Congress to regulate gold, I can use it when and if necessary."[8]

FDR's main argument for declaring that the gold clause was invalid was that there was not enough gold in the world to cover all contracts subject to it. This was flawed reasoning. The purpose of the gold clause—or of any such provision in contracts—was not that the creditor would necessarily receive physical delivery of the metal. Where was he to store bars upon bars? How would he move them from one place to the next? As most analysts acknowledged—including economists Irving Fisher and Edwin Kemmerer—the purpose of the clause was to make sure that the value of the debt would remain stable when measured relative to gold. Indeed, during the 1870s the Supreme Court had ruled that as long as the amount paid in paper money was consistent with the original value of the debt when expressed in gold, there was no violation of the clause.[9]

Payments on a number of foreign bonds—French, British, German, and other—that included the gold clause, and were denominated in U.S. dollars, were due during May. How would they be paid? Was the foreign issuer—often a foreign government—going to abide by the gold clause, or was it going to pay in depreciated dollars? There were arguments for and against honoring the clause. On the one hand, any Executive Order issued by the president, or any law passed by the U.S. Congress, was only valid in the United States. That meant that foreign countries didn't have to abide by them. On the other hand, most dollar-denominated securities floated by foreign entities had been issued in the United States and, supposedly, were subject to American regulations and laws. If they refused to pay in gold or gold-equivalent, foreign governments could harm their reputation, and find it more difficult to access international capital markets in the future. The problem was not a minor one, since the difference between the official and market value of the dollar had widened significantly. On May 2, the market price of the franc was $0.0463, considerably higher than the $0.0394 parity that had prevailed at the end of the Hoover administration. In merely eight weeks the dollar had depreciated by 15 percent with respect to the French currency; there was more to come, and by early July the franc would fetch $0.0564.

On April 30 the *New York Times* pointed out that "many [dollar-denominated] bonds of the French Government and municipal issues are held by French investors who prefer to receive payment in gold than in depreciated American dollars." The article then added that "as it is illegal for citizens of the United States to hoard gold, the benefit that would accrue to the holder of a foreign bond through payment in gold would be through its resale abroad."[10] Given the quotation of the franc in currency markets, in early May, payment in paper would have saved debtors almost 11 percent relative to paying in gold, as established by the original contract.

Around that time the Reichsbank stated that Germany would make payments in depreciated dollars. The argument was simple: according to the German authorities it made no legal sense for a country to use a legislative act to eliminate its gold-denominated obligations, "while at the same time maintaining the gold value of its claims."[11]

During the days that followed newspapers carried numerous stories arguing that the combination of the gold embargo and the depreciation of the U.S. dollar in international currency markets was not only confusing, but it was also costly to American investors. British financier Frederic H. Hamilton noted that the war debts owed to the United States and "nominally protected by the gold clause far exceed the amounts due by the United States to foreign bondholders."[12]

A few days later, three French municipalities announced that they were making payments on gold bases. In contrast, the Italian government paid coupons on its gold-clause-denominated debt using the market exchange rate, which meant a sizable discount with respect to gold. Four weeks later, on May 31, the French government announced that it was paying its 7½ and 7 percent bonds issued in the United States in 1921 and 1924 according to the gold value of the dollar. This meant that investors would get 18.7 percent more dollars than if the depreciated value of the currency was used to calculate the payment.

The fact that no one knew if foreign issuers would honor the gold clause on their dollar-denominated bonds created a paradox of sorts. Suddenly, securities issued by countries with a lower credit rating than the United States experienced price surges. The sheer probability that they could be paid in "gold coin" made them more valuable than U.S. bonds with similar coupons and maturities. But the main problem was not sovereign debt floated in dollars. The main problem was private debt issued by U.S. corporations. It was estimated that private securities subject to the gold clause amounted to $100 billion; in contrast, U.S. government debt with the escalation clause was approximately $20 billion. If private debtors in the United States were forced to pay in gold terms they would suffer immense losses, and most of them would be forced into bankruptcy.

GOLDEN CHARTS

On May 8, one day after the second Fireside Chat, Henry Morgenthau Jr., provided Roosevelt with a set of charts on the historical evolution of commodity prices, including gold. Although FDR knew exactly where prices stood in any particular day, and had a general sense of their level in 1932, he had not analyzed long historical statistical series. The author of these charts, which Roosevelt examined with great interest, was George F. Warren, a bespectacled and rather obscure Cornell professor of agricultural economics and farm management, who had advised Roosevelt on land issues while he was governor of New York.[13] Throughout the next weeks, Morgenthau would present FDR with new charts and memoranda prepared by Professor Warren. The overall message in these reports was clear, and coincided with the views that Roosevelt had slowly developed since Inauguration: If the price of gold increased—that is, if the dollar was devalued relative to the metal—so would commodity prices. But Warren argued more than that; according to him, if the government raised the price of gold, higher prices for cotton, wheat, corn, rye, barley, eggs, hogs, and other products would increase almost immediately and in the same proportion as the increase in the price of gold.[14]

In a short article published two days after the second Fireside Chat, and buried in the inside pages of the *New York Times*, Arthur Krock, a journalist who at some point had been very close to President Herbert Hoover, pointed out that in his presentation FDR had not specified with clarity the year to be used as a benchmark for calculating the appropriate value of debts; without that information it was difficult to understand what the president meant when he said that people should be "able to repay that money in the same kind of dollar which they borrowed." However, Krock continued, economists "have gotten the habit of choosing 1926 as the year to which it would be fairest to return for values and prices." Once the benchmark year was made explicit, the reporter concluded, any "good statistician with a pencil and pad . . . [could calculate] the point at which the president wants to shrink the purchasing power of the dollar."[15]

In late May, a *Wall Street Journal* editorial made the point that from the perspective of private parties—individuals, banks, and corporations—the prohibition to hold, buy, and sell gold was like "an act of God" that interfered with the willingness to make payments as originally contracted. Even if a debtor wanted to abide by the gold clause, and pay according to the original price of gold, it was not possible to do it. The *Journal* added that "it does not seem that a man should be held to a literal performance of a contract after the sovereign power has made performance impossible."[16]

A QUESTION OF NATIONAL DISHONOR

On May 22, ten days after the Thomas Amendment was signed into law, the first legal plea related to the gold clause made its way to the courts. It did not come from irate investors who wanted to get payment in bullion; it came from Craig B. Hazlewood, the president of a trust company that represented 94 percent of holders of a mortgage debt in New York City. The Irving Trust Company asked the New York State Supreme Court for guidance. On May 27, a payment worth almost $2 million was due on a mortgage that included a gold clause and had been issued by the Libby Hotel of New York. Since payment in specie was impossible, the Trust Company asked the Court whether it should consent to payment in paper dollars, and "not insist on gold."[17] The question was whether by accepting payment in legal currency the trust company was fulfilling its fiduciary obligation to protect bond holders.

Two days later, New York State Supreme Court Justice Phoenix Ingraham ruled that the payment could be made in paper dollars. In making his decision Justice Ingraham specifically stated that circumstances in 1933 were very different from those in the late 1860s, when the United States Supreme Court ruled that payment on a gold-clause mortgage had to be made in bullion or gold-equivalent—the famous *Bronson v. Rodes* case.[18] Justice Ingraham wrote that immediately after the Civil War "two varieties of money were in general circulation, the gold dollar and the paper dollar. The latter of a much depreciated value. At the present time [1933] there is but one lawful medium of exchange."[19]

Almost every analyst agreed that the New York State ruling would be followed by a long series of pronouncements by other courts on the validity of the gold clause, and on whether debtors—both private and public—could legally discharge their debts using paper money. The prospect of having a myriad of rulings—many contradictory between themselves—was troublesome. What would happen to the nation's capital market if the gold clause was not operational in New York, but it was valid, say, in Illinois?

On May 26, Secretary of the Treasury Will Woodin announced that the administration would ask Congress to officially void, through a Joint Resolution, the gold clause both for past and future contracts. He added that although the Supreme Court of New York had ruled that a gold coin obligation could be paid in legal paper money, "confusion may be created if the existing legislation is differently construed in different jurisdictions."[20]

The timing of the Joint Resolution was also important. On June 15 a number of government bonds were maturing, and it was necessary to roll them over. The administration was determined that the new securities would not include the gold clause. In order for the bond market to operate smoothly, and to print the new bonds correctly, it was of essence that the gold clause be voided before June 5. To the dismay of "sound money" members of Congress, this meant a restricted debate on the merits and consequences of the proposal.

Democratic Senator Carter Glass, who had already broken ranks with the administration by opposing the Thomas Amendment, was incensed. In spite of his failing health, he gave a press conference where he stated that "the proposal to repudiate all outstanding gold contracts is unconstitutional and the courts will so hold if there is any integrity left in the courts with respect to the sanctity of contracts. It is utterly worthless to enact this

FIGURE 7.2. Senator Carter Glass of Virginia, Secretary of the Treasury
Henry Morgenthau Jr., and Henry Morgenthau Sr. (*Source*: Harris & Ewing
Collection, Library of Congress)

legislation with 40 per cent of the world's gold in the United States." Republican senator David Reed from Pennsylvania stated that the resolution
meant "repudiation and will discredit this country for a hundred years."[21]

Prices of most agricultural products jumped as soon as it was known
that the administration had asked Congress to repeal the gold clause.
On May 31 cotton fetched 9.35 cents a pound, almost 50 percent higher
than on the first day of the Roosevelt administration. The *Atlanta Constitution* reported in a front-page article that the "President's message brings
flood of buying orders into market in closing hours." It added that "gold
mining shares started upward well in advance of the new measure suggesting that there may have been an intimation in the financial district
that something relating to the gold standard was coming."[22] As expected,
and as desired by the president, the dollar lost ground in international
markets relative both to sterling and the French franc. Sterling gained 2
percent, the franc 1.75 percent, and the Swiss franc 7 percent.

Congress decided to act quickly, and on May 27 the Banking Committees of both the House and the Senate approved the Joint Resolution nul-
lifying the gold clause. Senator Glass tried to introduce a motion that
would exempt government bonds and war debts owed to America from
the Resolution, but his proposal was narrowly rejected. During the debate on the floor, Senator Arthur H. Vandenberg, Republican from
Michigan, said: "I am inclined to wonder just how far we can go reducing
the obligations. If the government can cut 20 to 25 per cent off their
value, why can't it cut them down 100 per cent? Where will the line be
drawn and who will draw it?"[23]

A central issue in these debates was, as Senator Glass had anticipated,
whether the Resolution represented a "repudiation" of the government
debt, and thus unavoidably and in a serious way damaged the reputation
and the good credit of the United States. This was the position taken by
most Republicans and "sound money" people, including Ogden Mills, the
secretary of the treasury during the last years of the Hoover presidency.
Members of the administration and its supporters in Congress, in contrast, rejected the idea that this was either repudiation or partial default
of government debt. For them it was just a practical way of recognizing
reality, and acknowledging that there was not enough gold in the world
to pay all debts with the gold clause in bullion.

International markets and observers reacted with alarm to the proposed resolution. Lawyers in London stated that if it was passed they
would consider initiating legal action in the United Kingdom. British
economists pointed out that since gold clauses on all securities and debts
would be repealed, the UK would save millions of pounds in war debt
payments to the United States. Professor Gustav Cassel, from Sweden, one
of the world's foremost authorities on currencies, declared that the legislation violated the sanctity of contracts and would diminish property
rights around the world. This, he added, would reduce savings and investment and would be detrimental for the formation of capital and for
progress and economic growth. Officials in Chile lamented that with a
weaker dollar—the final goal of the Roosevelt administration—their
products would be at a disadvantage in world markets. In France, one of
the few countries still on the gold standard, the main concern was how
the nullification of the gold clause would impact the negotiations at the
upcoming London Conference to stabilize the exchanges. On June 1,
France made payments on its government 7 and 7.5 percent bonds issued

in the United States in 1921 and 1924 using the gold value of the dollar, thus fully honoring the gold clause in the contracts. [24] A few days later, the Swiss government announced that in spite of the abrogation of the gold clause in the United States, it would pay its sovereign dollar-denominated debt in gold or gold-equivalent.[25]

On May 29, 28 Republicans joined 250 Democrats, and the House approved the resolution abolishing the gold clause, both retroactively and for future contracts. Arthur Krock wrote that this augured severe international problems. According to him, it was likely that many European nations would choose not to pay their war debts. In his May 30 column in the *New York Times* he wrote: "If they [foreign nations] do not attack the move as repudiation, they will at least seek to justify war-debt defaults."[26]

The gold-clause repeal was passed by the Senate on the late afternoon of June 3 by an overwhelming margin. A number of Republicans joined their Democratic colleagues and supported the government's initiative to eliminate any reference to gold in past and future private and public contracts. Several motions to introduce amendments—to exclude government debt, or eliminate the clause retroactively only for government paper—were defeated. Before the vote, Senator William Borah, Republican from Idaho, who supported the measure, said: "We must cease to pay tribute to the gold standard at the expense of the citizens." He added that "these [gold-clause] contracts were taken by the purchaser with the understanding that the government had the right to change the monetary system. The citizen must take the loss, must accept whatever Congress says is money."[27]

Republican senator David A. Reed tried in vain to stop the resolution. He declared that this was "the most serious question of national dishonor" since he had entered the Senate. He then attacked the Administration's duplicity; he castigated it for having issued, a few weeks earlier, half a billion dollars of notes that included the clause and promised payment in gold coin. He then reminded his colleagues that in November 1932, just a few days before the presidential election, then-candidate Franklin D. Roosevelt said that the gold clause was a covenant between the government and the American people.

After the resolution was passed, a smiling Will Woodin said that with this vote Congress was acknowledging the reality and tacit understanding that "debts do not have to be settled in gold. It is . . . ratification of the abandonment of the gold standard, which was to all intents put into effect through the approval of the Thomas inflation amendment."[28]

After the signing of the Joint Resolution into law, agricultural prices moved sideways without a clear trend. On June 7 cotton fetched 9.25 cents per pound, down from 9.35 cents on May 31. Corn was also down; wheat and rye prices, in contrast, experienced small improvements. As expected, the dollar lost ground with respect to both the pound and the franc; 2.3 percent and 2.2 percent, relative to May 31, respectively. On June 7, the pound closed at 4.085 dollars, still shy of the 4.25 that FDR wished to see. On March 3, just before Inauguration the exchange rate had been 3.46 dollars per pound; with respect to that point, the dollar had lost 18 percent relative to the British currency.

Many years later, in 1938, when he commented on the dollar gyrations of 1933, this is what the president had to say about the abrogation of the gold clause: "This joint resolution was a necessary step in effectuating the Government's control of the monetary system. . . . [T]he holding of, or the dealing in, gold affects the public interest, and is therefore subject to public regulation and restriction. . . . The gold clauses in bonds obstruct the [Constitutional] power of Congress to regulate the value of money of the United States."

THE HUNDRED DAYS ARE OVER

Congress adjourned on June 16, a few days after FDR had anticipated. The "Hundred Days"—which in reality were 104 days—had generated a whirlpool of political activity never seen during times of peace. The president gave ten major speeches, signed a score of Executive Orders, gave two Fireside Chats, held nineteen press conferences, and met with representatives from over forty nations in preparation for the London Monetary and Economic Conference; more important, he sent fifteen messages to Congress and fifteen major pieces of legislation sponsored by him became law—see the timeline at the beginning of this book for details. The accomplishments of the period were many: the banking system was saved, investment and commercial banking were separated, and steps towards unifying state and national banking rules and regulations were taken; through the Farm Credit Administration and the Federal Home Owners Act, mortgage relief was provided to farmers and families.

The Agricultural Adjustment Act (AAA) represented a major effort—much of it on experimental bases—to raise agricultural prices by curtailing supply and paying farmers to leave their land idle. Originally, the AAA covered seven crops; in 1935 nine additional products were added to the list. Supply restrictions were complemented by an active government purchasing program aimed at providing support to commodity prices.[29] Throughout the years, scholars and historians who have studied the Great Depression have concluded that the AAA was a major distraction, and did not contribute in a significant way towards ending the crisis. Indeed, many scholars have argued that it created significant distortions and inefficiencies, and perpetuated protectionist practices that ended up hurting the poor and retarding the recovery in the agricultural sector.[30]

Through the National Recovery Administration (NRA or NIRA), the Administration tried to introduce some elements of planning into the functioning of the American economy. As in the case of agriculture, the main idea was to avoid "overproduction." Coordination and agreements between producers and the government were supposed to allow firms to plan their investment adequately, avoiding overcapacity. Prices were controlled, and "excessive competition" was avoided and even punished. Modern scholars have determined that instead of helping the recovery, this program hindered it by creating a vast bureaucracy, and by introducing severe inflexibilities in to the business world.[31] One of the earliest and most brutal criticisms of the National Recovery Administration (NRA) came from none other than John Maynard Keynes. In late December 1933, he addressed an open letter to President Roosevelt, where he wrote:[32]

I cannot detect any material aid to recovery in N.I.R.A. . . . . The driving force which has been put behind the vast administrative task set by this Act has seemed to represent a wrong choice in the order of urgencies. The Act is on the Statute Book; a considerable amount has been done towards implementing it; but it might be better for the present to allow experience to accumulate before trying to force through all its details. That is my first reflection—that N.I.R.A., which is essentially Reform and probably impedes Recovery, has been put across too hastily, in the false guise of being part of the technique of Recovery.

For the purpose of our story the most important action of the Hundred Days was the abandonment of the gold standard, and the efforts to generate "controlled inflation" through a depreciation of the dollar. By doing this, FDR ended a monetary system that, one way or another, had prevailed since Independence. It had not been easy. Getting off gold had required, in the first instance, using a doubtful legal authority—the Trading with the Enemy Act—to declare a gold embargo, and to force people to sell their gold holdings to the government. But more important, in order to abandon gold it was necessary to annul contracts worth over $120 billion, retroactively. It was not clear at the time if the abrogation of the gold clause would survive the challenges in the court system. In his 1939 memoir, Ray Moley, the man who during the Hundred Days was closest to Roosevelt, the man who could see the president unannounced and spent almost every morning at his bedside, the professor who presided over the Brains Trust, wrote this about the abandonment of the gold standard: "Roosevelt did not abandon the gold standard because of any positive theories about an "adjustable" dollar, but to prevent further deflation. . . . Roosevelt accepted the Thomas amendment only to circumvent uncontrolled inflation by Congress."

CHAPTER 8

⬦⬦⬦⬦⬦

A London Interlude

June 12, 1993–July 4, 1933

On April 19, when FDR announced that the United States was off gold, British prime minister Ramsay MacDonald was on the steamship SS *Berengaria* on his way to America. The purpose of his trip was to have preliminary discussions with the president regarding the London Monetary and Economic Conference, which was scheduled for June. For the United Kingdom, the most important goals of the Conference were to obtain some relief from intergovernmental debts and to discuss trade and exchange rate issues. In mid-1932, a one-year moratorium on European government debts had expired, and on December 15 Britain had reluctantly made the scheduled payment, on the understanding that the issue would be revisited soon and that a new moratorium would be negotiated. On the exchange rate front, the most important question to be discussed by the two leaders was whether Britain should return to the gold standard, and if so at which rate should it peg sterling.

When the British learned, through a cable delivered to the prime minister in the *Berengaria*, that the United Sates had officially abandoned gold, there was a sense of disbelief. In his memoirs Sir Frederick Leith-Ross, the respected adviser to the British Treasury who participated in almost every negotiation with the United States during this period, recalled the impact the news had on the delegation:[1]

We were approaching New York when, on 19ᵗʰ April, we heard that the President had suspended the sales of gold which meant that the dollar had gone off the gold standard. As the Americans at the Preparatory Committee [for the London Conference] and elsewhere had been consistently pressing us to return to gold, this was a surprise, indeed a shock to us. Unlike the United Kingdom, the U.S.A. had ample gold reserves and could undoubtedly have maintained its parity with comparatively small loss of gold. It looked as if they aimed at a competitive depreciation of the dollar with the pound. However, the dollar parity was the anchor on which all the schemes for currency stabilization had been fixed and the sudden abandonment of gold by America threw everything into the melting pot.

Herbert Feis, who attended the White House meeting where FDR told his intimates that the United States was going off gold, and who tried to convince the president to postpone the World Conference till the autumn, also wondered why the British prime minister had not been informed ahead of time: "[T]he President and Moley seemed to find amusement at the shock he [MacDonald], Montagu Norman [the governor of the Bank of England] . . . and sundry other foreign officials were going to experience."[2]

The British were so upset, that on arriving in the United States they considered to "transship to the *Mauritania* (which was due to leave New York the same day) and go home, as the American action made nonsense of all the plans for the conference."[3] But they didn't leave. Instead, they took a train to Washington, where starting on April 22, and during the next few weeks, British experts led by Leith-Ross would meet daily with their American counterparts to discuss a generally acceptable plan to "stabilize the exchanges," and for both nations to return to some kind of new, modified, and more flexible "international standard."

For the UK, the debt and the exchanges were intimately related. In Britain, most debts—both private and public—were in pounds and did not include gold clauses. Thus, they were not directly affected by fluctuating currency values.[4] However, there were two important exceptions: the intergovernmental debts owed to the United States were denominated in dollars. This meant that a depreciation of sterling with respect to the American currency resulted in a higher cost to the British Treasury of servicing that debt. In addition, there was a 1917 bond issue denominated in dollars, which had been placed with private American investors and that included a gold clause. A key question for the British, then, was whether payments on these bonds were to be made in depreciated paper dollars or in gold-equivalent. In the weeks to come, this issue would divide British politicians, and would linger in the background of the London Conference negotiations for stabilizing the exchanges.

The vessel SS *Ile de France*, also steaming towards New York, carried among its passengers France's former premier Edouard Herriot, who had also been invited to Washington, DC, for preliminary talks with the president and the secretary of state, Cordell Hull. Herriot held orthodox views about monetary policy and was firmly behind the gold standard and free trade. As one of the very few countries still on the gold standard, for France the forthcoming London Conference was meaningless if it didn't address, first and foremost, the currency issue. Herriot was accompanied by some of the most astute and respected "sound money" economists in Europe, including Charles Rist, the author of a detailed volume on monetary systems, where he exalted the virtues of the gold standard.

France had not made the scheduled payment on her war debts on December 15, 1932, and that issue hung over the delegation; for all practical purposes the country was in default. In contrast to the United Kingdom, which after the Great War had returned to the gold standard at the old parity of $4.87, France had adopted a new exchange rate with a much weaker currency. This had given the country an international advantage, as its producers could sell goods in the international market at lower prices than their competitors and still make a handsome profit. The weak franc had allowed the French to run large and systematic trade surpluses since 1929. As a consequence, large amounts of gold had found their way into the vaults of the Banque de France.

As soon as it was known that the United States was off gold, a number of questions emerged in Paris regarding the gold clause. Was it still valid? And if so, how would it be made operational? Many French investors held U.S. bonds, both private and public. Would they be paid in gold-equivalent, or would payments be made in depreciated dollars? Also, France had issued a number of bonds in the United States, and all of them included the gold clause. Whether payments were made (or received) in nominal dollars or in gold made an enormous difference to both creditors and debtors. In an article published on April 21, the (London) *Times* pointed out that French prime Minister Daladier expected that these thorny issues would be resolved at the London World Conference.[5] In a related note published the same day, the *Times* stated that according to banker

J. P. Morgan—a man who was not particularly popular among European politicians—"the embargo on gold exports was the best possible course in existing circumstances."[6]

After spending three days in Washington, Prime Minister MacDonald returned to London on April 26. During his stay, he met several times with President Roosevelt, but no progress was made regarding the stabilization of the exchanges, the debt, or any other topic of substance. The most important agreement was that the London Conference would open on June 12. This was the ideal date, it was concluded, since Congress would have finished its Extraordinary Session—the Hundred Days—and the grouse-shooting season would still be a few weeks away in England. Whether the Conference would address the intergovernmental debts was left in the air, as it was a highly divisive subject. FDR wanted to discuss it separately and in a bilateral fashion, while MacDonald thought that the debt overhang was a major impediment for global recovery. For him, it was fundamental to discuss it in an international forum, as many countries were involved. After all, in 1930, and as a result of the collapse of Austria's largest bank—the *Creditanstalt*—Germany had stopped paying reparations, and that had triggered the debt difficulties faced by the UK and France.

THE CONFERENCE OPENS

The London Monetary and Economic Conference was officially opened on June 12 by King George. His speech was short and to the point. Next, Prime Minister Ramsay MacDonald delivered his welcoming speech. To the American delegation's dismay, midway through his presentation MacDonald addressed the war debts issue. He said that in addition to the subjects in the agenda there was a key problem that needed to be solved with urgency: "I refer to the question of war debts, which must be dealt with before every obstacle to general recovery has been removed, and it must be taken up with no delay by the nations concerned."[7] As Ernest Lindley pointed out a few months later, the Americans should not have been shocked.[8] It was unthinkable that the leader of a country besieged by debt payments would not mention his country's plight in the opening speech of a conference he was hosting. Two days later the British made a $10 million partial payment on the debt. FDR issued a statement saying

FIGURE 8.1. Pound-dollar and franc-dollar exchange rates. Daily data, 1932–1934.

that he accepted it as an indication that the UK was willing to pay eventually the full amount owed. Officially, the UK had avoided default.

During his first speech to the plenary session, U.S. Secretary of State Cordell Hull stated that it was necessary that as many countries as possible would adhere to a "tariff truce." At least for the duration of the Conference no additional protectionist measures should be put in place by any nation. He then recited the virtues of free trade, and argued that it was important to go even further than the truce; it was imperative to reduce tariffs and get the wheels of international commerce moving again.[9] Towards the end of his presentation the secretary of state addressed the question of the monetary standard and exchange rates. He said that the Conference had to deal officially with the "problem of a permanent monetary standard, and determine the proper function of the metals gold and silver in the operation of such standard."[10]

In figure 8.1 I present the daily dollar-pound and dollar-franc exchange rates for 1932–1935. The figure captures some of the main currency events of the period. In particular, it is possible to see the depreciation of the dollar on April 19, the day the country went off gold. The duration of the London Conference is indicated by a shaded area. As may be seen, when the United States went off gold, sterling fetched $3.86 dollars. That same day the French franc was valued at 3.93 cents. By the time the Conference opened, on June 12, the exchange rates had moved to $4.18 per pound, and 8.6 cents per franc, representing a depreciation of the dollar of 8 percent and 23 percent, with respect to sterling and the franc, respectively. These figures should be kept in mind during the discussion that follows on the negotiations to stabilize the exchanges in the short run.

THE FRENCH AND THE CURRENCY WAR

In the morning of June 14, during the second plenary session, French premier Edouard Daladier stated that the first step to be taken—even before addressing trade, prices, credit, production, or recovery issues—was to "put an end to the currency war."[11] For the French, there was an urgent need to stabilize currency values for at least the duration of the Conference. In their view, if that did not happen it was not possible to make progress in solving the world economic crisis. A few days before the Conference was inaugurated, the dominant sentiment in France was one of skepticism. Frederic Jenny, the financial editor of *Les Temps*, summarized his countrymen's views as follows:[12]

> We are unhappily forced to admit the conference is going to open its labors under conditions just as deceptive as possible. The fall of the dollar and the American repudiation of the gold clause has already singularly complicated its task.

With respect to trade negotiations, the influential French deputy Paul Reynaud said that any "attempt to revive trade between the nations will be in vain as long as it is possible to nullify any customs agreement by manipulating their currencies. Two of the greatest currencies in the world [the dollar and the pound] are not being stabilized, this necessary condition is not fulfilled."[13] French sentiments were aptly summarized in a *New York Times* article published the day the Conference was inaugurated: "The formal opinion of France, which will be upheld by its delegates at the conference, is that there can be no question of talking about lowering tariff walls until an agreement is reached concerning [currency] stabilization."[14]

In June 1933, France was one of the few countries still on the gold standard. The Daladier government was concerned with exchange rate stability for two main reasons: First, with depreciated currencies, American and British exports were more competitive, and were beginning to crowd out French exports in the global marketplace. Second, in the absence of an "international standard" of some sort, there was a possibility of a series of competitive devaluations that would force France to devalue the franc once again. Premier Daladier and his associates were perfectly aware of the traumatizing experience of a major devaluation, and the last thing they wanted was to repeat the 1919–1926 experience. For them, it was essential that the Conference return things to "normality," and this meant fixed exchange rates.

The French position, "stabilization first," presented a major diplomatic and logistical problem. It was very difficult, if not utterly impossible, to negotiate the immediate stabilization of exchange rates in a meeting with sixty-four very different nations, such as Nicaragua, Haiti, the USSR, Switzerland, and the Netherlands. The only way to deal with France's demands was to have informal parallel talks, involving only the major players—the UK, the United States, and France. While the official gathering dealt with longer term issues through two formal working commissions, short-term stabilization questions were discussed in an unofficial and restricted conclave. The American negotiators in these shadow meetings were George Harrison, the chairman of the Federal Reserve Bank of New York, James P. Warburg for the White House, and Professor Oliver A. W. Sprague in representation of the Treasury; Sprague had been FDR's instructor at Harvard, and an adviser to the Bank of England. The British team was led by the governor of the Bank of England, Montagu

Norman, and by Sir Frederic Leith-Ross for the Treasury, while the French contingent was directed by Minister George Bonnet and senior officials Jacques Rueff and Jean-Jacques Bizot.

The parallel tripartite negotiations were launched on June 9, before the official opening of the Conference, and dealt exclusively with two questions: Was it possible to stabilize the exchanges immediately and, at least, for the duration of the Conference? And, if the exchanges were indeed stabilized temporarily, at what level should that happen? On June 10, two days before the Conference was officially launched, the British intimated that they would like to stabilize at $3.75, while the Americans mentioned $4.25 "with the expectation of striking a bargain around $4.00 to $4.10."[15] The gap between the two positions was nontrivial, but according to the U.S. negotiators it was possible to find a middle ground.

In the weeks prior to the Conference, FDR had said that he favored stabilization, but did not state at what rate. In his second Fireside Chat, on May 7, the president declared that one of the goals of the Conference was "the setting up of the stabilization of currencies, in order that trade can make contracts ahead."[16] On May 29, two weeks before the opening of the Conference, Roosevelt had some concrete ideas on what he considered to be an appropriate level for the dollar. He told Henry Morgenthau Jr. and the banker Bernard Baruch that he would like to see the dollar-pound exchange rate go to $4.25; on that day sterling was $3.99, implying a further devaluation of the dollar of 6 percent. He then said that "he would like to see the price of commodities be based on a 75¢ dollar." At the same time he wanted to make sure that speculative forces were kept under check: "I do not want the stock market [to] go up too fast."[17] In his memoirs Herbert Feis, the only professional economist who participated in the negotiations that eventually led to the official devaluation of the dollar in January 1934, said that "it was hard to tell what the president wanted [regarding exchange rates]. His ideas veered and waffled. Even now, with my records open, it is not easy to trace their gyrations."[18]

For the British, stabilization was important, but not as much as for the French. A serious issue was at which rate to steady sterling. In his memoirs, Leith-Ross (1968, p. 168) said the following about the preparatory meetings for the Conference, held during May in Washington DC: "While we did not question the desirability of the eventual return to a stabilized exchange rate, we felt that more experience was needed before we could decide what precise rate we would be able to maintain."[19] In early June, just before the Conference opened, he remarked that recent fluctuation in the currency market made the decision very difficult. "Sterling which not long ago had been worth less than $3.20 was now fetching over $4.20."[20]

RUMORS AND MORE RUMORS

Starting on June 10, rumors and counter rumors flooded London regarding the parallel negotiations on exchange rates. Some reporters said that an agreement on short-term stabilization was imminent, while others believed that it would only happen once Raymond Moley, FDR's closest adviser and the former head of the Brains Trust, arrived with fresh instructions from the president. On June 13, the dollar strengthened, and agricultural prices dipped. The U.S. stock market, which appeared to have found its footing during the previous weeks, faltered. While this happened, the members of the official U.S. delegation were busy trying to deflect the growing uproar about war debts. The next day, the dollar strengthened further as a result of rumors indicating that the parallel tripartite conference had reached an agreement and that the dollar would be stabilized at approximately $4.00 per pound.[21]

On June 14, Secretary of the Treasury Will Woodin decided to put an end to the rumors and released a statement in Washington stating that "any proposal concerning stabilization would have to be submitted to the president and to the Treasury and no suggestion of such a proposal has been received here."[22] His communiqué, however, had little effect on market sentiments. The next day, June 15, the dollar strengthened further to $4.02 per pound.

On June 16, there seemed to be some light at the end of the tunnel. After long and tortuous negotiations that went into the wee hours of the morning, the Americans reached a tentative agreement with their British and French counterparts. James P. Warburg, who was acting as a de facto head of the parallel U.S. delegation, immediately drafted a report, which he cabled to FDR for his comments and approval. The plan, he explained, was simple: the exchanges of France, the UK and the United States would be pegged for at least six weeks at the level where they stood the day the agreement was signed; that meant an exchange rate with respect to the pound in the vicinity of $4.10, and of approximately 4.68 cents with respect to the franc; in comparison to April 18 (the last day the

United States was under the gold standard); this meant a dollar devaluation of 17 percent relative to sterling, and 21 percent relative to the franc. The New York Federal Reserve Bank and the British Exchange Equalization Account would commit themselves to make sure that the exchanges would indeed remain at those levels. That implied, Warburg declared, that the Treasury would have to backstop the Federal Reserve in case any losses resulted from the stabilization effort.

The president's reply was short and precise, and came on June 17. He would not approve any plan that implied the possibility of gold shipments or Treasury losses. Negotiations should continue until a better deal was obtained. Warburg took the rejection in stride; they had to go back to the negotiating table and try something else. George Harrison, the president of the New York Fed, was not pleased. He would not be part of a proposal that exposed the Federal Reserve Bank of New York to losses. If the Treasury was unwilling to provide full cover for the Bank, he had no role to play in London. The next day (June 19) he sailed back on the SS *Bremen* to New York. The press and the financial markets took his departure as a bad sign. It meant that the negotiations had gone poorly; all there was to do now was wait for presidential envoy Raymond Moley's arrival. He, for sure, would come with authority to strike a deal that would allow the Conference to proceed with its official business. On June 21, however, the (London) *Times* cautioned that not much should be expected of Moley's trip. It was unlikely, the reporter wrote, that Moley would lead the American delegation "into greater cooperation. His personal isolationist views are too well known to require elaboration."[23]

On June 20, and according to schedule, Key Pittman, U.S. senator from Nevada, officially introduced an official U.S. draft resolution on a modified international monetary standard to the Monetary Committee of the Conference. This proposal referred to the long run and was, in principle, unrelated to the tripartite negotiations on short-term stabilization that were being conducted in parallel. The delegates took particular note of three aspects of the American longer-term plan. First, gold would continue to be at the center of the modified system. Second, gold (and silver) would only be used to settle international trade. That meant that "gold either in coin or bullion" would "be withdrawn from [private] circulation." And third, all nations would simultaneously reduce the cover ratio to 25 percent, allowing for an immediate expansion in credit and liquidity; at the time the cover ratio in the United States was 40 percent.

One of the advantages of this plan, which was the brainchild of James P. Warburg, was that by lowering the cover ratio significantly it allowed central banks to embark in countercyclical monetary policy.[24] Although the proposal was generally well received, not everyone agreed with every detail. The Swiss, for example, argued that an appropriate standard had to rely exclusively on gold. The Uruguayan delegation also expressed some misgivings about allowing a high percentage (up to 20 percent) of silver to back the monetary stock. And the Central European nations were leery of committing to a regime that could result in large losses of their already low gold reserves. During the next few days, the United States introduced two additional resolutions related to monetary and exchange rate issues to the Conference. One provided general principles for coordinating monetary and fiscal policies across countries, while the other advocated the removal of exchange restrictions in all nations.[25]

A WAITING MODE AND A BOMBSHELL

On June 22 the press noted that the Conference had entered into a "waiting mode." Speeches were still given, and meetings continued to take place, but nothing of substance happened. Everyone seemed to be waiting for the arrival of the presidential emissary, Raymond Moley, the former head of the by now mythical Brains Trust. Writing two months after the events, Ernest Lindley described the mood in London as follows:[26]

> [The] American delegation produces two resolutions. . . . Nobody pays much attention. Moley is coming with instructions from Mr. Roosevelt. The Conference marks time. The French decide to wait and see if Moley is bringing authority to peg the dollar. Stories that Hull is going to be displaced or resign fill London and other capitals. . . . [On June 26] the Dutch Guilder weakens. The French are in a panic. American commodities and stocks skyrocket. . . . Secretary Hull's patience is exhausted. . . . The President seldom consults him . . . [and] his friends feel he is at the point of resigning.

Raymond Moley arrived in London late at night on June 27. He immediately sensed that Secretary of State Cordell Hull was unhappy with his mission, and during the next few days Moley made every effort to appear as a loyal subordinate, as someone who took orders from the secretary, as a mere messenger without any power to negotiate or make decisions. But no one believed him. The French were convinced that he had the authority to stabilize the dollar.

It was at that point when gold-bloc countries led by the French decided to issue an ultimatum: "Stabilize or we quit."[27]

After conferring with James Warburg and Professor Sprague, Moley concluded that the only way to save the Conference was to issue a tripartite communiqué indicating that some agreement had been reached regarding the short-run stabilization of the exchanges. He was perfectly aware that it would not be easy to satisfy the three powers. The document had to be general and specific at the same time, both vague and detailed. He met with John Maynard Keynes and U.S. journalist Walter Lippmann, who was covering the Conference for the *Herald Tribune*, to get their opinion on the wording of the text.

Just before leaving the United States, Moley had met with FDR to get last-minute instructions. It was a dramatic rendezvous in the middle of the ocean. The fact that Moley had taken a seaplane to get to the president, who was on a vacation on his sailboat the *Amberjack II*, added to the myth that the former head of the Brains Trust had plenipotentiary powers. As he would tell later in his memoirs and in numerous interviews, he got precise instructions from the president: on arriving to London he was to communicate to every delegate from every country that the United States would not sacrifice domestic goals in order to address international ones. With respect to the global monetary system, he was to emphasize that the aim of the Conference—and of the parallel miniconclave, for that matter— was to raise commodity prices around the world, and not to merely stabilize the exchanges. The real question, the president insisted, was how to generate "controlled inflation."[28]

During the evening of June 30, a small group met at the American Embassy in London to draft a declaration to be submitted to FDR for approval. Raymond Moley, Professor Sprague, and James Warburg were in attendance for the United States and worked on the exact wording. The French secretary of finance and Sir Frederick Leith-Ross were there with their staffs. The group worked on a very general text. The draft communiqué stated that the United States and the UK (the nongold countries) were to make every effort to control currency speculation in the immediate run. That was as far as Moley was willing to go; the French seemed to understand that they were not going to get a deeper commitment, and agreed on the wording. The word "stabilization" was not in the text, nor was there a pledge to devote resources to stop speculators.

Almost at midnight, the new draft was sent to the president, who had just reached Campobello in his sailboat, for his reaction and approval. In its central part, the draft communiqué said: "Each of the government signatory hereto agrees to ask its central bank to work together with the central banks of the other governments which sign this declaration in limiting speculation and, at the proper time, reinaugurating an international gold standard."[29]

To everyone's surprise the president rejected the text of what was now known as the "Moley Plan." In FDR's view, there was the danger that the statement could be interpreted as a commitment and a moral obligation to stabilize the exchanges and ship gold in order to maintain stability. Moley was shocked, but after a few minutes collected himself and told the American delegates that they had to draft a new text that included the president's main concern: commodity prices should go up globally before a serious attempt was made at stabilizing currency values. It was a simple principle, the old question of the horse and the cart. The French understood that there would be no concessions by the Americans and agreed to drafting a revised version. A new statement was prepared, and on the night of July 1 it was cabled for FDR's revision and, hopefully, approval. By now the president had left Campobello and was on board the USS *Indianapolis* on his way back to Washington.

But instead of approving the new draft, as Moley and everyone else expected, the president cabled his own message to the delegates. This communication written on the *Indianapolis* was the bombshell that for all practical purposes sank the Conference.

The president opened his message by stating that the Conference's failure to address real long-term problems constituted a "catastrophe amounting to a world tragedy."[30] He continued by asserting that "a purely artificial and temporary experiment affecting the monetary exchange of a few Nations only" was a fatal diversion. He then added that "the world will not long be lulled by the spacious fallacy of achieving a temporary and probably an artificial stability on foreign exchanges on the part of a few countries only." From here he went on to state that the fixation with short-term stability responded to "old fetishes of so-called international bankers." Then came the paragraph that, in Cordell Hull's words, "threw the conference into an uproar":[31]

[T]he United States seeks the kind of dollar which a generation hence will have the same purchasing and debt-paying power as the dollar value we hope to attain in the near future. That objective means more to the good of other nations than a fix ratio for a month or two in terms of the pound or franc. . . . *Temporary exchange rate fixing is not the true answer.*

A few hours after receiving FDR's statement, the representatives of the leading nations, with the exception of the United States, drafted a declaration that in part read: "[T]he American statement on stabilization rendered it entirely useless to continue the conference."[32]

What made the delegates of the large nations particularly unhappy was that as recently as May 16, Roosevelt had stated in a letter to world leaders that a key objective of the London Conference should be to "establish order in place of the present chaos by *a stabilization of currencies,* by freeing the flow of world trade."[33] They wondered what had happened to the president. Why did he change his mind in the course of a few weeks? What prompted him to write such a harsh communiqué? What was his ultimate goal?

But not everyone was dismayed. In fact, in some intellectual and business quarters the bombshell was well received. John Maynard Keynes wrote in the *Daily Mirror* that the president's decision was "magnificently right," as it opened the way for a modern international system based on managed currencies. A few months later, however, Keynes would openly criticize the active exchange rate policy implemented by the United States after London. On December 31, 1933, he wrote in the *New York Times*: "The recent gyrations of the dollar have looked to me more like a gold standard on the booze than the ideal managed currency of my dreams."[34]

STILL A MYSTERY

The London Monetary and Economic Conference failed because FDR became convinced that stabilizing the dollar, even for a few weeks, would bring to an end the rise in commodity prices that had taken place since the gold embargo on March 6. This belief was based, first and foremost, on the fact that commodity prices and the stock market had escalated rapidly after the abandonment of the gold standard.[35] That is, in the president's mind unpegging the dollar from gold—and, thus, allowing for dollar "instability"—was associated with raising agricultural prices.

The president also thought that it was possible to eventually stabilize the exchanges at levels that were outside of the ranges considered during the discussions in London. As it turned out, he was right. Eventually, on January 31, 1934, the dollar was stabilized at $5.08 per pound, a level that was even higher than the historical parity between the two currencies ($4.87 per pound). And second, the president was increasingly influenced by Professor George F. Warren's theories on the relation of the price of gold and prices (see chapter 10 for a detailed discussion of George F. Warren's role in this story).

In addition to these factors, during the first few days of the Conference FDR became increasingly annoyed with the French obsession with short-term stabilization, and their neglect of other longer-term issues. His displeasure grew significantly after the French failed to make the scheduled war debt payment on June 15. Herbert Feis put it this way in his memoirs:[36]

[T]he default washed away any remnants of Roosevelt's tolerance for the French effort to cause us to return to the international gold standard at a fixed rate to the franc, and made him more determined not to let the British authorities ease him into an agreement about the relative pound-dollar value which might be to Britain's advantage.

Raymond Moley never recovered from the humiliation he suffered in London. Wherever he went, people would ask him why FDR had become so upset at him. Others asked him how he could have misinterpreted so badly the president's views and wishes. After he returned from London, the president seldom asked him to meet with him during breakfast. His reputation and star were irreversibly damaged. On July 30, the *New York Times* reported that there were imminent changes in FDR's "Bedside Cabinet." According to the story, after the rejection of his "international statement on currency stabilization . . . Dr. Moley is in partial eclipse."[37]

On August 27, Raymond Moley, the man who had been at FDR's side incessantly, the professor who had been called the American Rasputin, resigned his post as assistant secretary of state and left the administration. His letter of resignation to the president ended as follows: "Friendship for you as a great warrior and chief and a deep sharing of political ideals are precious. These remain and give me encouragement and hope as I undertake this new task [editing the weekly magazine that eventually became *Newsweek*]."

The London Monetary and Economic Conference marks a major turning point in FDR's policies towards gold and exchange rates; there is a "before London" and an "after London." Until that time, policy decisions on the currency had been largely dictated by financial and political events that were beyond government control. In fact, and as noted in the early chapters of this book, during the campaign neither Roosevelt nor his close advisers had developed a plan on what to do about the dollar. Furthermore, many observers thought that during its first four months the administration had been behind the curve. The gold embargo decreed on March 6 was the result of a banking crisis that exploded during the last three weeks of the Hoover administration; the banking holiday of March 6 through 13 was based on a plan drafted by departing Treasury officials; the abandonment of the gold standard on April 19 responded to Congress's inflationist demands, including to the amendments proposed by Senators Wheeler and Thomas; and the abrogation of the gold clause on June 5 was the administration's response to the barrage of legal cases. Not only that, the London Conference itself had been imposed on President Roosevelt. It had been suggested in mid-1932 by President Hoover to the European nations, as a follow up to the Lausanne Conference on debts, and as a way of making a concerted effort to deal with the economic problems of the day. As will be seen in the pages that follow, FDR's decision not to accept the French and British demands in London marked the beginning of a new attitude towards gold and exchanges; in many ways it was a defining moment. After July 1933, U.S. government policies towards gold and the dollar became significantly more assertive. Instead of reacting to events, the administration took a proactive stance, and implemented heterodox policies, many of them, as we will see, based on the ideas of Professor George F. Warren from Cornell.[38]

CHAPTER 9

◇◇◇◇◇

Order in Place of Chaos

July 4, 1933–August 29, 1933

On July 3, the day the "bombshell" stunned the American delegation in London, FDR was on the USS *Indianapolis* on his way back to Washington after a two week sailing vacation. Two days later, he invited the British and the French ambassadors for dinner. He wanted them to know that in spite of disagreements on exchange rate stabilization the three nations had important business to attend to. In addition to the diplomats and their wives, the guests included Undersecretary of State William Philips and his wife—Cordell Hull was still in London doing damage control—Mrs. Guernsey Cross, and Sidney Sheldon and his wife. There is no known record of what transpired on that occasion. I assume that the two diplomats expressed their governments' dismay about the tone of the president's message. He, on the other hand, probably talked about a communiqué prepared by John Maynard Keynes, Walter Lippmann, Ray Moley, and Herbert Swope, explaining the U.S. position on recovery, currencies, and stabilization. But this is only speculation. What we do know from the White House log is that the dinner lasted until past midnight and that the president retired to his private quarters at 0:45 in the morning.[1]

For the next few days the president continued to deal with the collateral effects of the London bombshell. Reporters were puzzled by what they considered a major change of heart and asked difficult questions. Some wondered about Ray Moley's future, while others inquired about Prime Minister Ramsay McDonald's reactions to the president's cable.

Most of them asked about the apparent contradiction between the London message and the May 16 statement, where FDR asserted that it was essential to "establish order in place of the present chaos by a stabilization of currencies."[2]

FDR, however, had no second thoughts about his London decision. He was now free to use the authority granted to him by the Congress, and he could concentrate fully on achieving the domestic goals of his administration. Overall, his successive policy choices were moving the country towards a new monetary system and, hopefully, higher prices: the gold embargo of March 6 had been followed by the requirement that all gold holdings be sold to the Federal Reserve; then, on April 19, came the abandoning of the gold standard, and on May 12 the Thomas Amendment authorized him to devalue the dollar by up to 50 percent. On June 5, the gold clauses were eliminated from all contracts, private and public, past and future. It was true that there were a number of legal cases looming on the horizon, but he would cross that bridge at the appropriate time. He was convinced that the decision to reject the French and British pressure to hastily stabilize the exchanges had left the country in the best possible position to move forward. He could now concentrate on his two fundamental goals: raising prices and reducing unemployment.

In Roosevelt's mind, the fact that commodity prices were much higher than when the London Conference was inaugurated, confirmed that he had done the right thing. In one month—between June 12 and July 12— the price of cotton had increased by 22 percent, from 9.4 to 11.5 cents a pound; the price of corn had gone up by 42 percent, wheat by 38 percent, and rye by a remarkable 55 percent. In addition, the dollar had depreciated very significantly with respect to the pound; the exchange rate had gone from 4.18 dollars per pound on June 12, to 4.75 on July 12, a depreciation of 12 percent. In relation to March 3, the day before Inauguration, the dollar had weakened by 30 percent relative to sterling. There were reasons for the president to be confident and satisfied.

A few days later he suffered a reality check.

Suddenly things started to move in reverse. The dollar strengthened quickly, and commodity prices began to fall at a surprisingly rapid clip. Between July 17 and July 31, the price of corn declined by 28 percent, that of cotton by 15 percent, and the price of wheat dropped by 24 percent. During the same period, the dollar strengthened by 11 percent with respect to the pound. It appeared that everything had been an illusion, and

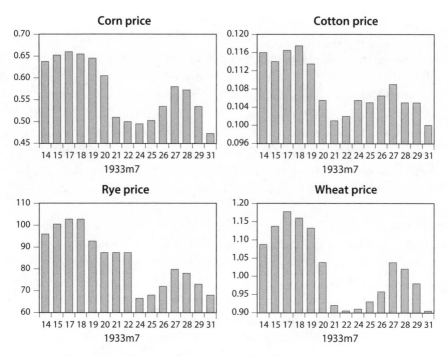

FIGURE 9.1. Commodity prices, daily, July 14 to July 31, 1933.

that the improvements of the last few weeks were just the handiwork of speculators. See figure 9.1 for details on the evolution of commodity prices during this period. The president had a major problem on his hands. The press was again questioning his decision to jettison the London Conference—which was still going through a charade of meetings and innocuous resolutions—and was wondering what he would do next.

The agricultural lobby reacted with fury to the collapse in prices. Many farmers detested the AAA and continued to demand rapid and real solutions. In Iowa, for example, everyone hated the idea of slaughtering baby pigs to raise prices. FDR was painfully aware of the situation. Indeed, he feared that if prices did not begin to increase again soon there would be an agrarian revolt, with hundreds of thousands of farmers marching on Washington. On July 22, he told Dean Acheson, the undersecretary of the treasury, that he was increasingly concerned about the news of farmers "stopping milk trucks and pouring their contents in the gutters."[3]

Meanwhile, there were significant and contradictory developments related to the abrogation of the gold clause and dollar-denominated foreign debts. While some countries, such as Switzerland, signaled that they would continue to pay their debts issued in the United States in gold-equivalent currency, others—including Germany—stated that the abrogation of the gold clause meant that they could make payments in paper dollars. Since the dollar had lost considerable value with respect to the gold-bloc currencies, paying in legal tender instead of gold implied significant savings. Many critics of the Administration's policy pointed out that the official price of gold was still fixed by the Gold Act of 1900, and continued to be $20.67 an ounce. To many leaders of the Republican Party this was a major contradiction that encapsulated FDR's duplicity.

On July 7, French government bonds denominated in dollars soared in price and commanded the highest price since they were issued. This was true both for sovereign bonds as well as for debt issued by French municipalities. This was a sign that market participants expected that, in spite of the Joint Resolution, France would continue to honor the gold clause in her bonds, and pay in gold-equivalent dollars.[4] Two weeks later, on July 21, the House of Commons approved a provision that cancelled payment in gold of UK World War I debts. Neville Chamberlain, the chancellor of the exchequer, said that the UK's legal position was abundantly clear. "The obligation that the British government undertook in 1917 has been abrogated by an alteration of the law of the land under whose jurisdiction the bonds were issued." The British government decided to exchange dollar-denominated bonds for sterling bonds at a depreciated rate. *The Economist* magazine severely criticized the move, and argued that the UK was being opportunistic and was departing from the original intent when issuing the debt.[5]

At home, suddenly, things didn't look much better than abroad. There was confusion and a generalized sense of the uneasiness, as everyone waited for legal challenges to the Joint Resolution to move through the courts.

CHARTS ON ONIONSKIN PAPER

Throughout these weeks, Henry Morgenthau Jr. continued to show the president Professor Warren's charts on prices, exchanges, and production. Morgenthau repeated again and again, that according to these theories, if the price of gold increased, higher prices for corn, wheat, and cotton would immediately follow. With growing fervor, he urged the president to try these policies. After all, Morgenthau pointed out, there was not much to lose. What was clear was that waiting for confidence to come back, as Budget Director Lew Douglas, Professor Oliver Sprague, and others recommended, was not an option any longer.[6]

On August 9, the president met in Hyde Park with James P. Warburg, George F. Warren, and Yale professor James Harvey Rogers.[7] The topics of conversation were gold, currency values, and commodity prices. The star of the meeting was, without any doubt, George F. Warren. FDR was fascinated by his elegant charts drawn on onionskin paper, which the professor displayed on the dining room table. At the end of the meeting Warren got most of the press coverage, and many newspapers barely mentioned the fact that Rogers and Warburg had also attended the gathering. At an improvised press conference, FDR showed reporters some of the professor's charts, and hailed the fact that prices had already returned to their 1914 level. When asked about the recent drastic and sudden collapse in agricultural prices, the president said that the move was "natural, normal and corrective."[8]

After the meeting, the president decided that he wanted Warren and Rogers close to him in Washington. He wanted to consult with them from time to time, get their views about specific aspects of his recovery policies, and discuss the evolution of commodity markets. He was particularly interested in having Warren near him. He had grown accustomed to looking at his weekly charts, and there was nothing better than having the professor himself explain them to him. It was arranged that Warren and Rogers would share an office in the old Commerce Building and that they would work with Treasury and Federal Reserve officials on ways to generate a permanent increase in prices.

According to the press, the Hyde Park conference and the professors' move to Washington were proof that the president would soon embrace policies aimed at attaining "the 1924 or 1926 price level in commodities." The *New York Times* added that the administration's ultimate goal was to adopt "a 'commodity dollar' which will fluctuate in line with general commodity movements instead of remaining as a constant factor through all periods of changing values."[9]

A NEW INTERNATIONAL STANDARD

Dean Acheson, the undersecretary of the treasury who was running the department because of Will Woodin's illness, became alarmed. He had a poor opinion of George F. Warren and thought that his ideas were based on statistical aberrations. He suggested the creation of a study group to produce concrete recommendations on how to generate higher prices and conduct monetary policy. He further argued that all polices aimed at reflation and prices should be coordinated by the Treasury.

The president thought that the idea of a study group had merit, as long as it met in secret and did not exist officially. Because the meetings took place in Manhattan it became known to its members as the New York Group. In addition to Secretary Woodin and Undersecretary Acheson, it was formed by Budget Director Lew Douglas, Professors Oliver Sprague and James Harvey Rogers, and George Harrison, Walter Stewart, and Eugene Black from the Federal Reserve. James P. Warburg was in charge of coordinating the views of the different committee members, and of drafting the group's proposal.[10] Warburg, a banker, was known universally as Jimmy. He was the son of Paul Warburg, the prominent banker who as early as March 1929 had warned his Wall Street colleagues of the imminent bursting of the stock speculative bubble. Jimmy was good-looking, well-traveled, and urbane. During the Great War he had been an ace pilot for the navy. He was married to Kay Swift, a gifted composer who after divorcing him in 1934 became George Gershwin's companion until his death. Warburg himself was a serious musician, and wrote the lyrics to some of Swift's more popular songs. Although he was not trained as an economist, he had a firm grasp of monetary policy and a rare ability to understand the way in which economic and financial variables interacted with each other. He had designed the U.S. official proposal submitted to the London Conference on a "modified international standard."[11]

During the next few weeks, the president received a number of memoranda and documents on monetary and exchange rate policies. George F. Warren touted his gold price plan, James Harvey Rogers advocated a devaluation accompanied by an intensive public works program, Oliver Sprague rejected both ideas and suggested patience, and Jimmy Warburg produced two plans on behalf of the New York Group. For the immediate future, the study group recommended that the Federal Reserve perform open market operations for eight to twelve weeks. Devaluation was to be postponed, and when implemented it should be done in a coordinated fashion with the British. The study group also recommended against buying and selling gold internationally, as a way of controlling the value of the dollar. According to the group, that policy—which had been promoted by Morgenthau for months—was very likely to trigger retaliation by foreign nations, including by France. For the longer run—what the group called the "ultimate program"—their proposal was very similar to the official draft resolution on monetary policy offered by the American delegation to the London Conference. It called for a devaluation of the dollar and for a major reform of the international financial system.

The new "modified standard" suggested by the New York Group would still be based on gold and stable exchange rates, but it would have a much lower and uniform cover ratio in all nations (in the 25 percent range). This would allow central banks to implement counter-cyclical monetary policy without being permanently concerned about the "free gold" issue. This "modified gold standard" had some similarities to a plan developed, around the same time (1933), by John Maynard Keynes.

In 1923 Keynes wrote what became a famous quote: "In truth, the gold standard is already a barbarous relic. . . . [I]n the modern world of paper currency and bank credit there is no escape from a 'managed' currency, whether we wish it or not."[12] However, Keynes's views on gold evolved, and by late 1932 they were much more nuanced. In 1933, he devoted chapter V of his pamphlet *The Means to Prosperity* to the possible adoption of a new gold standard and to the creation of an "international note issue" linked to gold. He wrote that the "notes would be gold-notes and the participants would agree to accept them as the equivalent of gold. This implies that the national currencies of each participant would stand in some defined relationship to gold. It involves, that is to say, a *qualified return to the gold standard*."[13]

THE INNOCENCE OF THE EARLY NEW DEAL

The president appeared to hesitate and to weight all options, but in his mind he was rapidly veering towards the Warren plan. In mid-August, he asked Dean Acheson to "try his hand at a draft (for discussion only) of an Executive Order offering to buy newly minted gold for 30 days at a fixed price say $28 an ounce and an offer to sell gold to the arts and dentists at the same price." Acheson wavered and dragged his feet, but Roosevelt insisted on seeing the draft as soon as possible. When the undersecretary tried to explain why he thought the plan was flawed, he was abruptly cut off by the president. Lawyers, FDR noted, were supposed to tell clients "what they could not legally do and not what they thought the client should do." [14]

On August 29, and in spite of Professor Sprague and James Warburg's opposition on political and economic grounds, Executive Order No. 6261 was issued. It invoked the economy's state of emergency, and authorized the secretary of the treasury to accept newly minted gold for sale on consignment. The metal could then be sold to individuals authorized to acquire gold—artists and dentists—and to foreigners. The purchase price would be "equal to the best price obtainable in the free market of the world after taking into consideration any incidental expenses such as shipping costs and insurance."[15]

By allowing newly minted gold to be sold at world prices, Executive Order No. 6261 cracked the gold door open, but no economist or serious observer thought that it was going to have any impact on U.S. inflation or commodity prices. There were two problems: First, by buying small amounts of gold inside the country only, the plan would have no effect on the world price, and second, the small purchases were made at existing world prices. Thus, there was no channel through which this buying program would affect the international price of the metal, exchange rates, the price of commodities, or of any other type of goods. Jimmy Warburg had tried to explain this to Warren, but every time the professor would turn to his charts and show the close relationship between two variables: the price of gold and the wholesale price index.

The press, almost unanimously thought that the main, if not sole purpose of the Executive Order No. 6261, was to assist gold producers.[16] Many years later, Walter Salant, a fervent New Dealer who joined the Treasury as an economist in 1934, referred to the policy as being part of "the economic innocence of the early days of the New Deal."[17]

CHAPTER 10

◇◇◇◇◇

The Gold-Buying Program

October 22, 1933–January 31, 1934

During the second half of 1933, George F. Warren was the most influential economist in the world. Almost every morning during November and December, he met with FDR while the president was still in bed, and helped him decide the price at which the government would buy gold during the next twenty-four hours. Henry Morgenthau Jr. who often attended these meetings, confined to his diary that the process had a cabalistic dimension to it. In selecting the daily price, FDR would, jokingly, consider the meaning of numbers, or flip coins. On one occasion, he decided that the price would go up by 21 cents with respect to the previous day. He then asked the group assembled around his bed if they knew why he had chosen that figure. When they said that they didn't, the president smiled broadly and remarked that it was a lucky number, "it's three times seven."[1] He would then write the new price on a piece of paper, which he handled to Jesse Jones, the chairman of the Reconstruction Finance Corporation (RFC). As noted, according to Warren's theories, higher domestic prices of gold would result in rapid and proportional increases in the price level and especially in commodity prices. The fact that today almost no one recognizes George F. Warren's name, let alone knows about his theories, illustrates how strange that period was.

The *New York Times Sunday Magazine* described Professor George Warren as "mysterious . . . , a sturdy man in his late fifties; not very tall, dressy or professorial; not remarkable in any outward particular except for his common-sense air and for a quiet, kindly dignity of the sort that comes from years of hard work."[2]

George Frederick Warren was born in a Nebraska farm in 1874. After college, he worked as a high school teacher and at age twenty-five he became superintendent of schools in Kearney County.[3] In 1902, he decided to pursue a doctorate in agronomy at Cornell, where he stayed for the rest of his life and where he had a distinguished academic career. In 1931 he published, jointly with his colleague the statistician Frank A. Pearson, *Prices*, a thick volume where they examined data for dozens of commodities for over two hundred years in a number of countries.[4] Soon after it was published, the book, which allegedly showed the close relationship between the prices of gold and other commodities, became the "Bible" for devaluationists from around the country. At around that time Warren became associated with the Committee for the Nation, the pro-devaluation lobbying group supported by Randolph Hearst, and during the next few years he helped the group develop some of its more technical arguments in favor of abandoning the gold standard.

FDR met George F. Warren in the 1920s through Henry Morgenthau Jr. who had a close connection to Cornell's farm management faculty. As governor, Roosevelt relied on Warren's advice on issues related to land conservation and reclamation. During the first part of his career, Warren focused on farm management techniques, on how to rotate crops efficiently, and how to grow alfalfa. He also devised way to improve hens' productivity, and to build better barns and stables. In 1913, he published the textbook *Farm Management*, which became required reading in almost every college that taught courses related to the agricultural sector. The book became a solid long-seller, and its royalties made Warren a fairly wealthy man—through its lifespan the book sold over 400,000 copies. *Farm Management* does not include a single word on gold, the gold standard, or the price level.

In 1923, as the agricultural sector suffered a fourth year of distress, Warren became interested in prices. A year later, he published an article in the *Quarterly Journal of Economics* in which he argued that farmers' standard of living would only improve if prices increased significantly. At the end of that year, he published, jointly with Frank Pearson, a book titled *The Agricultural Situation*, where they analyzed the causes and possible remedies for the sector's crisis. In chapter 25 they provided some evidence—mostly in the form of charts—of a tight connection between

FIGURE 10.1. From left to right, behind FDR: L. Oliphant, adviser to the president; Secretary of the Treasury Henry Morgenthau Jr.; Chairman of the Federal Reserve Eugene Black; Professor George F. Warren; President of New York Federal Reserve Bank George Harrison; and unidentified aide. During the signing of the Gold Act in January 1934. (With permission from Getty Images)

monetary gold and the price level, a connection that would become the basis for their devaluation recommendation in the 1930s.

Prices, the 1931 book, was impressive and a bit intimidating; it was full of charts and tables, and it contained long explanations of why there were price cycles. Warren and Pearson's conclusion was that prices went up and down because the world's stock of monetary gold increased and decreased through time. These fluctuations were the results of new gold discoveries and of increased demand for nonmonetary purposes. Price jumps were also the consequence of countries going in and out of the gold standard. This meant that the solution for the deflation that had gripped the nation for so long was rather simple: the availability of monetary gold had to increase dramatically. The easiest ways of doing this was by increasing the dollar value of the existing physical stock of gold through a devaluation of the currency.

Warren and Pearson further argued that future price cycles could be avoided by frequently adjusting the value of the metal. The relation between the dollar and gold would not be rigid any longer; it would "slide" up or down depending on the availability of monetary gold in the world. There was a similarity between the Warren-Pearson "sliding dollar"—often ridiculed by their opponents as a "rubber dollar" or "baloney dollar"—and Irving Fisher's "compensated dollar." But the similarities were superficial. As may be seen in the appendix to this book, the two professors had very different mechanisms in mind when they recommended unhinging the currency from gold. For Fisher this was only one component in a complex plan with many parts; for the process to operate properly the Federal Reserve needed to "cooperate" through the provision of the right amount of liquidity (credit and money). For Warren and Pearson, on the other hand, raising the price of gold was enough to unleash the forces required to end deflation; there was no direct role for the Fed or for traditional monetary policy. In the appendix to this book, I present a more detailed discussion of the differences between Warren and Fisher proposals to adopt a "sliding" or "compensated" dollar.

By September 29, one month after the president had authorized the purchase of newly minted gold at world prices, the commodity markets continued to be depressed. The price of corn was 28 percent lower than on July 15; the price of cotton, rye and wheat had declined by 13 percent, 30 percent, and 21 percent relative to that date. The plan was not working as the president had anticipated.

In the meantime, and almost by stealth, the government was making changes to its public debt policy. On October 11, the Treasury retired 30 percent of the Fourth Liberty Loan—which had been originally issued with the now defunct gold clause—and replaced it with twelve-year bonds with a 1 percent coupon. The new offer was vastly oversubscribed, suggesting that contrary to what many conservatives had argued, the abrogation of the gold clause had not generated serious damage to the government's reputation, or to the demand for government securities. Moreover, the low interest rate on the new debt signaled that expectations of inflation continued to be depressed.

Meanwhile, the legal machinery continued to move forward. On October 11, the Advisory and Protective Committee for American

Investments was formed in London. Its purpose was to take part in legal actions that would protect British investors from the "default in gold payment and gold-clause situation."[5] This body was supposed to complement the work of the International Committee against the Repudiation of the Gold Clause that had been formed by French, Swiss, and Belgian debt holders on July 4, a day after FDR delivered his bombshell message to the London Conference.[6] The main concern of these committees was to get the courts to protect their rights and rule that debts that carried the gold clause had to be paid in gold-equivalent.

THE FOURTH FIRESIDE CHAT

On Sunday October 22, the president delivered his fourth Fireside Chat. He opened by summarizing his administration's accomplishments. He talked about public works and the legislation passed during the Hundred Days; he praised the National Recovery Act and the AAA; and he told the American public that things were improving. He asserted that since Inauguration four million people had found work. He reiterated that the definite goal of the government was to "restore commodity price levels, [and] to make possible the payment of public and private debts more nearly at the price level at which they were incurred." With regard to currency values, he stated that "when we have restored the price level, we shall seek to establish and maintain a dollar which will not change its purchasing and debt-paying power during the succeeding generation." It was important, he asserted, not to put the cart before the horse. [7]

He said that his government was building an "edifice of recovery" with many columns, and that "the work on all of them must proceed without let or hindrance."[8] He then declared that one of these columns, monetary policy, was less developed than the others and that it was time to strengthen it.

Towards the end of the presentation, the president said that in order to raise prices he was adopting a new policy: he was establishing a market for gold in the United States. The Reconstruction Finance Corporation (RFC) would buy newly minted gold at prices determined after consultation with the secretary of the treasury and the president. If needed, the RFC would also buy and sell gold in the world market at these prices. It was important, the president declared, that people understood clearly

FIGURE 10.2. Dean Acheson and Felix Frankfurter. (*Source*: Harris & Ewing Collection, Library of Congress)

what he was doing: "This is a policy and not an expedient. It is not to be used merely to offset a temporary fall in prices. We are thus continuing to move toward a managed currency."[9]

FDR then turned to his critics: "Doubtless prophets of evil still exist in our midst. But Government credit will be maintained and a sound currency will accompany a rise in the American commodity price level." He ended with an emotional note: "I have told you tonight the story of our steady but sure work in building our common recovery. In my promises to you both before and after March 4th, I made two things plain: First, that I pledged no miracles and, second, that I would do my best." [10]

The news of the new gold-buying program was received both in the United States and in world financial centers with calm bewilderment. No one knew exactly how the program would work, or how the purchase price would evolve through time. More important, no one knew if the new buying program would be able to move the international market for gold, exchange rates, or prices. Markets did not panic; they waited.

After reviewing the president's speech, lawyers determined that there were three main differences between this new gold-buying program and the one established on August 29 through Executive Order No. 6261. First, while in the original program gold purchases were at ongoing world prices, the new program permitted the government to set any price it wanted and to alter it as frequently as it desired. Second, by explicitly allowing buying and selling gold in the global market, this program recognized that what mattered was the international price of the metal. As noted, this issue had been a source of contention between George Warren, who believed that all that counted was the domestic price, and James Warburg who insisted that any such program had to change world prices of gold, and through that channel exchange rates. Only then would commodity prices be affected. What wasn't clear, however, was how large these foreign purchases would be, and if they would indeed alter the world market for bullion. And third, under the new plan, payment to sellers was to take place through a complex procedure that involved the issuing of short-term RFC debentures at significantly below par.

A STUMBLING BLOCK

On October 22, the day FDR delivered his fourth Fireside Chat, the official price of gold was still $20.67 per ounce. This posed a serious legal problem for the newly announced gold-buying program. It was unlawful for the government to use public funds to purchase gold at a higher price than the one established by law. This was the case independently of the merits and desirability of the policy. Herman Oliphant, the head lawyer at the Treasury, found a way around this impediment: instead of paying in cash, the Corporation would pay with its own debentures, which it would issue at a discount. The Treasury would immediately buy these securities at face value from the gold producer or from the foreign dealer selling the metal. This back-to-back operation would amount to paying a discretionary and higher price to the gold seller, and at the same time the law would not be broken. If on a particular day the president wanted to pay $31.32 per ounce of gold, the debentures would be issued at 66 percent of par: 20.67 divided by 0.66, is exactly 31.32.

FDR and Henry Morgenthau Jr. believed that this clever system effectively allowed the government to circumvent the Gold Act of 1900. However, there was a problem. Dean Acheson, the acting secretary of the treasury and the official in charge of implementing the program, did not agree with them. He believed that the government did not have the authority to pay any price different from the one set by statute, and that price was $20.67 per ounce. In his view "the sale was a sham and a violation of the law which, since the Treasury must redeem them [the debentures] at face value, contemplated a sale at full market value."[11]

Dean Acheson was a lawyer by training, and until he became undersecretary of the treasury in April 1933, he did not have much experience in financial or economic issues. He was tall and famous for his wit. He often dressed in tweeds and cut a dashing figure with his well-kept moustache. In many ways he was a typical representative of the Eastern establishment. Like FDR, he had attended the Groton School in Massachusetts. He then went to Yale College and Harvard Law School, where he became one of Felix Frankfurter's protégés. After graduating with top honors he clerked for Justice Louis B. Brandeis for two years. It was from Brandeis that he got a keen interest in constitutional law, and a desire—never fulfilled—to serve one day as the nation's solicitor general. According to Sir Frederick Leith-Ross, Acheson could be mistaken for a British gentleman, a fact that could "prejudice his prospects in American political life."[12] The son of an Episcopalian bishop, Acheson was highly principled, a characteristic that would occasionally get him in trouble. In 1949, for instance, when he was Harry Truman's secretary of state, he was violently attacked by Republican members of Congress for refusing to condemn alleged spy Alger Hiss, a friend of many years. It was because of these principles that in October 1933 Acheson decided not to go along with the gold-buying program, a program that he considered to violate the law. In a tense meeting with the attorney general—the atmosphere was close to "open warfare"—he told Homer Cummings that he would only authorize the program if he got written instructions, either from the secretary of the treasury or from the president.

On October 24, two days after the fourth Fireside Chat, Acheson received a telegram from Secretary Woodin, who was still recovering in New York. The communication left no room for interpretation:[13]

I hereby direct and instruct you in my behalf and in my name to approve the issuance of ninety day debentures by the Reconstruction Finance Corporation to be sold at a discount basis in accordance with its resolution of October 20th and further to approve such prices of said debentures to be payable as stated in the said resolution in gold as the Corporation may determine after consultation with the President.

From that point on the relation between Acheson and FDR became strained, cold, and distant. Three weeks later, on November 15, Secretary Woodin asked Acheson for his resignation. In a short letter to the president, the undersecretary expressed his thanks for having been allowed to serve during "stirring times." Two days later Henry Morgenthau Jr. was inducted as his replacement. Before two months, when Woodin's health took a turn for the worse, Morgenthau was promoted to secretary of the treasury, a post he held for over a decade, until July 1945.

BUYING GOLD IN THE INTERNATIONAL MARKET

On October 25, the first day of the new gold buying program, the RFC paid $31.36 per ounce of gold, 27 cents above the world price. During the next 45 days or so, FDR, with George F. Warren's assistance, determined every morning the price at which the RFC would buy gold during that day; almost always at a premium over the world price. In figure 10.3 I present the daily RFC and world prices of gold for the period October 25 through December 31, 1933.

In a column published two days after FDR's announcement, Walter Lippmann argued that the Roosevelt administration was trying to manage the dollar in a way similar to the way the British had taken control of the pound. While the British used their Equalization Fund, the United States had decided to put in place a gold-buying program. In a subsequent piece published on October 27, Lippmann declared that this was not a first step towards a system of fiat money. On the contrary, he said, the ultimate goal of the experiment was to find the appropriate level of the dollar, a level at which the gold standard would be re-established. In the same piece, Lippmann warned against impatience. He argued that it would take a few months to find out if the experiment worked.[14]

The RFC made its first international transaction on November 1, when it bought a small batch of gold in France at $32.36 an ounce. according to the *New York Times* the size of the deal was not known exactly. However, "the amount was understood to have been small." The reporter added that in the view of international experts, as long as the purchases continued to be insignificant it was "virtually certain that the French authorities will offer no objection."[15]

As days went by, bankers and reporters began to wonder about the scale of the program. The administration, however, was secretive regarding international transactions, as it feared that too many details could trigger retaliation by foreign governments, something the New York Group had warned about in its August report. Anonymous sources confirmed that "purchases would be kept within bounds which would not provoke counter-actions by other nations."[16] On November 9, Jesse Jones, the chairman of the RFC, informed the press that since the launching of the program the corporation had bought 213,000 ounces of newly minted gold domestically. He once again stated that the amount of gold bought in global markets was modest, and once again refused to divulge the exact amount.[17] That day the price offered was $33.15 per ounce, 10 cents higher than the international market price. On November 15, an informed source who did not want to be identified stated that to that date purchases abroad had amounted to only $6 million.

At the end of November, University of Chicago professor Jacob Viner, who would soon join the Treasury as an adviser, wrote a long memorandum to Henry Morgenthau Jr. in which he explained that the gold-buying program was not working as promised. A serious problem, Viner asserted, was that the purchases abroad were too small, and did not really change the international price of gold. In addition, the discretionary changes in the price of gold and the absence of a clear program geared at stabilization, were generating uncertainty, encouraging speculation, and negatively affecting investment decisions.[18]

The rest of the world continued to react to the decision to abrogate the gold clause and to the policy of deliberately pushing the dollar value down. On November 28, the Tokyo Electric Bond Company cancelled the provision that allowed debt holders to collect payments on gold bases. The measure was justified "by the cancellation by the United States of the gold clause on contracts." That same day, the Italian government announced that it was paying $3 million corresponding to the 1925 7 percent Morgan

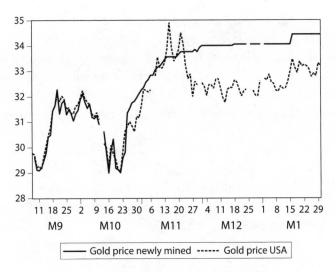

FIGURE 10.3. Daily RFC prices for gold and London
market price in dollars.

loan in paper dollars. A story in the *New York Times* reported that the loan
contained a gold clause "but Italian governmental officials contend that
since the loan was contracted under United States law, the gold clause is
not obligatory. . . . The payment in paper, however, will mainly affect Ital-
ians, since they repurchased more than half the loan."[19] On the same day
the Brazilian government cancelled contracts with gold clauses, allowing utility companies to make payments on their debts in milréis.[20]

THE GOLD RESERVE ACT OF 1934

In mid-November 1933, enthusiasm for the gold-buying program began
to wane. Walter Lippmann pointed out that relative prices—or "price
disparities" as he called them—had moved in the wrong direction. Agricultural prices were now lower, in relation to industrial goods, than in
July. He asserted that this was a severe problem, and that the "country
felt it instantly." He added that the "doubt and discontent of the past
three months have reflected it [the relative decline in agricultural prices]."
In his view, the problem had two components: on the one hand, the
gold-buying program was not affecting agricultural prices as anticipated
by its promoters, and in particular by George F. Warren, and on the other

the NRA was pushing up prices of manufactured goods in an artificial fashion, through price agreements.[21] He added that neither the president nor Warren realized that the mechanics at work were complex and that, as the New York Group had pointed out in its August 29 report, any change in the value of the dollar would have to be supported by other policies, including fairly massive open market operations undertaken by the Federal Reserve.

Even those members of Congress who favored inflation became disappointed with the gold-buying program. On November 23, Senator George W. Norris, the Progressive Republican from Nebraska, pointed out that after three months of intervening in the gold market the administration had little to show for it. Gold had been purchased at increasingly higher prices, and commodity prices were still significantly below their 1926 level. He argued that it was time to try something different; it was time for the president to use the authority given to him by the Thomas Amendment and officially devalue the dollar. Commenting on the resignation of Professor Oliver Sprague, a declared opponent of devaluation, from his post as adviser to the Treasury, Senator Morris Sheppard of Texas said that this was good news, since the door was now open for official deliberations on an official increase in the price of gold. Senator Key Pittman from Nevada, who had been at the London Conference with Sprague, added that now the president could move forward with a program of generating "controlled inflation."[22]

In the meantime, there were important legal developments on the international front. On December 18, the House of Lords ruled that the Belgian utility *Societé Intercommunale Belge d'Electricité* had to make debt payments on its 1928 bonds on the bases of gold-equivalent. The decision, which overturned a lower court ruling, had no effect on British dollar-denominated debts, since their payment in paper money rather than gold was the result of legal changes in the United States, the country where these bonds were issued in 1917. In spite of this, legal experts thought that the ruling by the House of Lords could play a role as a precedent in the gold-clause cases that were looming in the United States, and that everyone expected would be taken by the courts any day now.[23]

On December 31, 1933, the *New York Times* published John Maynard Keynes's open letter to President Franklin D. Roosevelt. The final part of the note contained the sentence that many people remember today: "The recent gyrations of the dollar have looked to me more like a gold standard on the booze than the ideal managed currency of my dreams."[24]

Most analysts interpreted Keynes words as asserting that during the gold-buying program the dollar exchange rate was excessively volatile, and that this volatility was harmful for the recovery. Keynes told the president that it was time to make policy changes. He wrote:

> In the field of gold-devaluation and exchange policy the time has come when uncertainty should be ended. This game of blind man's bluff with exchange speculators serves no useful purpose and is extremely undignified. It upsets confidence, hinders business decisions, occupies the public attention in a measure far exceeding its real importance, and is responsible both for the irritation and for a certain lack of respect which exists abroad.

At the end of 1933, almost coincidentally with the publication of Keynes open letter to the president, the program was effectively ended.[25]

On the first day of the year 1934, the press reported that the president would finally move forward on the currency issue. The *New York Times* pointed out that as a result of the gold-buying program there had been a "slight speculative increase in the commodity price level temporarily." The main achievement of the initiative, the *Times* continued, had been to "prevent further deflation." The reporter pointed out that according to well-informed sources the president had "decided to recommend that Congress chart the course to be pursued in the devaluation of the dollar and decide what is to be done about any profit on gold held by the Federal Reserve Banks."[26]

On January 16, the Gold Bill was introduced in Congress. The *New York Times* reported that its "enactment will permit the President to take all powers of currency issue from the Federal Reserve Board, and lodge them exclusively in the government." The article explained that the proposed regime would be a modified "bullion standard," where international trade would be settled in gold. However, private parties would not be allowed to own, buy, or sell the metal: "There is nothing in the plan to set up a free or open gold market, and, while the President in his message spoke sympathetically of the increased use of silver . . . he did not promise any, further pro-silver legislation soon." The bill gave the president authority to fix a new official value for the dollar between 50 and 60 percent of the original par of $20.67 per ounce of gold. Further, in the future the president could change the value of the currency at his will within that 10 percent window or band. Towards the end of the long article, the reporter pointed out that one of the key purposes of this legislation was to remove one of the main criticisms of the administration's gold policy: "that it was uncertain and no one knew what the new value of the dollar was to be."[27]

On January 30, 1934, and after a heated debate in both chambers of Congress, the Gold Reserve Act of 1934 was signed into law. The next day the president set the new official price of gold at $35 an ounce. The Treasury announced that it was willing to buy and sell any amount of metal at that price, internationally. U.S. residents, however, were still not allowed to hold gold. This official price of $35 an ounce was in effect until August 1971, when Richard Nixon closed the Treasury's "gold window."

An important and controversial component of the Gold Reserve Act was the creation of an Exchange Stabilization Fund at the Treasury.[28] The Fund was, to a large extent, tailored after the British Exchange Equalization Account, and its main objective was to intervene, under well-defined circumstances, in the global currency markets. The purpose of these interventions—either buying or selling dollars—was to assure that the exchange rate would indeed stay within a very narrow window around $35 per ounce of gold. The Stabilization Fund was originally funded with $2 billion, corresponding to the Federal Reserve profits from the revaluation of the price of gold from $20.67 to $35 an ounce. What made the Stabilization Fund so controversial was that the legislation that created it moved the property of all gold held by the Federal Reserve System to the Treasury. On January 17, Homer Cummings, the attorney general, delivered an opinion in which he stated that the government had the authority to take over the Federal Reserve's gold stocks "in exercise of its right of eminent domain." The attorney general added that "such power extends to every form of property for public use," including gold.[29]

Almost ten months after Franklin D. Roosevelt had been inaugurated, the second shoe had dropped. The majority of the population seemed to think that the devaluation was a good thing. Through his many speeches and Fireside Chats the president had convinced the American public that this was a required step to raise prices, end the Depression, and create jobs. But, not everyone agreed. To many investors, bankers, lawyers, and politicians, the devaluation of the dollar and the abrogation of the gold clauses constituted a violation of contracts, an outright transfer from the creditor to the debtor class, and an outrageous expropriation of wealth. All there was left to do now was wait for the highest court in the land to rule on the constitutionality of these Rooseveltian policies.

CHAPTER 11

The Path to the Supreme Court

January 1, 1934–December 1, 1934

On March 24, 1934, Wilder Hobson, an associate editor at *Fortune*, wrote to the new secretary of the treasury and requested his help for an article that he was writing. He asked some clarifying questions about Henry Morgenthau's upbringing and about his farm business. He attached an eighteen-page "rough and tentative" draft of the piece. A barely legible carbon copy of the manuscript can be found in the Morgenthau Papers at the Roosevelt Presidential Library. In the archives there is also a seven-page commentary written by Henry's wife, Elinor, in which she argues that the text is so inaccurate and misleading that it would be better not to run it. The draft article opens as follows:[1]

> Henry Morgenthau, Jr. is about the most obscure Secretary of the Treasury this country has ever had. . . . Mr. Morgenthau is a rank amateur who has done none of the things which are usually regarded as prerequisites for his job. Today, of course, there are lots of minds elastic enough to endorse the idea of trying mere lawyers in our banks and mere professors in our cabinets and mere farmers in our treasuries. But so far Mr. Morgenthau is a beginner in his post, and it is impossible to give a cold opinion on his value until more results have been shown.

Hobson then tells the story of the secretary's grandfather, Lazarus, a German cigar trader who immigrated with his eleven children to

FIGURE 11.1. Attorney General Homer S. Cummings leaving
the White House in late January 1935, just before the Supreme Court's
ruling on the gold cases. (*Source*: Harris & Ewing Collection,
Library of Congress)

Brooklyn in 1862, where he suffered serious financial difficulties. His
ninth child was Henry Morgenthau Sr., a brilliant and hardworking boy
who would become a lawyer and make a fortune in real estate. Henry
Sr. got involved in Democratic Party politics, and in 1913 Woodrow
Wilson appointed him ambassador to the Ottoman Empire. From
there, Hobson's article moves to Henry Jr.'s schooling—three years at

Exeter, and two stints at Cornell, with no degree earned—and his lack of sporting abilities. Hobson then writes of how, prodded by his father, young Henry became interested in farming and purchased the Fishkill Farms in upstate New York. The farm was only thirty miles from Hyde Park, where the Roosevelts had a large property. According to the manuscript, this geographical coincidence was at the heart of Morgenthau's political career: "If Mr. Morgenthau had done his farming in Texas or Oregon he would probably not be secretary of the Treasury today. . . . Mr. Morgenthau's whole public sector career has followed on the fact that he and the President became Dutchess County neighbors twenty years ago."[2]

Of course, it was true that the president and Morgenthau were neighbors and close friends. They had comparable interests, they loved farming, their wives liked each other, and they shared a similar sense of humor. But, as the secretary would soon show, he was not a mere "yes man"; on occasions he would confront FDR and resist his directions. Henry Morgenthau Jr. led the Department of the Treasury through tumultuous times, including the 1937 recession, World War II, and the Bretton Woods Conference, which set the bases for the international monetary system that was in operation for nearly three decades. He was secretary of the treasury for eleven years, the second-longest of anyone in U.S. history.[3] One of Morgenthau's first major tests was the gold-clause cases heard by the Supreme Court during the second week of January 1935. At the time, these cases were considered to be so important that some analysts argued that if the abrogation of the gold clause was ruled to be unconstitutional, the country would sink into a catastrophic crisis.

Hobson's biographical essay on Morgenthau was published in the May 1934 issue of *Fortune*, with very few changes with respect to the "rough and tentative" draft that was sent to the secretary. That issue of *Fortune* also included articles on the Air Mail service provided by the U.S. Post Office, and on the Federal Reserve, as well as a portfolio of color photos by Stanley Woods on the Boulder Dam—later the Hoover Dam—which was still under construction.

THE YEAR WHEN GOLD FLOWED IN: 1934

The first full year of recovery was 1934. Output was up in almost every sector, unemployment declined, and prices began to recuperate. Of course, the Depression was not completely over, but the freefall had been arrested, and there was hope. As Milton Friedman, Ben Bernanke, and Allan Meltzer, among others, have emphasized, the most important factor behind these developments was a profound change in monetary policy. For the first time since 1927, the broadly defined quantity of money increased throughout the year. At the heart of this policy change was the decision by the Federal Reserve to allow large inflows of gold to be translated into higher liquidity and credit. That is, the central bank made no attempt to "sterilize" gold inflows by selling securities to the public, and in that way mopping up liquidity from the system. With an expansion in money and credit came a jump in confidence, higher investment, enhanced sales, and a reduction in unemployment. The New Deal policies, including the more controversial ones, such as the National Recovery Administration (NRA) and the Agricultural Adjustment Act (AAA), also contributed to the change in mood and renewed optimism, by making clear that the government was willing to try anything in order to bring the Depression to an end.[4]

In figure 11.2, I present the evolution of Gross National Product (GNP), in monetary terms, between 1919 and 1944. The year 1934 is presented by the shaded area. As may be seen during that year, there was an important expansion in national income. This increase was the result of both higher prices and higher real output. In figure 11.3, I display the Wholesale Price Index and some of its most important components. This figure clearly shows that, although prices increased relative to their lowest point, in 1934, they were still below their 1926 level. In fact, FDR's goal of raising prices back to that golden year was gradually abandoned; reporters, politicians, and economists spoke less and less about that specific objective. Perhaps the most interesting feature of this figure is that by late 1934 the gap between farm prices and prices in other industries had narrowed significantly.[5]

Between January and December 1934, the stock of monetary gold more than doubled in the United States; it went from $3.9 billion to $8.1 billion. Part of this increase—a little over $2.5 billion—was the result of the devaluation of the dollar, which allowed the Treasury to reprice its stock of

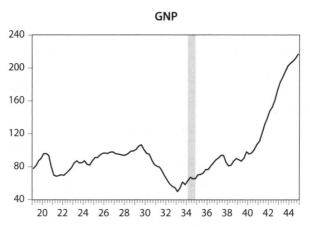

FIGURE 11.2. Gross National Product (GNP),
1919–1944 (quarterly data in nominal terms).

bullion (which it had received from the Federal Reserve) at $35 an ounce. But more important than repricing were the large amounts of gold that came into the country immediately after the Gold Reserve Act was passed in late January 1934. More than $750 million flowed in during February alone—$239 million from London, $124 million from Paris—another $262 million in March, and $155 million in April.[6]

Several factors were behind these very large shipments of metal. First, as required by the newly passed Gold Reserve Act, the Treasury was willing to buy unlimited amounts of gold in foreign markets at $35 an ounce. This was a significant difference with respect to the Warren-inspired gold-buying program of late 1933, in which international purchases were strictly limited to small amounts in order to avoid foreign complaints and retaliation. Second, although the devaluation was smaller than what was permitted under the Thomas Amendment, it was large enough to give investors confidence that there would be no additional adjustments in the medium term. This meant that the dollar was seen as stable currency, at least for some time. Third, most people believed that the United States was in a path towards recovery. In the public's mind, there was, finally, an all-encompassing attempt to bring the crisis to an end. This general optimism regarding the policies of the New Deal was reflected by the Democratic Party's overwhelming victory in the 1934 midterm election, where it picked up nine seats in the Senate, and was able to amass a super majority of 69 out of 96 senators.

There was also an increasing feeling in financial centers around the globe that the gold-bloc countries were in an untenable position, and that sooner rather than later they were going to abandon the gold standard and devalue their currencies. Under these circumstances, an obvious defensive move was to seek refuge in the one country that offered stability and a very attractive price for gold. After the devaluation and the fixing of the official price of bullion at $35 an ounce, the United States had become a clear safe haven for investors.

The decision to allow gold inflows to be reflected in higher liquidity was momentous.[7] This change in policy, however, was not due fully to the Federal Reserve. As noted, after the Gold Reserve Act of 1934, it was the Treasury and not the central bank the one that controlled the policy towards gold and exchange rates. The Treasury paid for bullion by issuing gold certificates, which were deposited at the Fed. After receiving the certificates, the central back "printed money"—fresh dollars—which were then used by the Treasury to pay foreigners for their gold.[8] It was this "printing of money" that resulted in higher liquidity. As Allan Meltzer has noted, Fed officials—including Marriner S. Eccles, the new chairman who took over from Eugene Black in late 1934—continued to be concerned about possible bouts of inflation, and were leery about the rapid increases in liquidity. When it came to monetary policy, between 1934 and 1941 the Federal Reserve was in the backseat; its leaders "opposed devaluation, silver purchases or increases in money unless they increased consumers' purchasing power."[9]

PAYABLE IN UNITED STATES GOLD COIN?

The official devaluation of the dollar on the last day of January 1934 was followed by a period of legal and judicial upheaval. Initially, one of the most confusing issues was related to bonds whose coupons were payable in one of several currencies. Given the circumstances, the vast majority of holders selected one of the gold-bloc currencies. The *New York Times* reported that in the case of the St. Louis Southwestern Railway Company, many investors had asked for payments in Dutch guilders or Swiss francs. This meant a hefty premium over those who were paid in dollars. A growing number of companies, including the Pacific Gas & Electric and Bethlehem Steel notified the New York Stock Exchange that in the future they planned to make payments only in dollars. It was not clear, however, whether their decision was legal and would survive in court.[10]

On March 1, 1934, a diplomatic problem erupted when the government of Panama returned to the U.S. Treasury a check for $250,000 dollars corresponding to the rent of the Canal Zone. According to the Panamanian government, payment was due in gold or gold-equivalent, and that meant that the number of paper dollars paid had to be raised by 69 percent relative to the original agreement. Panama's lawyers made the simple point that in this case the gold clause was part of an international treaty, and not of a simple loan contract. Thus, it was not affected by the Joint Resolution of June 5, 1933. They noted that the 1904 Canal Treaty clearly stated that "the United States agrees to pay the Republic of Panama the sum of $10,000,000 in gold coin of the United States . . . and also an annual payment during the life of this convention of $250,000 in like gold coin."[11] Arthur Krock, the influential journalist, pointed out in a March 7 column that although the sums in dispute were miniscule ($250,000), the case was extremely important for the two precedents it could create. On the one hand, if the Treasury refused to pay Panama the revised amount, it would signal that the United States was ignoring clear stipulations in international treaties when dealing with smaller nations. This, undoubtedly, would hurt the credibility and reputation of the country. On the other hand, there was a domestic angle to the problem. If the United States agreed to make the payment in gold coin equivalent, this would create an incentive for holders of U.S. debt to challenge the abrogation of the gold clauses in the courts.[12] The disagreement between the Treasury and Panama lingered until mid-1939, when the United States decided to pay a higher lease of $430,000 per year, retroactive to March 1934. The difference between the new and old leases corresponded, almost exactly, to the amount by which the dollar was devalued in 1934 with respect to gold. This was an implicit, albeit delayed, recognition that the United States would, after all, respect international treaties.[13]

Meantime, a number of legal cases were brought to the courts by investors who demanded to be paid according to the new gold price of $35 an ounce. A case involving Iron Mountain bonds issued in 1903 caught the immediate attention of the media, due to its complexity. Iron Mountain was a subsidiary of the Missouri & Pacific Railroad, and was in bankruptcy procedures. The question in front of the court was how different creditors would be paid. Senior bondholders, represented by Bankers

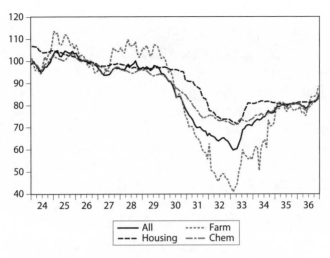

FIGURE 11.3. Wholesale price index and some of its key
components, monthly, 1924–1936.

Trust, demanded payment in gold-equivalent. Other creditors—including
those with junior and unsecured debts—disagreed, and argued that if senior bondholders were paid in gold coin equivalent, the amount of funds
available for servicing other debts would be greatly diminished. The fact
that the RFC was one of the junior creditors—it had made a $25 million
loan to Iron Mountain—made the case particularly interesting. Payment
to bondholders using the new higher price of gold, as requested by Bankers Trust, would result in a large loss for the RFC, and would hurt tax-
payers. Because of this, the government decided to get directly involved
in these proceedings.[14]

There was a lot at stake in the Missouri & Pacific case. A ruling that
payment had to be made in gold-equivalent dollars would set an important precedent, and would likely result in an increase in the debt burden
of thousands of companies by 69 percent. During most of May and June,
the media followed the case with great expectations and speculated on
the consequences of a ruling that would declare the Joint Resolution to
be unconstitutional.[15] On June 20, and to Wall Street's relief, Federal Judge
C. B. Faris ruled in St. Louis that the Joint Resolution was valid. As soon
as the ruling was known, the lawyer for Bankers Trust, the trustee of Iron
Mountain Senior bondholders, announced that he was appealing and
would take the case all the way to the Supreme Court.

Two weeks after the Missouri Pacific decision was announced in St. Louis, on July 3, 1934, the District Court in New York ruled on the case of *Norman v. the Baltimore and Ohio Railroad*. The court pointed out that according to the Constitution, Congress had the power "to coin money, [and] regulate the value thereof," and that the Joint Resolution had altered the type of money with which debts could be discharged. According to the original contract, the court continued, the Baltimore and Ohio debt was payable in money and not in commodities (gold, of course, being a commodity), and thus came under the power of Congress. Therefore, the court ruled, the debt could be discharged in any type of paper money that was declared by Congress to be legal tender. As soon as the decision was read, Emanuel Redfield, the lawyer for the plaintiff, announced that he was willing to take the case on appeal all the way to the Supreme Court.[16]

Investors trying to recover their money in gold also sued in state courts, across the country. The outcomes were similar to those in federal court. For instance, on August 29 New York Supreme Court Justice Leary dismissed a suit by a certain Charles M. Levy who tried to have the Asbestos Ltd. Company make payment in gold.[17]

Meanwhile, there continued to be developments abroad. On July 7, Poland abolished the gold clause in all contracts, past and future, in domestic and foreign currencies. This had a direct and negative effect on U.S. loans, including the Dillon & Reed loan of 1925 to the Republic of Poland, and on the Stone & Webster 1929 loan to the City of Warsaw. A few days later, the Imperial Bank of Bahamas sued the Illinois Central railroad, in order to receive payment for a bond coupon in gold coin. [18]

It soon became evident that the profusion of federal and state gold cases were creating heightened uncertainty and slowing down business decisions. Investors did not know if they should purchase new bonds without the gold clause, or if it was more convenient to purchase old ones in the secondary market, on the hope that the courts would invalidate the Joint Resolution.[19]

As a way of dealing with this uncertainty, on November 15 the administration announced that it was asking the Supreme Court to consolidate a number of cases related to the abrogation of the gold clause and to hear them together. Attorney General Homer Cummings declared that he would personally argue in front of the Court.[20] Three days later,

J. Crawford Biggs, the solicitor general, informed the press that he had presented a motion to have four cases heard by the Supreme Court jointly on January 8. Two were related to private railroad debts, and two involved government debts. The private ones were the Missouri & Pacific Railroad case, which was now pending for appeal in the Eighth Circuit Court, and the *Norman v. Baltimore and Ohio Railroad* case, which came from New York.[21] Since the RFC was a junior creditor of Missouri & Pacific, the government was part of that specific private debt case; the government, however, was not involved in the *Norman* case.[22]

The government cases were related to a Liberty Bond and to a gold certificate. John H. Perry of New York City had presented a Liberty Bond with a face value of $10,000 for payment. He expected to get $16,921, corresponding to the original amount recalculated at the new official price of gold. The second public debt case was brought up by F. Eugene Nortz, who owned a Treasury Gold Certificate, series of 1928, with a face value of $106,300. He asked for a payment of $170,634. The government argued that according to the law he was only to get the face value of the Certificate, $106,300. These cases came to the Supreme Court through the Court of Claims for consultation and guidance. The Court of Claims was—and still is—the only court where the U.S. government could be sued by private individuals or corporations. In the *Perry* case, the Court of Claims forwarded the following two very specific questions to the highest tribunal in the Nation (the questions in the *Nortz* case were similar):

1. Is the claimant, being the holder and owner of a Fourth Liberty Loan 4¼ percent bond of the United States, which was payable on and after April 15, 1934, and which bond contained a clause that the principal is "payable in United States gold coin of the present standard of value," entitled to receive from the United States an amount in legal tender currency in excess of the face amount of the bond.

2. Is the United States, as obligor in a Fourth Liberty Loan 4¼ percent bond, series 1933–1938, as stated in Question One, liable to respond in damages in a suit in the Court of Claims on such bond as an express contract, by reason of the change or impossibility of performance in accordance with the tenor thereof, due to the provisions of Public Resolution No. 10, 73rd Congress, abrogating the gold clause in all obligation?

THEY ARE NOT BANKERS

Before proceeding with the details of the Supreme Court hearings, it is useful to analyze the role played by the Federal Reserve System, both in the unleashing of the crisis as well as in the incipient recovery observed during 1934. This discussion will provide the proper background for fully understanding the reasoning used by the government in the briefs it presented to the Court, as well as the thinking of the Supreme Court justices when rendering the decisions.

In figure 11.4, I present the evolution of the four monetary variables between 1929 and 1937. The figure includes data for (a) the stock of monetary gold; (b) the Federal Reserve base money (or high-powered money); (c) the broader monetary aggregate that economists call M1; and (d) the "money multiplier," a variable that reflects the banking sector's ability to expand credit; this multiplier connects the monetary base—which is the aggregate directly controlled by the central bank—and the more general monetary aggregate M1.

Several aspects of this diagram deserve attention. As may be seen, the stock of money in circulation (M1) began to decline in 1929. As economists now know, this monetary squeeze was at the center of the Great Depression. It is important to notice that this collapse in the monetary stock happened at a time when the narrower aggregate, monetary base (high-powered money), was still increasing. In the late 1920s and early 1930s monetary experts—including senior officials at the Fed—focused exclusively on the base (which is a reflection of the Federal Reserve System balance sheet). For them, as long as this variable continued to expand it was not possible to talk about a situation of monetary restriction or liquidity squeeze.

Why did these two variables—the monetary base and the broad monetary aggregate M1—move in opposite directions? Why, did one increase while the other shrank? The answer is given by the multiplier. When the public hoards currency and banks accumulate excess reserves, the banking system sees a great reduction in its ability to expand liquidity. Under normal circumstances, when the Federal Reserve injects money through, say, open market operations, people that receive that initial monetary injection, deposit the new monies in their banks. Thus, banks' ability to make loans increases. Under most circumstances banks would, then, increase credit. The recipients of these loans will deposit the money they

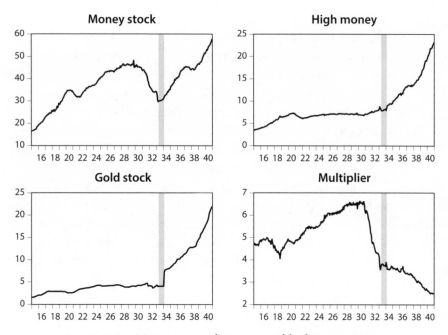

FIGURE 11.4. Monetary conditions, monthly data 1914–1940.

obtain from the banks in their own banking institutions, and these banks will, in turn, increase their own loans, and so on. This chain reaction continues for many additional rounds, and the initial action by the Federal Reserve gets "multiplied." However, if the public is facing heightened uncertainty and banks are encountering difficulties, this process breaks down. Instead of depositing their money in banks, people hoard currency, and instead of lending, banks increase their reserves. The multiplier, then, collapses and normal central bank actions become futile. This process, which today is well-known by undergraduate students of monetary theory, was not understood fully by central bankers in the late 1920s and early 1930s.[23]

Most scholars who have studied the Great Depression agree that the Federal Reserve played a central role in the crisis. The received wisdom is that instead of alleviating the situation, the Federal Reserve System was partially responsible for the depth and duration of the crisis. Due in large part to the Fed's actions what would have been only one more serious recession—a "panic" to use the terminology of the time—became the worst economic crisis in the history of America, a crisis that changed the nature of the country, and deeply affected the relations between the federal government and the states.

Of course, the Fed was not the only responsible institution for the downfall of the American economy. Throughout the 1920s the comptroller of the currency, and more importantly, the state regulatory agencies had been very liberal in granting banking licenses, and helped create a system that to a large extent encouraged speculation. Banks of all sizes and from every corner of America invested in shares and provided ample credit to those who wanted to make a quick buck in the stock market. People in all walks of life and of every economic condition—dentists, housewives, bellboys, farmers—could borrow substantial amounts on margin from their bank and then play the market. While things worked out and the market kept going up, everyone was ecstatic; it had never been easier to become rich in America—or anywhere else in the world, for that matter. The United State was the true land of opportunity.

By 1930 the country had close to 20,000 banks, many of them very small, poorly capitalized, and poorly run. Senator Carter Glass described the state of affairs vividly in a speech in the Senate floor in March, 1933: [24]

> Little grocerymen who run banks who get together $10,000 or $15,000, as it may be, and then invite the deposits of their community, and at the very first gust of disaster topple over and ruin their depositors! . . . If a struggling young man wants to get a place here in Washington as a stenographer or typist, he has to have a civil service examination; and yet we have people all over the country from one end to the other calling themselves "bankers," and all they know is to shave notes at an excessive rate of interest. They are not bankers.

And from here, the august Virginian, whose name is attached to banking legislation that continues to be discussed well into the twenty-first century, went on to state that unlike the United State, in countries such as Canada and Great Britain bankers were careful, avoided speculation, and knew the business of their clients well.

After the Crash of October 1929, the Fed's policies changed significantly. The Fed now reduced liquidity, and most of its senior officials sided with the view that the excesses of the 1920s had to be dealt with through the liquidation of investments. At the time, this perspective was popular among many economists, including luminaries such as the Austrian economist and Harvard professor Joseph Schumpeter—the man behind the "creative destruction" theory of economic growth and progress under capitalism—and the London School of Economics professor Lionel Robbins. Many members of the Federal Reserve tended to agree with Andrew W. Mellon, the long-serving secretary of the treasury, who in 1930 told President Herbert Hoover that the answer to the Crash and the slump was to "liquidate labor, liquidate stocks, liquidate farmers, liquidate real estate . . . it will purge the rottenness out of the system. High costs of living and high living will come down. People will work harder, live a more moral life. Values will be adjusted, and enterprising people will pick up from less competent people."[25] Fed actions during this period have been examined exhaustively by Milton Friedman and Anna Schwartz and Allan Meltzer, among other. With the exception of a brief period during 1932, when open market operations were pursued to increase liquidity, the Fed either stood passively on the sidelines or contributed to the malaise.

★   ★   ★

In late 1934, when government lawyers were frantically preparing the briefs to be presented to the Supreme Court, commodity prices were significantly higher than in March 1933, when Roosevelt had been inaugurated. In particular, the price of cotton had just crossed the 12.5 cents a pound threshold, which FDR considered to be the acceptable floor. Between March 1933 and December 1934, the price of corn quadrupled, that of cotton almost doubled, the price of rye doubled, and that of wheat increased by 114 percent. During the same period, the Dow stock market index had increased by 67 percent. In spite of the fact that there were choppy legal waters ahead, the president was happy and convinced that the nation was well on its way to full recovery.

CHAPTER 12

◇◇◇◇◇

Nine Old Men and Gold

December 1, 1934–January 7, 1935

In 1935, the Supreme Court was made up of "nine old men" and was deeply divided.[1] With four conservative and four liberals, the decisive vote was often provided by Charles Evans Hughes, a seventy-two-year-old progressive Republican with a distinguished career in public service. Before being appointed chief justice by President Herbert Hoover in 1930, Hughes served as secretary of state during the Harding and Coolidge administrations, and as Governor of New York during two terms. He was also an associate justice of the Supreme Court between 1910 and 1916, a position he resigned in order to run for the presidency in 1916. He lost to Woodrow Wilson by one of the slimmest margins in U.S. history (277 to 254 electoral votes). A graduate of Brown University and of Columbia Law School, Hughes was the top student in his class. As a justice, he was known for his efforts to find common ground and forge compromise. His opinions were well written, beautifully reasoned, and tended to be on the long side. In 1907, while he was governor of New York, he made a remark that was not well received by conservatives, and that would come back to haunt him later in life: "We are under a Constitution, but the Constitution is what the judges say it is."[2]

Chief Justice Hughes had an ample forehead, and a perfectly kept white beard. Although he dressed impeccably, his dark three-piece suits were slightly out of fashion. He was of medium height and had watery blue eyes; a strong nose and thick eyebrows gave his face a sense of determination. His voice was somewhat nasal, and he spoke in short, commanding sentences. His views about politics and social issues are captured succinctly in a short speech he gave in 1940, after receiving an award from National Conference of Christians and Jews: "Rancor and bigotry, racial animosities and intolerance are the deadly enemies of true democracy. There can be no friendly cooperation if they exist. They are enemies more dangerous than any external force, for they undermine the very foundations of our democratic effort."[3]

There is somewhat of a controversy on who coined the term "nine old men" to refer to the Hughes Court. According to the historian William Leuchtenburg, the term was first uttered, in passing, by the Brains Trust member Adolf A. Berle in 1933. The expression became part of common usage after a column by Drew Pearson and Robert S. Allen published in 1936.[4]

The liberals in the Court included some of the best legal minds in the country: There was Louis Brandeis, a man whose legal views on privacy were extremely influential during the early twentieth century. Brandeis was very critical of conglomerates, large corporations, and trusts, and believed that the best way to ensure a just society was by breaking them down into smaller units. This approach was controversial among many FDR early advisers, including Rex Tugwell, who believed that instead of breaking trusts down, they should be regulated and their activities coordinated through some form of planning. Then, there was Justice Benjamin Cardozo, one of the most elegant legal writers of his generation. During his eighteen years as a judge in the New York Court of Appeals, Cardozo had built a reputation as a wise, considerate, and kind man. He was appointed to the Supreme Court in 1932 by Herbert Hoover, as a successor of Justice Oliver Wendell Holmes, an icon of America's legal world. Everyone agreed that Cardozo was the perfect appointment, and his nomination was confirmed by the Senate on March 1, 1932, by a unanimous voice vote.

The third prominent member of the "liberal contingent" was Harlan Fiske Stone, a former dean of Columbia Law School and a former attorney general, who in 1941 would rise to the position of chief justice. Stone frequently agreed with Brandeis, although he often produced a separate short opinion. Today, Harlan Stone is mostly remembered for an important footnote he penned in a 1938 opinion. In the so-called footnote four, written at a time when the Court was trying to forge some kind of peace agreement with the Roosevelt administration, Stone pointed out that judicial scrutiny should be more rigorous and exacting when the statute in question dealt with individual rights and liberties than when it was concerned with economic and social policy legislation; this approach is today known as "strict scrutiny."[5] These three liberal Justices were sometimes referred to as the Three Musketeers.

Owen Roberts, a Philadelphia lawyer and former prosecutor, was appointed to the Court by President Herbert Hoover after the Senate rejected his first choice, John J. Parker. Although Roberts was a Republican, he was considered a swing vote. With time he sided more and more often with the liberal wing of the Court. In 1937, when FDR was seriously pushing his Court packing plan, Roberts provided the key vote in the *Parrish* case, which ruled that women were protected by minimum wage legislation. Many analysts believe that with this vote Owen Roberts saved the Court from an all-out war with the president, and helped avoid a major political and Constitutional crisis.[6]

Throughout the New Deal, Justices James Clark McReynolds, Pierce Butler, George Sutherland, and Wills Van Devanter were known as the Four Horsemen. They were deeply conservative and almost always voted as a group in opposition to the Roosevelt administration. In his memoirs Charles Evans Hughes referred to the Four Horsemen as follows: [7]

> When I became Chief Justice, I was well aware of the cleavage in the Court. [These four Justices] generally acted together. They had similar views as to the construction of constitutional provisions, and were classed by many as a conservative *bloc*. . . . The disposition of these Justices to work together was strengthened by their common disagreement with certain views held by Justice Brandeis, and his elaborate and forceful exposition intensified opposition.

James Clark McReynolds, a native of Kentucky and a "gold Democrat," was the most colorful and memorable of the Four Horsemen. He was a staunch conservative, a perfectionist, and a racist; among other things, he refused to talk to his two Jewish colleagues in the Court, Justices Brandeis and Cardozo. He favored bow ties, was a loner with a gloomy personality, and was a lifelong bachelor. He ardently believed in the sanctity of contracts and in the inviolability of private property. In 1913 he was appointed attorney general by Woodrow Wilson, and a year later, after the president learned firsthand about his difficult personality, he decided to "promote" him to the Supreme Court, where he served until 1941, at age eighty-two. His opinions were to the point and very brief; he often spent hours looking for the word which would precisely capture the intensity of his views.[8]

The second member of the conservative wing was Justice Pierce Butler, a Democrat who had made a fortune as a railroad lawyer in Minnesota, and who was appointed to the Court in 1922 by President Harding. He was extremely skeptical of the constitutionality of most business and utilities regulation, and in many cases sided with Justice McReynolds. Butler was a self-made man, born in a family of poor Irish immigrants, and raised in a farm in Minnesota. He was Catholic, and his ability at cross-examination was legendary. In college he was a wrestler, but what he really enjoyed was boxing. According to some, he was a bully who loved to humiliate lawyers who argued cases in front of the Court.

The third conservative in the 1935 Court was George Sutherland, also appointed by President Warren G. Harding. Sutherland was born in England in 1862, a year before his father decided to immigrate with his family to the United States. George Sutherland earned a law degree from the University of Michigan, and served in Congress as both a representative and a senator for Utah. He had protectionist views—he backed the Smoot-Hawley tariff—and was a solid supporter of private property. He abhorred the idea of a federal minimum wage, and in 1938, he wrote a passionate thirteen-page dissent—also signed by the other Horsemen—in the *Parrish* case. Justice Sutherland was succeeded on the bench by Stanley Reed, who in 1935, as head lawyer of the RFC, argued one of the gold-clause cases in front of the Court.

The final member of the "Four Horsemen" was Justice Willis Van Devanter, a native of Indiana who had been a successful railroad lawyer and had served as chief justice of the state of Wyoming. He was appointed to the Court by Theodore Roosevelt, and by 1935 he had served in the bench for over thirty years. He was kind and friendly, although somewhat reserved. Throughout his long career—he retired in 1937—he wrote very few opinions, as he had a tremendous difficulty in putting his thoughts on paper. According to the Chief Justice Charles Evans Hughes, Van Devanter was not at heart an ultraconservative. As time passed, however, he relied more and more on the views of Justice McReynolds to form his own opinions.[9]

In January 1935, these nine men had the future of the nation's monetary system in their hands. It was plainly clear that without the Joint

FIGURE 12.1. Chief Justice Charles Evans Hughes. (*Source*: Harris & Ewing Collection, Library of Congress)

Resolution that abrogated the gold clause the devaluation of the dollar would create havoc, including millions of bankruptcies across the country. If the Joint Resolution was ruled to be unconstitutional, debts originally expressed in gold coin would automatically increase by 69 percent. Many analysts believed that if that were to happen the devaluation would have to be rolled back, and the old official price of gold of $20.67 an ounce would be reinstated.

CONTRARY TO PUBLIC POLICY

During the last months of 1934, an army of lawyers in the Department of Justice worked on the three briefs that the government would submit to the Court. The legal team was assisted by a number of economists that came from several government departments. The archives of Attorney General Homer Cummings at the University of Virginia contain voluminous correspondence, memoranda, and reports pertaining to the cases and to the government strategy.[10] Assistant Solicitor General Angus D. MacLean pointed out in a 1937 article, that this was the first time briefs submitted to the Court provided elaborate macroeconomic reasoning and included diagrams and graphs on variables such as price indexes, and time series on interest rates for different securities. MacLean, who would argue one of the cases, wrote that these "graphs and tables [were incorporated] to demonstrate that complete financial disaster was likely to ensue unless the resolution was upheld."[11] The briefs also cited prominent economists such John Maynard Keyes and Edwin Walter Kemmerer.[12]

Although the three briefs submitted by the government addressed the peculiarities of each case, they were all based on common principles. The most important primary argument was that according to the Constitution, Congress had the power to coin money and regulate the value thereof. This meant that Congress could "pass a law prohibiting gold clauses in future obligations."

According to observers, reporters, and analysts, there was no doubt that Congress had the authority to change future contracts. The difficult issue was whether Congress had "this power in respect [to] outstanding obligations," which emanated from contracts written in the past.[13] The Administration tried to convince the Court that Congress indeed had this power, as expressly stated in Article I, Section 8 of the Constitution, and as confirmed by the Supreme Court in the Legal Tender Cases in 1870s.

In the Missouri & Pacific brief the government declared that "the discretion of the Congress in enacting the Joint Resolution was exercised in a way which has been considered by broad and informed opinion to be indispensable to the proper and effective exercise by the Congress of its monetary and other powers." According to the government lawyers this meant that Congress had the authority to annul contracts—both public and private—retroactively. This contention was at the very heart of these cases. The administration also claimed that there was no "taking" and that the Government had not violated the Fifth Amendment. According to its lawyers in no way could Congress's actions be described as "unreasonable, arbitrary, and capricious."[14] In the *Perry* brief (p. 56) the government specified: "There is no depravation of property within the meaning of the 5th or 14th Amendments when a contract with the government is affected by a statute enacted in the exercise of paramount power."

The government went further and argued that the abrogation did not violate Section 4 of the Fourteenth Amendment, as alleged by Perry in his brief. This section of the Fourteenth Amendment states:

> The validity of the public debt of the United States, authorized by law, including debts incurred for payment of pensions and bounties for services in suppressing insurrection or rebellion, shall not be questioned.

The government argument relied, chiefly, on the idea that in the Fourteenth Amendment the word "validity" refers to the mere existence of the obligation. The abrogation did not question the existence of public debts; all it did was regulate the type of money that could be used to discharge them. The government added that an analysis of the history of the Fourteenth Amendment showed unequivocally that it referred to a complete repudiation of the public debt, something that, of course, the abrogation did not consider. [15]

In arguing that there was no "taking," and thus no damages, the government went even further, when it pointed out that if one entertains the idea that there was "taking" this would have happened on June 5, 1933, when the Joint Resolution was passed. It was at that point that an intangible attribute of the contract—its gold clause—was modified. In the Perry brief the government asked what the value of the gold clause was on June 5, 1933. It answered as follows:

> Clearly it had absolutely no value, for the bond was worth just as much with that right withdrawn or abrogated as it was worth when

that provision still formed part of the obligation. This is conclusively demonstrated by the fact that there was no drop in the market price of the bond upon the passage of the resolution.

In addition, the government continued, if Perry had received gold coin for his bond, he would have been required by the Emergency Banking Act of March 9, 1933, to deliver the bullion to a Federal Reserve Bank or to the Treasury at the then official price of $20.67 an ounce of gold.[16]

In his own brief, John Perry agreed that the government had the power to determine what legal tender was; that was not the pertinent question. According to him, the real question was "as to the amount of legal tender required to satisfy the claimant's bond." In his opinion he was due $1.69 for each dollar of face value of his Liberty Bond. He contended that on June 5, 1933, gold-value obligations were at a premium with respect to paper money, and that the dollar had declined in value as a result of the government action.[17] Perry's claim was difficult to prove, since at the time of the Joint Resolution—on June 5, 1933—all obligations of the United States had, by law, to include the gold clause. Consequently, it was not possible to compare the price evolution of government bonds with and without the gold clause. In addition, most traded corporate bonds incorporated the clause; the Dow index of thirty corporate bonds included only one security without it. Thus, even today it is difficult to ascertain whether Perry's contention was indeed valid.

On this point, however, the government lawyers were very clear: Perry did not provide convincing proof that gold dollars were at a premium at the time the Joint Resolution was approved. In its brief the government stated that: "If he [Perry] fails to prove this [that gold dollars were at a premium], his entire argument falls." The government then pointed out that the only citation made by Perry in support of his claim was that the U.S. dollar had fallen in value with respect to the gold-bloc currencies in international currency markets. But this, asserted the government, was completely "irrelevant, since the Executive Orders effectively prevented the claimant and those similarly situated from exporting gold or otherwise realizing on any increased value of gold in terms of United States dollars in foreign markets."[18]

An important point made by government lawyers was that all U.S. gold-clause bonds were domestic bonds, and that none of them was marketed "especially to nonresident aliens."[19] This is a fundamental difference with the Argentine dollarization cases of the 2000s. Argentina deliberately marketed its securities internationally. Indeed, they were issued under foreign countries' jurisdictions—mostly in New York and London—and the Argentine economic authorities participated actively in road shows aimed at convincing foreign investors—both institutional and retail—to purchase these bonds.

In all three gold-clause briefs, the Roosevelt administration lawyers forcefully made the point that the gold clause was "contrary to public policy," a legal term that implies that certain actions, regulations, or contracts are harmful and injure the public and citizens at large. According to the government, the gold clause was "inconsistent with our present monetary system."

NECESSITY AND CONSTITUTIONALITY

A fundamental component of the government's legal argument was that in 1933 Congress faced the "necessity" to take action and to bring the Depression to an end. This necessary "action," which included devaluing the dollar with respect to gold, would only be effective if the gold clause was eliminated from future and past contracts. According to Assistant Solicitor General MacLean,[20]

> if the gold clauses were maintained . . . this meant bankruptcy on a national scale. This was the situation which impelled Congress, confronted by a deep recession, a banking collapse and a money panic to adopt the Joint Resolution annulling all such clauses. . . . [T]he Supreme Court was virtually obliged to sustain the action of Congress . . . in order to save the country.

In an article published in the *Yale Law Journal* in 1934, before the government submitted (or even drafted) its briefs, the legal scholar Arthur Nussbaum explored international precedent and argued that the Supreme Court could indeed consider the argument of "necessity" or *ordre public* to support the constitutionality of the Joint Resolution. After reviewing international evidence and constitutional history, he concluded that the "sharpest weapon against the abrogation of the gold clause would be retaliation" by foreign countries.[21]

The concept of "necessity" has been used repeatedly in trying to justify modern episodes of sovereign defaults and debt restructurings. This was the fundamental legal argument made by Argentina in the early 2000s. According to its lawyers, in the face of an unprecedented crisis unleashed by external forces, the Argentine government had no alternative but to end the convertibility law that had fixed the value of the peso at one dollar, and to devalue the national currency. In brief after brief, lawyers for Argentina declared that the combination of lower export prices, a stronger dollar in international markets, heightened aversion for risk in international capital markets, higher interest rates in the United States, and a crisis in Brazil resulted in a "perfect storm." Without major action, including the devaluation of the peso and the retroactive abrogation of contracts that had originally been written in dollars, there was a high probability of irreparable damage to the state itself. What was at stake, they argued, was the survival of the nation. In many ways one can think of the Argentine arguments in the early 2000s, as an amplified and Latin American version of those used by the Roosevelt administration.

In its three gold-clause briefs, the U.S. government also used a "secondary argument," to support its position. This came in two parts. First, there was the notion of "impossibility." Even if debtors—including the U.S. government—wanted to make payments in gold coin, this was impossible as there was not enough gold in the entire world to cover the amount of debts written with gold clauses; these were estimated to be between $100 billion and $120 billion in the United States. This argument, which had been used before by FDR in one of his public speeches—the second Fireside Chat—was a weak argument, to say the least. As the plaintiff lawyers explicitly declared, debtors did not ask for physical gold, nor did they deny the power of Congress to control monetary policy. What they argued was that there existed a contract that stipulated payment in gold-equivalent, and that not doing so meant that their property was being taken without due process. In the words of the assistant solicitor general, "those who attacked the resolution contended that they were entitled to be paid in lawful money the equivalent in value of what their contracts called for."[22]

The second component of the government's secondary argument had to do with damages, and went as follows: since the country had been subject to a significant deflation, plaintiffs could not claim to have suffered any damages; in fact, the same amount of paper dollars bought more goods and services in 1934 than a decade or two earlier. This point was made in the briefs through a detailed analysis—using graphs, diagrams, and tables—of the evolution of index numbers of prices. Assistant Solicitor General MacLean explained the administration's position:[23]

> [The government] contended that no damage had been sustained or could be shown since legal tender currency would buy just as much and pay as many debts as gold coin—one dollar being equal to every other one in value—and if a man had to give up a gold bond or gold certificate for other lawful money he was equally as well off as before, at least in this country, export of gold to any other being prohibited.

In the *Nortz* case, involving a gold certificate, the government took the position that gold certificates were not "warehouse receipts"; they were monetary obligations, and as such they came under Article 1, Section 8, of the Constitution, which gives Congress the power of coining money. It followed that Congress could change the type of money used to pay those certificates.

The government argument on gold certificates was based on the fact that the Act of March 3, 1863, which allowed their issuing, expressly stated that they could not exceed 120 percent of the amount of gold held by the Treasury as reserve. It is impossible, the government said, to believe that there would be mere warehouse receipts in excess of the thing warehoused (in this case gold). The fact that the Act set the limit at 120 percent, was clear proof that the certificates were a type of money and not a simple warehouse receipt; if the certificates were indeed money, then they could be regulated by Congress, and Nortz did not have a case.[24]

ECONOMIC EMERGENCY AND THE MINNESOTA MORATORIUM CASE

In early 1935, there was an immediate precedent for considering the argument of "economic necessity" when deciding on the constitutionality of certain public policies. On January 8, 1934, a divided Supreme Court ruled that a Minnesota statute declaring a moratorium on mortgages was constitutional. What made this ruling particularly controversial was that in Article 1, Section 10, the U.S. Constitution expressly states that "No

state shall . . . pass any Bill . . . or Law impairing the Obligation of Contracts." In April 1933, the Minnesota senate passed by a unanimous vote
a law declaring a one-year moratorium on mortgages. Part 1, Section 4
of that Act authorized district courts to extend the period for initiating
foreclosure procedures "for such additional time as the court may deem
just and equitable," but not exceeding one year. The Act clearly stated that
its provisions were temporary in nature and that they could only be in
effect while the economic emergency lasted: "only during the continu-
ance of the emergency and in no event beyond May 1, 1935."[25]

This case pitched the Four Horsemen against the more liberal members
of the Court. At the end, the Court ruled 5 to 4 to uphold the constitutionality of the Minnesota statute. Chief Justice Hughes wrote the majority's
opinion, where he stated that "While emergency does not create power,
emergency may furnish the occasion for the exercise of power." In his
view, some provisions of the Constitution—each state has two senators,
for example—are not affected by crises, while other are affected by emergencies, both natural (fires and earthquakes) and economic. The chief
justice explained his reasoning, by adding that situations may arise "in
which a temporary restraint of enforcement may be consistent with the
spirit and purpose of the constitutional provision and thus be found to
be within the range of the reserved power of the state to protect the vital
interests of the community."[26]

Justice Harlan Fiske Stone was troubled with the chief justice's reasoning in the Minnesota moratorium case. He thought that Hughes was
making too much of the fact that the Minnesota Act dealt with temporary emergencies only. In a note to the chief justice he wrote that in the
not too distant future the Court "may yet have to deal with cases . . . where
the law itself is made applicable for longer periods . . . whether they could
be regarded as temporary or not is, of course, a relative matter."[27] That
was indeed, what would happened almost exactly a year later, when the
gold-clause cases were argued in front of the Court. In those cases, the
federal government was not defending a temporary decision, but a permanent one; according the Joint Resolution of June 5, 1933, the gold clauses
were permanently annulled.

Justice Sutherland, one of the Four Horsemen, wrote a strong dissent
in the Minnesota Moratorium case, vehemently criticizing the chief justice's interpretation of the Constitution. For Sutherland and his three com-
rades, there was not such a thing as an "emergency," and an economic

crisis certainly did not provide a justification for relaxing the strict interpretation of the Constitution. Sutherland wrote, "The current exigency is not new. From the beginning of our existence as a nation, periods of depression, of industrial failure, of financial distress, of unpaid and unpayable indebtness, have alternated with years of plenty." But the most vitriolic part of his dissent was directed to Hughes's words on the relation between constitutional power and emergencies. Sutherland wrote:[28]

> I can only interpret what was said as meaning that while an emergency does not diminish a restriction upon power it furnishes an occasion for diminishing it; and this, as it seems to me, is merely to say the same thing by the use of another set of words, with the effect of affirming that which has just been denied.

Although there were many differences between the Minnesota Moratorium and the gold-clause cases—the former referred to state law that suspended contracts temporarily, while the latter concerned a Congressional Resolution that altered contracts permanently, both in the future and retroactively—members of the administration got comfort from the fact that the Court was sympathetic to the necessity and emergency arguments. It was true that the constitutionality of the Minnesota Moratorium had been upheld by the slightest of majorities, but it had been upheld, and that was what mattered.[29]

THE LEGAL TENDER CASES AS PRECEDENT

In its three briefs the government made several references to the legal tender cases from the 1870s. The question at that time was whether "greenbacks," or currency unbacked by gold or silver and issued by the Treasury during the Civil War, could be used to discharge debts that were written before the passage of the Act and were payable in gold coin or gold coin equivalent.

On February 7, 1870, in *Hepburn v. Grinswold*, the Court ruled in a 4 to 3 decision—at the time the Court had two openings—that the Legal Tender Act, insofar as it referred to debt contracts written before its passage, was unconstitutional; debts contracted before 1862 had to be discharged in metal coin or its equivalent.[30] This ruling affected nearly $450 million of greenbacks issued during the Civil War that were still in circulation.

The same day the decision was handed down, President Ulysses S. Grant nominated two new members to the Court: William Strong and Joseph P. Bradley. They were promptly confirmed by the Senate, and took their seats on March 14 and March 23, 1870. Five weeks later, on April 30, the Court heard two new Legal Tender cases, *Knox v. Lee* and *Parker v. Davis*. On May 1, by a vote of 5 to 4, the Court reversed itself, and ruled that the Legal Tender Act was, after all, constitutional with regards to debt contracts written before its passage by Congress; the two new justices voted with the majority. Debts incurred before the Civil War, the Court now said, could be discharged with greenbacks. The conservative press reacted very negatively, and accused President Grant of having packed the Court in order to have the ruling reversed. Opponents to the president pointed out that both Justices Strong and Bradley had been prominent railroad lawyers, and pointed out that the railroads were the main beneficiaries of the decision, as they could now pay their large debts in depreciated greenbacks.

In 1935 the Roosevelt administration argued in the three gold-clause briefs submitted to the Supreme Court that the Legal Tender cases provided important precedent. The government reasoned that *"Hepburn v. Grinswold* was overruled by the later Legal Tender cases, in which the Court . . . made use of the expression 'Whatever power there is over the currency is vested in Congress. If the power to declare what is money is not in Congress it is annihilated.' "[31] Whether in 1935 the Hughes court would be persuaded by these arguments was still to be seen.

BAD NEWS

During the last few weeks of 1934, while an army of lawyers got ready for the hearings, Henry Morgenthau Jr., the man labeled by *Fortune* magazine as the most obscure secretary of the treasury ever, was busy. One of his main concerns was to restructure the public debt; bonds that included the gold clause were being retired and new securities with relatively low coupon rates were issued to replace them. Morgenthau was also preoccupied with making sure that the new monetary system inaugurated with the Gold Reserve Act of 1934 functioned properly. In particular, he spent a significant amount of time on the phone with overseas Treasury agents in order to make sure that the dollar exchange rate relative to other currencies stayed within the gold points or narrow corridor established by the new monetary system.[32]

On January 7, one day before the gold-clause hearings were to begin, the Roosevelt administration got very bad news. That day the Court ruled against the government in the "hot oil" case.[33] The question in front of the justices had been whether the government could restrict interstate shipments of oil in excess of predetermined state quotas. These restrictions had been imposed by the NRA as a way of avoiding the effect of dumping across state lines on oil prices. From a policy point of view, and in line with the overall philosophy of the NRA, the administration sought to reduce competition and encourage producers to cut supply as a way of keeping prices relatively stable. This policy was perhaps the clearest manifestation of the administration's desire to introduce some form of planning into the U.S. economy.

From a constitutional perspective the question was whether Congress could delegate its power to the executive. By an overwhelming vote of 8 to 1—Justice Cardozo was the lone dissenter—the Court ruled that Section 9(c) of the National Recovery Act was unconstitutional, since "Congress, without laying down proper rules to guide the Chief Executive, had delegated undue power to Mr. Roosevelt."[34] The Court gave no opinion regarding the Oil Code itself, but ruled that Congress could not delegate legislative power without limit. In his dissenting opinion, Justice Cardozo brought up the issue of emergency and necessity, an issue that was central in the government's position regarding the gold-clause cases. He wrote:[35]

what can be done under cover of that permission [the delegation of power] is closely and clearly circumscribed. . . . The statute was framed in the shadow of a *national disaster*. A host of unforeseen contingents would have to be faced from day to day. . . . The President was chosen to meet the instant *need*.

This time, however, Cardozo's views found no echo among his colleagues.

The Court's decision on the "hot oil" case was a hard blow for the administration. Although government officials, including the president, had considered the possibility of a negative vote, they thought that it would be a close call. The fact that even Justice Brandeis, considered to be a dependable ally of the administration and a supporter of the overall policies of the New Deal, voted with the majority was very disturbing. It was a bad omen on what could happen during the upcoming gold-clause cases.

CHAPTER 13

Embarrassment and Confusion

January 8, 1935–January 11, 1935

On January 12, 1935, after an eighteen-hour solo flight over the Pacific, Amelia Earhart landed in Oakland. It was the first time an aviator had crossed that ocean unaccompanied. After landing, she eased the Lockheed Vega towards the hangars. Without waiting for the propeller to come to a full stop, she emerged from the cockpit, smiled and rearranged her short hair; she then waved to a huge adoring crowd estimated to be close to ten thousand. After getting off the monoplane, she told reporters that it had been an uneventful flight, and credited her support staff for making it possible. The *New York Times* carried the story prominently on the front page of its Sunday, January 13, edition. There was a map with details about the route and a first-person account written by Earhart herself. The second-most-important story in that Sunday's edition of the *Times* referred to the upcoming trial of Bruno Richard Hauptmann, the man accused of kidnapping and murdering Charles A. Lindbergh's baby son. Also on the front page, sandwiched between the Earhart and Lindbergh stories, was an article on the recent Supreme Court hearings on the gold clause. It was titled, "Capital debates gold issue; justices confer for 5 hours." The piece explained that government lawyers, including Attorney General Homer Cummings, had done poorly at the hearings held on the 8, 9, and 10 of January, and that it was possible that the Joint Resolution abrogating the gold clause would be declared unconstitutional.

The story noted that the Court was expected to rule in the next few weeks, and captured the mood among analysts, legal experts, and politicians. According to the reporter, members of Congress belonging to the "inflationist bloc" were panicking. A reversal of the abrogation meant that for every dollar of original debts with the gold clause, debtors would now have to pay $1.69. This would generate tremendous financial stress and bankruptcies across scores of firms and farms, and would have serious deflationary effects.

Senators Elmer Thomas and Burton Wheeler stated that if the Court declared the Joint Resolution unconstitutional, they would introduce whatever legislation was required to avoid a return to the gold standard and deflation. Some senators, whose names were not provided in the article, were even considering adding two to three members to the Supreme Court, a move that President Roosevelt would attempt in 1937, at the beginning of his second term. According to the *Times*:

> The consensus was that [if the Court annuls the Joint Resolution] some offsetting action would at once be taken. Some Congressional inflationists were studying the possibility of increasing the membership of the Supreme Court from nine to eleven or twelve within the twenty-five days elapsing between the decision and the court ruling upon a government appeal for reconsideration. . . . President Roosevelt would leave nothing undone to offset a decision which would destroy the new monetary system built up by the administration. . . . [The President may assert] control over the currency under the old wartime laws which he invoked in bringing order out of the banking and financial disruption which existed when he took office.

THE HEARINGS

January 8, 1935, was the first of three days of arguments at the Supreme Court. From the early hours the small chamber in the Senate building, where the Court operated in those days, was filled with spectators. There were prominent lawyers, reporters, executives from railroad companies, CEOs from large manufacturing firms, bankers, and politicians. Hundreds of people who wanted to witness the arguments could not get in and were turned away at the doors. In the front row sat Senators Connally of Texas, Wagner of New York, Robinson of Arkansas—the majority leader in the Senate—Gore of Oklahoma, and Buckley of Ohio. The distinguished, silver-haired John W. Davis, the Democratic candidate for the presidency in 1924, was also there, as was Jesse Jones, the chairman of the Reconstruction Finance Corporation.[1]

Homer S. Cummings, the attorney general, opened his argument by making a general plea involving all cases. He presented, in a succinct fashion, what the government had argued at length in its three massive briefs. The tall, distinguished, and soft-spoken lawyer noted that the Joint Resolution was undertaken in the midst of the worst crisis that the nation had ever faced, "an industrial and financial crisis of the most terrifying character," a crisis where "failures and bankruptcies were attaining unparalleled proportions, [where] our people were slipping to the lower level of civilization."[2]

Given the depth of this emergency, the attorney general continued in a grave tone, the government faced the obligation and the necessity to act and bring relief. Monetary policy was a key component of the administration's relief policy, and within monetary policy, raising the price of gold—or devaluing the dollar—played a crucial role. It was a required step in the effort to bring the deflation to an end and to raise prices. He then asserted that "failure of Congress to act in 1933 would have made impossible the carrying into effect of the relief program. The government could not have effected this relief if all these gold-clause contracts had been written up 69 per cent."[3]

Cummings continued his presentation by stating that the gold clauses were contrary to public policy. Abrogating contracts was necessary in order for the devaluation of the dollar to be effective and to contribute successfully to bringing deflation to an end. If enforced, the attorney general argued, gold clauses would "interfere with recent monetary measures adopted to protect the gold reserves of the United States." In addition, their enforcement would deprive the Congress of its power to regulate the value of the dollar. He added that a decision against the government's position would reduce the balance in the Treasury by $2.5 billion and would result in a $69 billion increase in the private and public debts of the nation. To put things in perspective, in 1935 this was almost as high as the country's GNP.[4] The attorney general closed his argument by predicting that if the gold clauses were let to stand there would be generalized financial chaos, not only in the country but in the whole world.

During the second day, the government position was argued by RFC head lawyer Stanley Reed (who in 1938 would join the Supreme Court as an associate justice) and by Assistant Solicitor General Angus D. Mac-Lean.[5] They carefully and punctiliously followed the script laid out by the three government briefs, and expanded on many of the points made by the attorney general the previous day. They argued that the Joint Resolution was grounded on the powers that the Constitution gives to Congress. They added that the Joint Resolution was not capricious; on the contrary, it responded to an economic necessity, given the deep crisis that prevailed in the country. Congress, they said, had a strong basis to determine that the gold clause was contrary to public policy, inconsistent with the monetary system in which all currency and coins are legal tender of equal value.

Stanley Reed, who according to a news report was tall, spruce, tense, keen, factual, and tended to eschew oratorical methods, summarized, in his closing remarks, the government's position very clearly. He repeated what had been said before by his colleagues: given the emergency, a new monetary policy was required. This, as had been the case in other nations in the early 1930s, implied devaluing the currency as a way of raising prices. However, Congress could not in effect undertake this policy effectively if a dual monetary system prevailed, a system with two types of money, gold coin and lawful U.S. money. Under that dual system, he repeated, a devaluation would result in such a large increase in debt values that, without any doubt, there would be massive bankruptcies and the economy would come to a halt. He said that the gold-clause contracts were entered with the knowledge that Congress had the power to fix the value of the dollar. Reed declared that this was a "risk the bondholders assumed when they purchased these securities." As Reed spoke, Justice James Clark McReynolds asked a page boy to go and fetch for him a copy of *Who's Who in America*; he wanted to know who was this man who dared question the sanctity of contracts.[6]

The plaintiffs' positions were argued by James H. McIntosh and Edward W. Bourne, in representation of the Missouri & Pacific bondholders; by Emanuel Redfield, who represented Norman in his suit against Baltimore & Ohio; by Otto C. Sommerich in representation of F. Eugene Nortz, who owned a gold certificate; and by John H. Perry, a lawyer, who represented himself in the case involving a Liberty Bond. They all made similar points: neither Congress nor the government had the power to annul contracts retroactively. Property rights were protected by the Constitution, and the abrogation of the gold clause was a form of taking property without compensation. This was in clear violation of the Fifth Amendment of the Constitution. Moreover, by abrogating the gold clauses Congress was infringing the rights of states and municipalities. They all recognized that there was a difference between being paid in actual bullion—something their clients did not expect—and receiving the amount in paper dollars corresponding to the face value of the security calculated at the new price of gold. It was this type of gold-equivalent payment that their clients were seeking. They believed, as Redfield put it to the Court on January 8, that "because payment in actual gold was impossible, since the government had seized all stocks of that metal, the obligation to pay the equivalent was not . . . reduced."[7] The lawyers for the plaintiffs disputed the attorney general's assertion that reversing the abrogation would bring chaos to the nation. Edward W. Bourne, who represented bond holders of the Missouri & Pacific Company, argued that paying these debts at $1.69 per original dollar would have no serious effect on monetary policy. He contested the idea that gold had a public interest, like light, water and air. Bourne closed by saying: "If it [gold] has any public interest it is as a standard of value; and this being so, why should it not be used in gold clause contracts?"

McIntosh, the lawyer for the Missouri & Pacific creditors, gave a long explanation of the meaning and purpose of the gold clause. From today's perspectives, his arguments sound extraordinarily modern, not very different from the arguments used recurrently in litigation involving sovereign debt and contracts repudiation, including the numerous cases involving Argentina during the first decade and a half of the twenty-first century. McIntosh explained that the railroads inserted the gold clause in their bonds because the companies were aware that they would not be able to raise money for a long period of time (say, thirty years) without protecting creditors against the possible depreciation of the currency. If one replaces "railroads" with "Argentina" one would get, almost word by word, one of the legal arguments made by plaintiffs in the Argentine cases heard by different arbitration tribunals during the 2000s.

McIntosh, a tall, impeccably dressed white-haired gentleman, went on to say that the gold clause "has been essential to the building up of this

FIGURE 13.1. Attorney General Homer S. Cummings tells Senator
Duncan U. Fletcher (D. of Florida), that the "gold clause" legislation was a
"legitimate and inevitable outcome." (*Source*: Harris & Ewing Collection,
Library of Congress)

country. It has been the only method of borrowing money for long
periods of time." The lawyer got so caught up with his own rhetoric that
at the height of his discourse, at the time his voice thundered in the august chamber, he lost the upper plate from his dentures. The *Chicago
Daily Tribune* reported that he "caught it, however, and replaced it without loss of dignity." He was then able to finish his argument.[8]

Observers and legal analysts were surprised that no questions were asked from the bench during the first day of proceedings, something extremely uncommon in the Hughes Court. Things, however, changed dramatically on days two and three, when the justices interjected their questions frequently. The barrage of questions started when the chief justice interrupted Mr. McIntosh, counsel for the creditors of Missouri & Pacific, and asked what the meaning of "value" was? What a dollar can buy at any moment in time, or is it the metal content of the currency in question? McIntosh answered without hesitating: it was, as contracts specified, a gold coin of certain weight and fineness. Justice Butler asked whether in the opinion of the government lawyers Congress could make "the dime a dollar." Stanley Reed, in representation of the RFC, answered that, although it could appear strange, contradictory and against logic, that action was, indeed, within the power of Congress.[9]

But the most important questions, the questions that shocked analysts and had rapid repercussion in Wall Street, came during the last day of the arguments. According to news analyses published on January 11, these questions "seemed to indicate that some members of the court were in grave doubt as to the constitutionality of the abrogation laws and resolutions." Perhaps the most difficult question came from Chief Justice Hughes. After Assistant Solicitor General McLean stated that by abrogating the gold clause in Liberty Bonds, Congress was exercising the sovereign power that the Constitution vested on it, Justice Hughes leaned forward and in his slightly nasal voice asked:[10]

Here you have a bond issued by the United States Government, issued in a time of war and in the exercise of its war powers. A bond which the government promised to pay in a certain kind of money. Where do you find any power under the Constitution to alter that bond, or the power of Congress to change that promise?

MacLean answered by saying, once again, that Article 1, Section 8, gave Congress the power to coin money and regulate the value thereof. He then added that after the British devaluation of 1931 the House of Lords had upheld payment in sterling rather than in gold. He was brusquely interrupted by Justice Van Devanter who interjected: "What England can do, what Germany or any other nation can do has no controlling influence here." [11]

Other questions asked by Justices McReynolds, Butler, and Sutherland, revolved around a similar issue: Where did the Constitution give Congress the power to alter a solemn contract, a promise to pay the government debts in a certain way, the power to take property without proper compensation?

Justice Harlan Fiske Stone asked if the government could fix a value in his farm and then take it away from him without just compensation. And Justice Sutherland inquired, in reference to the gold certificate, "Isn't this certificates both a receipt and a contract, as well as a promise to pay in gold of a given amount and standard of fineness?"[12] Although the questions were varied, the government lawyers stuck to their prepared answers, and stated repeatedly that the Constitution allowed Congress to coin money. At one point Justice McReynolds became visibly exasperated and scolded Stanley Reed: "It seems to me that you assert that right over and over again without giving me any reason to support it."[13]

During the last day of arguments, and towards the end of his presentation, Assistant Solicitor General MacLean said that the government "cannot bind itself in contracts in such a way as to limit its authority." At that point the chief justice, once again, interrupted, and asked:[14]

Is it not the very essence of sovereignty to be able to bind a sovereign State in a contract to borrow money? Does not the validity of international law depend, as a matter of international law, on the power of the sovereign State issuing obligations to bind itself to repay those obligations and to fix the conditions of the repayment? Is it not the very essence of sovereignty to be able to contract, since it may be necessary to do so in the interest of its own security?

Acute analysts and old-time Court observers noticed that throughout the proceedings not a single question was asked by two of the "Three Musketeers." Justices Brandeis and Cardozo sat quietly, and followed the arguments intently; they took notes, and never smiled or frowned. Justice Roberts, the jurist who was usually the swing vote, did not ask any questions either.[15]

Every observer agreed that counsel for the government had not handled the questions in the best of ways. According to the *Chicago Daily Tribune*: "at least four of the justices . . . indicated impatience with the New Deal theory that Congress, by declaring an emergency, can wipe out the gold clause in 100 billion dollars of contracts." The article then added: [16]

> the astute questions from the bench led to embarrassment and confusion on the part of the lawyers and for the second time in the course of considering New Deal legislation the learned justices joined in the laughter of the spectators. The last time the justices laughed, an almost unprecedented thing for that august bench, was in the NRA "hot oil" case, which was decided against the government in an 8 to 1 decision on Monday [January 7, 1935].

The next day the Chicago daily was even more critical. It said that "it was the third day of arguments in this most vital of New Deal legislation and the third day on which government counsel palpably suffered in comparison to its adversaries."[17] The *Washington Post* pointed out that government lawyers "did not have smooth going," and wondered whether that explained their late emphasis on the consequences of a reinstatement of the clause, of "what would happen if the court ruled adversely."[18]

The justices' pointed questions generated a sense of despondency among administration lawyers. Suddenly things did not look so bright, and an adverse ruling seemed highly probable. Many of them remembered that only a few days earlier the Court had ruled against the government in the *Panama Oil* case. As the proceedings were coming to an end on January 10, the attorney general asked for an additional half hour on the next day, when he was to say a few words—a "prayer" in legal terms—to the Court. The petition, which was granted, was unusual and did not escape analysts' attention. In his final presentation, Cummings was emotional and asked the Court to consider the "general welfare" of the nation. He also pointed out that he was ready to go back to the Court if the justices thought that he had not presented an adequate or convincing case. The *Chicago Daily Tribune* pointed out that according to veteran members of the bar "such a statement, which they interpreted as tantamount to a confession of weakness, to be without precedent in the nation's highest court."[19]

CHAPTER 14

◇◇◇◇◇

The Waiting Game

January 12, 1935–February 25, 1935

The markets reacted to the government's lukewarm performance in the Supreme Court with extreme nervousness. Many analysts believed that an adverse ruling meant a return to the gold standard, and a new bout of deflation. Prices declined across the board for stocks, corporate bonds, and commodities. The only exception was for government securities with the gold clause. One problem, however, was that the supply of that type of paper was extremely low, since the administration had deliberately retired large amounts of Liberty Bonds and had replaced them with conventional securities. On January 12 the *Los Angeles Times* ran a lengthy story titled "Sharp break on market. Fight over gold clause factor." Similarly, the *New York Times* pointed out in a front-page article that markets had been "wrenched" by the gold cases. Pessimism was so deep that the market had completely ignored good news, including the improvement in the number of freight cars loaded for the week—a record in recent history—and the fact that the National Steel Corporation had declared an extra dividend. This was the first time an extraordinary dividend was paid by a listed company in many years.[1]

On January 13 the *New York Times* pointed out that due to "the speculative fever for 'gold'" the price of Liberty Bonds had reached their highest since their issuance in 1917. According to the article, "should the gold-clause case now before the United States Supreme Court go against the government, a complete reclassification of prices of gold and nongold State and municipal bonds would be in order." [2] That same day another article in the *Times* noticed that it was ironic that the Supreme Court was considering the gold-clause cases at a time when the United States held almost 40 percent of all the monetary gold in the world; official holdings of the metal were at "an exceedingly high level, measured in terms either of 'old' dollar or the 'new.'"[3] Eugene M. Lokey pointed out in his popular Saturday column that the federal government debt subject to the debt clause held by the public was roughly $10.2 billion, about one half of what it had been in June 1933. This significant reduction was the result of refinancing operations initiated by then secretary of the treasury Will Woodin, and expanded by his successor Henry Morgenthau Jr. Lokey added that most people were unaware of the fact that "nearly all of the $20,000,000,000 of obligations of States, municipalities, &c., was theoretically payable in gold, and that an invalidation by the Supreme Court of the clause-revocation act would, also theoretically, add about $13,000,000,000 to that debt."[4]

During January, commodity prices declined across the board, as depicted in figure 14.1. These price movements happened in spite of the fact that a few days earlier the president had unveiled the most inflationary budget of his administration. Global markets were not indifferent to the Supreme Court hearings and to the, now, nontrivial probability that the Joint Resolution would be voided. On January 15, the international value of the dollar rose significantly, as international speculators considered the consequences of a return of the dollar to its old parity of $20.67 per ounce of gold. At the end of that day the franc was still 2.7 percent below its parity. The U.S. Treasury intervened promptly, and sold dollars massively in the UK, France, and the other gold-bloc countries.

In spite of significant changes in the international price of gold, no large bank wanted to engage in gold commerce. According to a news story, "Yesterday the margin of profit on gold imports from Europe reached fabulous dimensions, but no banks engaged gold. They feared that while it was on the way here, the government might revalue the dollar and instead of receiving $35 an ounce they might get only $20.67 an ounce, the old statutory price."[5] In spite of the Treasury's massive intervention, during the days that followed, the gold-bloc currencies continued to be under pressure.

Foreign governments also faced great uncertainty. Germany, for example, had taken the view that since Congress had voided the gold clause, it could pay its own dollar-denominated debt to U.S. creditors in paper

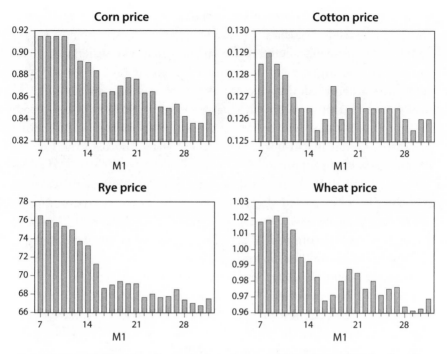

FIGURE 14.1. Daily prices for agricultural commodities, immediately after the Supreme Court hearings, January 7 to January 31, 1935.

dollars. Thus, an adverse Supreme Court ruling would result in a 69 percent increase in German debts; the amount affected was estimated to be in the order of $750 million. This was particularly serious, since Germany "was trying to renegotiate its debt with private Wall Street banks . . . [and] all of Germany's old long term bonds included the gold clause."[6] A news report wired from Berlin pointed out that "to the Nazi mind the idea of a mere court's undertaking to review the Executive's action is virtually inconceivable. The Nazi Government is a government of one man to whom all others owe blind obedience."[7]

As the days passed, speculation on what could happen became wild. The fear among many politicians was that the main effect of a decision voiding the Joint Resolution "would be to raise gold bonds and gold-clause contracts to 169 percent of their face value." According to a press report, many economists believed that if the Court's ruling was adverse to the government, "an act of Congress revaluing the dollar upward [to its old parity] not only would be the simplest but possibly the most politic thing to do."[8] Not surprisingly, the inflationist bloc in Congress did not like the idea, and considered a series of possible remedies. For the bloc a strong dollar was to be avoided at all costs. Senator Burton Wheeler, one of the faction's leaders, argued that if the Court decision was adverse, Congress could pass a constitutional reform giving the government the right to alter contracts retroactively. After being passed by Congress, the amendment would be submitted quickly to the state legislatures. In Wheeler's view, thirty-six legislatures would ratify it at once. Another idea that was floated in Washington was to "levy a tax of 69 cents on each $1.69 of devalued currency collected per unit of old-gold dollar, putting the extra 69 cents on each government contract back in the Treasury, and reimbursing private corporations in the same degree." Legal scholars, however, pointed out that it was highly likely that this scheme would be challenged in court for violating the "due process" clause.[9]

In an effort to gain some insight on the upcoming decision, the press scrutinized every movement by every justice. On Saturday January 19, it was noticed that after the routine "conference" of the Court, six of the members stayed behind for an informal gathering. According to some reporters this was clear indication that a decision on the gold cases had been reached and that on Monday January 21 it would be handed down.

Monday came and went, without a pronouncement by the Court.[10] Uncertainty mounted significantly, and market participants were not quite sure on how to proceed. Suddenly, logistical difficulties intervened. On January 25, the press reported that international gold operations had almost halted due to "the growing scarcity of shipping facilities for landing gold here before Feb. 4, when the United States Supreme Court is expected to hand down its decision in the gold clause cases."[11]

During the first week of February, rumors grew at an alarming pace. According to news stories, the Court's decision would uphold the abrogation for government bonds held by U.S. nationals, but require the government to make payments at the old parity to foreign creditors.[12] The situation was considered to be so serious and unstable that the Securities and Exchange Commission released a statement saying that it would ask the president for authority to close the nation's exchanges, if needed.[13] On February 4, the governors of the New York Stock Exchange announced that the Exchange was prepared for any eventuality in case the Supreme Court decision generated abnormal volatility; trading would be suspended, if necessary.

By February 8, it was still unclear when the Court would announce its decision. However, almost every observer believed that following the precedent established in the "hot oil" case, the decision would be "deferred until the stock market has closed for the day."[14] The same day, reporters noted that the traditional, annual White House dinner in honor of the Supreme Court had taken place the previous night. Seven of the nine Justices attended, as did a score of other dignitaries, including Attorney General Homer Cummings, and Solicitor General James Crawford Biggs. The event was pleasant; gold, commented the press, was not one of the subjects of discussion. Some reporters noted that it was significant that one of the guests at the traditional dinner was none else than former Brains Trust head and former assistant secretary of state, Raymond Moley. His relations with the president seemed to be improving.[15]

FDR DOES NOT GIVE UP

As soon as the hearings were over on January 11, the White House began to prepare for the worst. It was eminently possible that the ruling would be adverse, and that at least some aspects of the Joint Resolution would be declared unconstitutional. From the first moment, the president decided that that he would not allow the nation to go back to the old parity; he asked his advisers to look at every possible way out, in case the Court overturned the Joint Resolution.[16]

On January 16, the secretary of the treasury and the attorney general met for several hours to devise a strategy for the days to come. It was decided that opinions from several prominent jurists would be sought on possible courses of action. When asked about the meetings, Secretary Morgenthau replied that his department was "doing its homework."[17] A few days later, when asked about the imminent handing down of the decision, Attorney General Cummings said, "We are ready for any emergency."[18] According to press reports, one of the most important points discussed by the two senior officials was what to do if the Court ruled that payment in gold-equivalent had to be made to foreign holders of government bonds.[19] On January 29, Senator Pat Harrison, the chairman of the Finance Committee, said that if the gold cases were decided against the government, the Senate would likely "be here getting out of our troubles." He declined to be more specific on what he, or his colleagues, had in mind.[20] Less than a week later, the *Los Angeles Times* reported, in a front-page article, that the president had "definitely decided against the restoration of the former gold value of the dollar, even if the Supreme Court would rule adversely."[21]

On Saturday, February 9, the Court's clerk released a statement saying that no decisions would be announced during the coming Monday. This type of announcement was unprecedented in the history of the Court, and was interpreted as an explicit effort by the chief justice to avoid excessive and unnecessary market volatility. The press speculated that the rulings might be handed down on Tuesday, as the stock market would be closed to honor Lincoln's birthday. The *New York Times* reported that the White House continued to be very concerned about the decisions. In a front-page story, it reported that the highest government officials were spending immense amounts of time getting ready for the rulings:[22]

> Emerging from the White House after a two hours' meeting with President Roosevelt, Attorney General Cummings would say nothing. . . . Silent as he was, it became known that the conference related almost solely about the gold issue. . . . As there are a number of possible decisions in the four gold cases argued in the Supreme Court precisely thirty days ago, a very comprehensive defense program has been formulated by the government, involving many eventualities. Steps of all kinds which either the state or Congress might quickly take, have been studied and charted and could be swung into action with surprising speed, it is stated in authoritative quarters.

A few days later, it was Henry Morgenthau Jr.'s turn to calm the markets. He declared that "the country can go about its business with assurance that we are prepared to manage the external value of the dollar as long as necessary."[23] He then added that during the previous month the Treasury had used the $2 billion Exchange Stabilization Fund to keep the dollar steady. This was the first time in over a year that the administration acknowledged using the fund created by the Gold Reserve Act of 1934, and funded with the profits from the devaluation of the dollar from $20.67 to $35 an ounce. Market participants asked themselves what would happen next.

Immediately after the hearings, President Roosevelt's inclination was to create enough market turmoil, so the members of the Supreme Court would understand that if they ruled against the government there would, indeed, be "chaos," as the attorney general had anticipated. On January 14, merely three days after the hearings, FDR had lunch with Henry Morgenthau Jr. and with the attorney general. The secretary of the treasury confided to his diary that Roosevelt said: "I want bonds to move up and down. . . . [I]f we keep things in a constant turmoil if the case should go against us the man in the street will say for God's sake, Mr. President, do something about it."[24] Both Cummings and Morgenthau were horrified at the suggestion of deliberately generating market volatility, and tried to persuade the president that the plan was a very bad idea. The following evening, at a dinner at Vice-president Garner's residence, Roosevelt was in good spirits and told those in attendance that he wanted markets to stay calm, independently of the Supreme Court decision. He smiled broadly and looking at Morgenthau said that he had taken "the side of the opposition in order to bring out the various points but of course I didn't believe in these [market turmoil] arguments." The plan was filed, new defensive moves were analyzed, and new strategies were devised by an army of advisers and high-ranking officials.[25]

Seymour Parker Gilbert was a respected lawyer with ample experience in financial issues. He was undersecretary of the treasury during the Harding administration, and in 1924, at age thirty-two, he was appointed agent general of reparations. In that position, he supervised the implementation of the Dawes Plan, and became an expert in all aspects of international finance. In mid-January 1935, and in light of the shaky performance of the government team at the Supreme Court, the secretary of the treasury asked him for his legal opinion on what the administration could do if the Court voided the Joint Resolution. On January 17, Parker Gilbert produced a six-page memorandum on the options open to the government. His first point was that in case of an adverse decision the Treasury had to "announce, without more than a few minutes' delay, its program for dealing with the situation. Otherwise there will be danger of severe panic, and of serious setback to recovery."[26] From here Parker Gilbert moved to the issue of damages, and argued that in case of a negative decision the object of the government's action should be to deprive claimants "of any measure of damage." There was a potential problem with this strategy, he noted, since the fact that the new paper dollar was worth 59.06 cents of the old dollar, provided a "ready-made measure of damages."[27]

On February 12, Henry Morgenthau Jr. had a long telephone conversation with George Harrison, the president of the New York Federal Reserve Bank, on a possible statement by the secretary aimed at calming the markets. The gist of the potential message was that independently of the Supreme Court decision the Treasury was "prepared to manage the external value of the dollar as long as it may be necessary."[28] Harrison was troubled by the notion of providing too many details on how the Treasury had operated in the last few months. In particular, he resisted the idea of saying whether the Treasury intervention had been in the gold or currency markets. He then wondered what would happen if there was a strong speculative spike in the demand for dollars after the decision. In his view, a strong commitment on what the Treasury might do was "a mistake." For the next few minutes the two officials talked about the degree of assurance that the government should provide, and on the exact language to use in the statement. A few days later, the secretary called Harrison to inform him that when the Supreme Court decision came, the Treasury would "operate both in London and Paris with the objective of trying to keep gold within the gold points."[29]

AN AGENDA FOR IMMEDIATE ACTION

By mid-February the White House had developed an elaborate contingent plan that considered eight possible outcomes. A carbon copy of the strategy is in Henry Morgenthau's papers held at the Roosevelt Presidential Library. The summary strategy has the suggestive title "Alternative Agendae [sic] of Immediate Action."[30] The first outcome considered was that all cases were favorable to the government. Under those circumstances the immediate action was to "rejoice and be thankful." The other seven options in the document considered all possible combinations of positive and negative decisions by the Court on the three cases where the government took a part.

The second numeral in the "Alternative Agendae" document referred to the worst possible outcome for the administration: decisions on all cases were "adverse on the merits." Under this contingency the strategy considered six actions, including a proclamation by the president, a message to the Congress asking it to pass legislation that would correct the situation, a press release, and two resolutions: one withdrawing the right to sue the government on gold-related claims, and the other withholding appropriations to make gold-clause-related payments to bond holders.

The other alternative outcomes considered in the "Alternative Agendae" plan included the case where the Liberty Bond case was adverse, but the rest were favorable, or if the private bonds cases were adverse, but the Liberty Bonds and gold certificate cases were favorable to the government.

The language and aim of the different components of the administration's contingent plan are so extraordinary, that they merit to be quoted at length. The draft proclamation by the president indicated that the state of emergency defined by the Emergency Banking Act of March 9, 1933, still existed. As a consequence, the president would impose a ninety-day stay on any debt payment in excess of the nominal dollar amount of the obligation. The draft read:[31]

I, Franklin D. Roosevelt, President of the United States, by virtue of the authority vested in me, do thereby declare that the national emergency hitherto found and declared to exist, continues, and, in order to permit a period of adjustment to prevent the bankruptcies and the destruction of credit which would result from immediate attempts to realize upon claims arising from provisions declared by said Public Resolution to be against public policy, I do hereby proclaim, order, direct and declare that until the expiration of a period of 90 days from this day, or the earlier revocation of this proclamation by me, every payment by any banking institution organized or doing business in the United States . . . is prohibited in every case where such payment or transfer, or any part thereof, is made or . . . will be applied, in full or partial payment of any obligation in an amount over and above the steed dollar amount thereof because of any claim arising from any provision declared in said Public Resolution to be against public policy.

A series of messages to Congress, asking for new legislation to deal with the consequences of the Court's decisions were also drafted. The first such draft message was simple and confined to one page. It asked the legislative branch to pass legislation withdrawing the right to sue the government on claims arising from the gold clause, and asked it not to appropriate any funds for making those payments. In its core part it read:[32]

I [Franklin D. Roosevelt] recommend legislation to the Congress withdrawing the right to sue the United States on its bonds, currency or similar obligations, withholding appropriations for the payment of more than the face amount thereof and making it unlawful for any officer of the United States to pay in excess of such amount. The passage of bills for this purpose becomes immediately necessary because of the decision of the Supreme Court just announced in the *North* and *Perry* cases.

Subsequent drafts of the president's message to Congress extended the length of the stay, during which payments on government debts could not exceed the nominal dollar value, from ninety days to one year, and asked Congress to reaffirm the proclamation withdrawing the right of individuals and corporations to sue the United States in the Court of Claims for debts related to the gold clause.

A report prepared by the Office of the Solicitor General explained that since 1855, the type of cases against the government that could be taken by the Court of Claims had changed many times. In particular, the report noted, after the Civil War the right to sue the government for actions by the army in its effort to fight rebellions was withdrawn. In subsequent reforms, the government also limited the right of citizens of other nations to sue the government.[33] Along these lines, during the first half of February 1935, while waiting for the Supreme Court's decisions, the Roosevelt administration produced a detailed draft bill amending Section 24, Subsection 20, of the Judicial Code, which established which type of claims against the United States may be considered by the Court of Claims. The proposed amendment to the relevant Section of the code read as follows:[34]

[The Court of Claims has no] jurisdiction to hear and determine claims arising out of bonds, contracts or other obligations for the repayment of money made, issued or guaranteed by the United States, or *arising out of gold or silver bullion, or any coin or currency of the United States*, or out of the surrender, requisition, seizure or acquisition of any such coin, bullion or currency.

If passed by Congress, as it was very likely to be the case, it would become impossible for holders of gold-clause government bonds to obtain their money back from the government. This amendment of the Code, however, would do nothing for private debtors. In that sense, an adverse decision in the *Norman* case would generate significantly more havoc in financial markets than in the *Perry* case, on the Liberty Bond.

The draft legislation declaring a one-year moratorium on payments arising from the (supposedly) adverse Supreme Court decision stated that the reason for Congress taking such action was to "establish justice, insure domestic tranquility, provide for the common defence, promote the general welfare, and securing the blessing of liberty to ourselves and our posterity."[35]

THE NIGHT OF THE DAY

A key element in the White House strategy was a direct appeal from the president to the American people. On Monday, February 11, during lunch, FDR told Henry Morgenthau Jr. "you eat and let me read my proposed radio speech to be given on the night of the day the court hands down the decision." As he read, the president smiled and chuckled, very "pleased with himself and with the statement." When he finished reading, the president told the secretary of the treasury that "Joe Kennedy thinks that the statement is so strong that they will burn the Supreme Court in effigy."[36]

There is a draft of the speech in the Roosevelt Presidential Library. At the top of the first page, FDR wrote in black ink: "File—Private. This is a rough draft of radio address I *would* have made if the Supreme Court decision in the Gold Cases had gone against the Gov." He then signed his full name and dated it "Feb 18 1935." [37]

In the opening paragraphs of this draft speech, which was never given, and that, with a high degree of probability, would have generated a deep constitutional crisis, the president described his administration's efforts to defeat deflation. The main objective of these policies, he wrote, was to bring the inflation-adjusted value of debts back to what they had been when contracted. This, he pointed out, required "a dollar of stable purchasing power." The president then explained that significant progress had been made since his accession to power: "We have brought about present dollar value which is within twenty percent of what it was when the majority of debts, private and governmental, were incurred."

However, the draft speech went on, by rendering decisions "based on the legal proposition that the exact terms of a contract must be literally enforced," these efforts were being derailed by the Supreme Court rulings. Then the president provided a series of examples of the effects of the Court's decisions. He wrote that "if the letter of the law is so declared and enforced, it would throw practically all the railroads of the United States into bankruptcy." He then referred to the effects on mortgages and families. Here he wrote that as a consequence of the Supreme Court decisions "home owners, whether city workers or farmers, could not meet such a demand [paying 69 percent more on their mortgages]."

The next part of the proposed speech dealt with the consequences of a negative Court decision on public debt. The president recognized that the "actual enforcement of the gold clause against the Government will not bankrupt the Government." But making payments in gold-equivalent coin would require an additional $9 billion effort, an effort that would be paid by all Americans, an effort that would hurt, in particular, those with fewer means. He then went back to one of his favorite arguments: all the gold in the world was not enough to pay the debts that included gold clauses. The fact that none of the plaintiffs had asked for payment in gold, but wanted to be paid in gold-equivalent legal money, did not appear to bother him.

Towards the end of the draft speech, the president quoted Abraham Lincoln at length: "if the policy of the government . . . is to be irrevocably fixed by decisions of the Supreme Court . . . the people would have ceased to be their own rulers." President Roosevelt then wrote: "To stand idly by and to permit the decision of the Supreme Court to be carried through to its logical, inescapable conclusion would so imperil the economic and political security of this nation that the legislative and executive officers of the Government must look beyond the narrow letter of contractual obligations."

The draft speech ended with a reference to the Bible and with a brief summary of his proposed course of action:

> For value received the same value should be repaid. That is the spirit of the contract and of the law. Every individual or corporation, public or private, should pay back substantially what they borrowed. That would seem to be a decision in accordance with the Golden

Rule, with the precepts of the Scriptures, and the dictates of common sense.

In order to attain this reasonable end, I shall immediately take such steps as may be necessary, by proclamation and by message to the Congress of the United States.

On February 11, the day he read the speech draft to Henry Morgenthau Jr. the president didn't know what the Supreme Court decisions would be. What he did know was that he would not stand idle while a majority of those "nine old men" tried to wreck one of the most important accomplishments of his administration.[38]

CHAPTER 15

◇◇◇◇◇

The Decisions, at Last

February 16, 1935–February 25, 1935

On February16, the Court held its traditional Saturday conference. At the end of the meeting, the chief justice made no announcements. This was taken by the press as a clear indication that on Monday, February 18, the Court would finally hand down the long-awaited decisions on the gold cases. This was the last chance for doing so during February, as the Court was about to begin its two-week winter recess. According to a newspaper story, "eight of the justices went calmly to their automobiles when their meeting was ended. After that, close watch was kept on the small chamber where Mr. Hughes remained apparently alone. . . . The gold cases have now been before the Court for more than five weeks." The reporter then pointed out that a decision adverse to the government would, with all likelihood, rattle financial markets in the United States and abroad. "How much the court will take the stock market in consideration when it promulgates its decision is subject to speculation. Chief Justice Hughes did delay announcing the "hot oil" opinion until the market had been closed for the day, and perhaps a similar course will be taken on the gold case."[1]

On Monday morning, February 18, the secretary of the treasury and his main legal adviser, Herman Oliphant, walked into the Cabinet Room in the White House a few minutes past 11 o'clock. They had installed a special phone line connected to the Treasury's "gold room." A minute past noon a second line rang. It was Joseph Kennedy, informing the secretary that the decision was coming. Henry Morgenthau Jr. had agreed with

Kennedy that "as he got word from his men who had a phone in the Supreme Court he should phone me. I felt the President would get a greater kick out of it if he talked to Kennedy directly so from then on I turned over the phone to him."[2]

A STIRRING VOICE AND A ROLLERCOASTER

At eight in the morning, a long line had already formed outside of the Supreme Court. Hundreds of people wanted to witness the historic decision. According to court functionaries, never in living memories had there been such a massive interest in any issue. At 11:55 A.M. the justices slowly entered the small room, with a capacity for barely 300 people. According to the press the room was full of "notables." The wives of the chief justice and of Associate Justices Butler and Roberts were there, as was the wife of the secretary of the treasury, Mrs. Elinor Morgenthau. A score of senators were in the front row, including Elmer Thomas from Oklahoma, the undisputed leader of the inflationist bloc. Dean Acheson, not in government any longer, was also present. One of the "lookers-on noted that the scene resembled a first night at a Washington theater."[3] The attorney general, who had led the government team during the hearings five weeks earlier, was absent. He decided that it was best to wait for the decisions in his office. Solicitor General J. Crawford Biggs and Assistant Solicitor General Angus D. MacLean, who had handled a barrage of difficult questions from the justices on January 9–10 hearings, sat at the government's table.

When the justices entered the room, "the audience rose as if on puppet wires."[4] The justices "found great difficulty in making their way through the crowded corridors."[5] Once the nine men, in their solemn black robes, took their seats, the chief justice took a piece of paper, and without any preamble, he began to read. Breaking with historical precedent, instead of plunging into the rulings, he decided to deliver first a summary of the Court's findings.[6] After the summary he explained, with a clear voice, the grounds for the decisions. He accentuated his "points with gestures as he proceeded." [7]

Meanwhile, at the White House, the president had joined the small group in the Cabinet Room, and listened intently to Joseph Kennedy's rendition, over the phone, of what was going on in the Court. Everyone was nervous, and feared that the decisions would be adverse. At one point, FDR's secretary, Missy LeHand, asked the president "whether she could find out how her gold stock was doing. . . . The President told her quite firmly 'no.'"[8] During the next few minutes the small group went through an emotional rollercoaster.

There was a great sigh of relief among government officials and supporters when in his summary the chief justice said that in the private debt cases it was clear that "these [gold] clauses interfere with the exertion of powers granted to the Congress [by the Constitution]."[9] The decision on the constitutionality of the Joint Resolution for private debts was reached by a 5–4 vote, with the "Four Horsemen" in the minority. The abrogation of the gold clauses for private contracts was constitutional, and debtors could discharge their debts using legal currency.

Elation turned to deep concern when Chief Justice Hughes read the summary for the two public debt cases. In a clear, stirring voice he said:

> We conclude that the joint resolution of June 5, 1933, in so far as it attempted to override the obligation created by the bond in the suit, went beyond Congressional power. . . . The Congress . . . is endowed with certain powers to be exerted on behalf of the people in the manner and with the effect the Constitution ordains. . . . Having this power to authorize the issue of definite obligations for the payment of money borrowed, the Congress has not been vested with authority to alter or destroy those obligations.

It was a defeat for the government. The majority of the justices—eight out of nine—had voted for declaring the abrogation of the gold clause, as it applied to federal debt, unconstitutional. It seemed that the administration's contingent plan would have to be activated after all, and that the draft speech prepared in great secret to be used "during the night of the day" of the decision, would have to be delivered by the president. And then, when everything seemed lost, came the last part of the decision. The chief justice, declared that according to the majority, the "plaintiff [John Perry] has not shown or attempted to show that in relation to buying power he has sustained any loss whatsoever. On the contrary . . . payment to the plaintiff of the amount which he demands would appear to constitute not a recoupment of loss in any proper sense, but an unjustified enrichment."[10]

There it was: by a vote of 5 to 4 the Court had accepted the government's secondary argument that the abrogation of the gold clause had not produced any damages to bond holders; in terms of purchasing power over goods and services, bondholders were at least as well off in 1933, as they had been at the time the Liberty Bonds were issued. Although Congress and the Executive branch were scolded by the Court for passing an unconstitutional statute regarding public debt, bondholders could not sue in the Court of Claims for damages. Thus, there was no practical economic consequence for having passed an unconstitutional law. The new dollar policy—including the Gold Reserve Act of 1934, and the Exchange Stabilization Fund created by it—would continue to operate. To the relief of administration officials, there was no need to consider any of the contingent plans, or to start a war with the Court—that war would begin in earnest on May 27, "Black Monday," when the Court rejected by unanimous votes three New Deal statutes.

It took the chief justice almost three quarters of an hour to read the Court's arguments for the *Norman* case. At 1:25, after Justice Harlan Stone read his own concurring opinion, the two government debt cases—*Perry* on Liberty Bonds and *Nortz* on gold certificates—were completed. Later, reporters would write that it was 1:40 P.M. when Justice James Clark McReynolds began his peroration and explained the views of the minority.

EUPHORIA AT THE WHITE HOUSE

While the grounds for the decisions were being read by the chief justice, Secretary Morgenthau monitored the currency markets. Around 12:10 P.M., he noticed that as a result of the news coming from the Court, sterling was beginning to move upward. This meant that there was an opportunity for the Treasury to make a profit. He picked a phone at the other end of the Cabinet Room and gave an order to Treasury operators "to sell Sterling every time it went up a little." A few days later he wrote in his diary: "Subsequently history proves that I am right and I am only sorry now that we could not have sold more [sterling]."[11]

The secretary of the treasury was not alone in monitoring markets. As soon as the wire services announced the decisions, investors from around the country placed orders for stocks, commodities, and industrial goods. As the *New York Times* pointed out in a front-page story published the next day, the Supreme Court's decisions provided "impetus" for trade. The reporter declared that share prices had reacted immediately, and emphasized the fact that the end of uncertainty would result in "advance in general activity." The *Times* stated that "active stocks soared from 1 to 10 points between Noon and 1 o'clock. . . . The decision yesterday was hailed on all sides with deep satisfaction as a definite aid to the restoration of confidence."[12]

The next day, newspapers from around the country covered extensively the historical decisions by the Court; every paper carried the story in the front page:

The *Atlanta Constitution's* headline said, "'New Deal' Upheld in High Court."

The *Chicago Tribune's* headline read, "Roosevelt Policy is Upheld by 5 to 4 Division of Court."

The *Los Angeles Times* wrote, "Government Wins Gold Victory in 5–4 Supreme Court Ruling," and then highlighted the fact that the chief justice had been "on side of liberals."

The *Wall Street Journal* emphasized the fact that the government had been rebuked on the constitutionality of the Joint Resolution with respect to government debt. Its headline read, "Moral Defeat, Practical Victory, for Government."

The *Washington Post* was concise and effective in its headline: "New Deal Abrogation of Gold Clause Upheld as Supreme Court Splits 5–4."

The *New York Times* headline read: "Court Backs Government on Gold; 5–4 Bond Payment in New Dollar; Business Surges Forward; Stocks Rise."

The foreign press also reacted to the Court's rulings. The *Times of London* provided, in one of its editorials, a succinct and lucid explanation of the consequences of the decisions: "Yesterday's judgement . . . leaves the Administration free to act as if what is declared unconstitutional were in fact constitutional. There will be thus no necessity for any remedial legislation."[13]

Henry Morgenthau Jr. one of the few people who were with President Roosevelt while the judgments were read, described in his diary the mood in the White House:[14]

As the decisions came over the phone we would have general discussion and I was interested to see from the President's questions that he was not really familiar with the case any more than I was and he had to get Oliphant to interpret each decision for him. We were in the Cabinet Room all together about an hour—the atmosphere was very jolly—the President was very natural, laughing and smiling practically all the time. It certainly was one of the big moments of my life and it was an experience to be with him.

POWER, NOT POLICY

The ruling in the *Norman* case, on private contracts, made clear that the Court was not evaluating the appropriateness or the merits of the Roosevelt administration's decision to abandon the gold standard, devalue the dollar, eliminate the private market for gold, and adopt a new dollar-based international standard. The chief justice said, "We are not concerned here with the wisdom of the steps [the devaluation and related policies]. We are concerned with power, not with policy."[15]

The majority's opinion in *Norman* dealt directly, and appropriately, with the economic aspects of the abrogation. The Court said:[16]

It requires no acute analysis or profound economic inquiry to disclose the dislocation of the domestic economy which would be caused by such disparity of conditions in which, it is insisted, those debtors under gold clause should be required to pay one dollar and sixty-nine cents in currency while respectively receiving their taxes, charges and prices on the basis of one dollar of such currency.

That is, the Court recognized that the gold clause would cause tremendous economic harm ("dislocation") to different segments of society. In that sense, the Court appeared to agree with the government's argument of the "necessity" to abrogate private gold contracts, in order to pursue an effective monetary policy that would help the country get out of the Depression. More important, the Court said, the clauses would have generated a dual monetary system, with one currency linked to gold, and the other set in nominal terms. Congress, the majority opined, had the constitutional power to determine if the monetary system would be based on only one type of money, and there was nothing in the Fifth Amendment that would curtail that power.

It is important to notice that even the justices in the minority acknowledged that Congress indeed had the power to regulate what money was and the value thereof. In his dissent Justice McReynolds wrote, "Congress may adopt a [monetary] system." But then he added the crux of the Four Horsemen argument: "it doesn't follow that this [power] may be enforced in violation of existing contracts."[17]

JUSTICE HARLAN STONE IS TROUBLED

In the *Perry* case, the Court pointed out that according to existing legislation, there was no private market for gold in the United States. Further, private parties were not allowed to export the metal and in this way get for it the market price in, say, London. This meant that although, in the opinion of the Court, it was unconstitutional to annul public debt contracts, there were no damages: If Perry had received gold for his bond, he would have been forced to sell it to the Treasury for $20.67 an ounce. The majority then pointed out that since the Court of Claims could only deal with cases where there was a possibility of redress, it could not take Perry's case. This reasoning was so intricate that for a few minutes after the decision was read, many analysts were confused. So much so, that some reporters reported that the government had "lost," and that payment on government debt would have to be made in "gold equivalent."

In crafting his opinion, Hughes was following Chief Justice John Marshall's approach in the famous *Marbury v. Madison* case, which established judicial review in the United States. In early 1801, at the end of his presidency, John Adams appointed William Marbury as justice for the peace for Washington, DC The appointment, however, was not officially made—that is, the commission was not delivered—even though Marbury's papers were properly signed and sealed. A few months later Marbury brought a law suit against the new secretary of state, James Madison, under Section 13 of the Judiciary Act of 1789. Marbury asked the Supreme Court to issue a *writ of mandamus*, or order, to Madison to deliver the commission to him. The key constitutional question was whether the Supreme Court had "original jurisdiction," and could consider this case. The opposite view was that the Court had only "appellate jurisdiction" over these type of appointments, and thus was only allowed to "revise and correct" the proceedings of a case already visited by a lower court. In 1803, Chief Justice Marshall penned an opinion where he stated that although Marbury had the right to make the petition, and the right to the commission, the Supreme Court could not issue the *writ of mandamus* that Marbury requested. The reason for this, Marshall argued, was that the statue in question—Section 13 of the Judiciary Act of 1789—was unconstitutional. In passing this Act, said Marshall, Congress had exceeded its power by extending "original jurisdiction" to cases that were not contemplated in the Constitution. According to Section III of the Constitution, Marshall wrote, the Supreme Court had "original jurisdiction in all cases affecting ambassadors, other public ministers and consuls. . . . In all other cases [including justices for the peace] the Supreme Court shall have appellate jurisdiction."[18] If an act of Congress contradicts the constitution, Chief Marshall concluded in his 1803 opinion, it was the role of the Supreme Court to declare it void.[19] As Richard A. Epstein has noted in his treaty on constitutional law, by refusing to accept jurisdiction over the *Marbury* case, the Court did not have to provide a remedy. By taking this approach, Marshall avoided a political clash with the new administration of Thomas Jefferson. That is exactly what, in 1935, Chief Justice Hughes's decision in the *Perry* gold case did: by separating constitutionality from damages, it avoided—or delayed—a clash between two of the branches of government.[20]

Justice Harlan Stone was disturbed by the chief justice's reasoning in the *Perry* public debt case, and decided to write his own concurring opinion. According to Stone's judicial philosophy, the Court should always stay within the narrow confines of the questions at hand; it should not opine on related or broader issues. In his view, having determined that there were no damages, the Court should have stopped there, without addressing the issue of constitutionality of the Joint Resolution. He wrote in his opinion, "I cannot escape the conclusion, announced for the Court, that in the situation now present, the Government, through the exercise of its sovereign power to regulate the value of money, has rendered itself immune from liability for its action. To that extent it has relieved itself of the obligation of its domestic bonds, precisely as it has relieved the obligors of private bonds."[21] According to Stone, the most serious problem in *Perry* was that the Court had "imposed restrictions upon the future exercise of the power to regulate the currency."[22]

The fact that Stone did not side with Chief Justice Hughes' reasoning, and instead wrote a concurring opinion, resulted in an interesting judicial outcome. Strictly speaking, the Court had not provided an opinion that could be used in the future as a strong precedent. In a letter to his son, Harlan Stone explained:[23]

> most of the papers seem to have missed, that there is no opinion of the Court in the Government Bond cases. The Chief Justice wrote one, in which three of his brethren concurred; I wrote another, and the dissenters wrote another, so the Court has not declared, decided, or adjudged that the Government is bound by the Gold Clause. Besides my desire not to agree to an opinion which seemed to look both ways, you will see that there was method in my madness.

THE CONSTITUTION IS GONE

After Justice Stone read his short concurring opinion on the Liberty Bond case, it was the turn for the minority to present its views. In yet another departure from historical precedent, Justice James Clark McReynolds, who until that time had been leaning back on his leather seat with his eyes closed, delivered a rousing speech, a peroration "bristling with scorn and indignation."[24] His southern drawl became more pronounced as he proceeded without once looking at notes; at times, and to emphasize a point, his voice quivered with anger.[25] The speech was replete with irony and sarcasm. What the majority had done, he said, was "abhorrent," and amounted to "repudiation of national obligations." As he spoke, the public was spellbound, and leaned forward in order to hear every word. The chief justice and the associate justices in the majority sat silently and looked forward as McReynolds proceeded with his bitter statement. He declared: "The Constitution as many of us understood it, the instrument that has meant so much to us, is gone." He then made a pronouncement about the sanctity of contracts, government obligations, and repudiation under the guise of law. He ended his speech in a tone that the Court had never heard: "Shame and humiliation are upon us now. Moral and financial chaos may be confidently expected."[26]

Since McReynolds spoke extemporaneously, there was no official transcript of what he said. Members of the press tried to capture every one of

FIGURE 15.1. Chief Justice Charles Evans Hughes and Associate Supreme
Court Justice James Clark McReynolds.

his words, but at times he spoke so rapidly that complete phrases were
missed.[27]

In the written dissent—which deviated in tone, but not in substance
from McReynolds speech—the minority pointed out that since the government had contributed to the situation where payment in gold was not
possible, it could not use that argument to deny payment. "Congress
brought about the conditions in respect to gold which existed when the

obligations matured. Having made payment in this metal impossible, the government cannot defend by saying that if the obligation had been met the creditor could not have retained the gold." The justices in the minority argued that this behavior is similar to that of a private debtor who seeks "to annul or lessen his obligation by secreting or manipulating his assets with the intention to place them beyond the reach of his creditors."[28]

A BAFFLING PRONOUNCEMENT

The Court's decision in *Perry* was immediately criticized by constitutional experts on several counts. In particular, a number of scholars argued that in his effort to satisfy both the government and those who thought that repudiation was abhorrent, the chief justice had created significant confusion. Many observers sided with Justice Harlan Stone, and believed that the chief justice had made a mistake by declaring the Joint Resolution unconstitutional with regard to public debt; they felt that this was not needed. As pointed out by Stone, it was enough to declare that there were no damages and, thus, that Perry was not entitled to remedy.

In May 1935, barely three months after the judgments were handed down, the *Harvard Law Review* published a long article by the noted constitutional scholar Henry M. Hart Jr. titled "The Gold Clause in United States Bonds." Hart went on the attack from the first paragraph:

> Few more baffling pronouncements, it is fair to say, have ever issued from the United States Supreme Court. . . . Seldom has a legal controversy been touched with ramifications so various and so extensive. . . . Almost the only thing which it is possible to say with assurance is that the plaintiff in the particular suit did not recover.[29]

Professor Hart then proceeded to criticize the core of the Hughes argument; in doing so he sided with the views expressed by Justice Stone in his concurring opinion:[30]

> the Court violated two of its most frequently repeated canons of constitutional decision. It decided a constitutional question when it was not necessary to do so; and it permitted the question to be raised

by a litigant who was able to show no interest in its outcome. Probably also it violated a third, and much more important canon by deciding a constitutional question which upon the facts was not presented for decision.

Hart also criticized the Court for not addressing the issues of devaluation and the price of gold, issues that were at the very center of the four cases. He argued that the Court could have explored the ways in which the mere existence of the gold clause could have "prevented the dollar from being devalued," and in this way contributed to the threat and extent of "economic dislocation." Moreover, according to Hart, the Court should have discussed the arguments "for devaluation itself, which as a matter of constitutional law is an impressive one, whatever it may be as a matter of economics." Devaluation, he pointed out, affected—in reality or potentially—interstate and foreign commerce and international relations, all subjects covered by the Constitution. He then wrote: "Had devaluation been directly forbidden, or had it been indirectly defeated by enforcement of the gold clause, the United States would have been deprived of what may be reasonably deemed its most effective weapon for redressing the balance of both the internal debt structure and foreign exchange."[31] These arguments are remarkably similar to the ones made by Argentina in the arbitration and legal cases involving the abrogation of the dollar clause from her own contracts in the 2000s. Indeed, in many ways, reading the article by Professor Hart is like reading some of the briefs presented by Argentina in the early 2000s to the arbitration courts that considered the legality of its own annulment of contracts.

In his memoirs, or "Autobiographical Notes," Chief Justice Charles Evans Hughes is almost silent with respect to the gold cases. He briefly noted that he wrote the three opinions, and that on the unconstitutionality of the Joint Resolution with respect to government debt he was supported by eight justices—Stone being the sole exception. He also pointed out that Justice Cardozo, who was the only dissenter in the "hot oil" case, explicitly supported his reasoning in *Perry*. Cardozo wrote a note to Hughes on the margins of the draft opinion where he stated: "I agree, and I think that it has been finely worked out."[32] Merlo J. Pusey, Hughes's first biographer, points out in his 1952 two-volume book that during the proceedings the chief justice had contemplated assigning the opinions to

Stone. However, when he realized that Stone favored a very narrow ruling that excluded declaring the Joint Resolution unconstitutional, he decided to write the *Perry* opinion himself.[33]

In a column published on February 26, 1935, Walter Lippmann remarked that the gold decisions could be seen as "a victory but not as a vindication of the government." He then delved into the morality of the decisions, and raised many points that were in people's minds. He argued that although there were practical reasons to support the Court's rulings—they would ensure that the course followed by the administration until then would be maintained—that did not mean that the judgments were morally acceptable. "The abrogation," he stated, "destroys a vested right. It repudiates a contract. . . . And unless one is prepared to argue that legitimate rights can never be extinguished, the gold clauses cannot be dealt with on the theory that contracts are absolute."[34]

THE MARKETS AND THE COURT

In spite of the constitutional and moral issues raised by the decisions, the fact of the matter was that once they were handed down, the nation let out a sigh of relief. Markets reacted, in the immediate run, with enthusiasm. The demand for stocks and nongold bonds skyrocketed, and orders for industrial goods increased significantly. Demand for commodities was so strong, that twenty minutes after the chief justice began reading the decisions prices had jumped from their previous levels. According to traders in the Chicago Board of Trade the wheat market started to get out of hand, with prices running up 3.8 cents relative to the very low levels they had attained after the hearings. Activity was so chaotic that the directors of the Board decided to close the exchange for the rest of the day. Observers pointed out that "the suspension of the Board of Trade was the first ordered in trading hours in the memory of operators."[35]

Figure 15.1 presents the evolution of four commodities analyzed throughout this book in the days leading to the decisions, and two days after the rulings. As may be seen on February 18, there was an important to jump in all prices. The surge continued during the following day, February 19.

The data in figure 15.3, on Liberty Bonds and Treasury Bonds of similar maturities and coupons are particularly interesting. As may be seen,

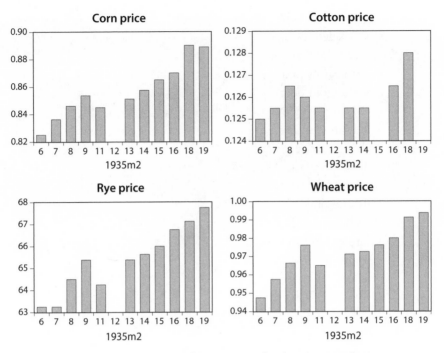

FIGURE 15.2. Commodity prices in the days surrounding
Supreme Court decisions.

on the day of the Supreme Court decisions these prices moved drastically
and in opposite directions. While the price of Liberty Bonds collapsed—
the reason was that after the resolutions the gold clause was valueless—
the price of Treasury Bonds that did not include the gold clause advanced
rapidly. Those investors and speculators who had sided with the president
and had bet on the Court supporting the president and his policies reaped
large gains.

Overall, the Court's ruling was well received in Europe, and in particular in Germany. According to financial experts in Berlin, a defeat of
the government would have resulted in further havoc and uncertainty
in international markets, "most of all in Germany where all public debtors, banks, industrial and shipping corporations long since have compiled
their debt returns and balance sheets in depreciated dollars."[36] The reaction in France was mixed, with many analysts arguing that the decision
included a strong scolding of the government. This, they declared, was a
positive development that made further devaluation of the dollar with

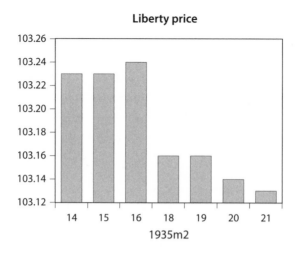

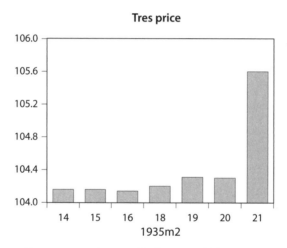

FIGURE 15.3. Prices of Liberty and Treasury
bonds the days following the Supreme Court
rulings.

respect to gold less likely. In a dispatch from Paris, a reporter pointed out
that in France, "nobody risks formulating an opinion, as it is felt that, in
view of the impulsive character of decisions frequently made in the United
States, it is impossible to foretell what will happen the next day."[37] This
quote captured quite accurately the fact that after the London Conference fiasco, European and other global market participants had grown
to mistrust the Roosevelt administration's intentions and actions.

A few days after the decisions were handed down, the United States received very large shipments of gold. Most of the metal came from England and France. Analysts and reporters pointed out that it appeared that the Treasury's Stabilization Fund had "been purchasing large amounts of sterling as well as francs in holding down the dollar. The sterling purchased was evidently used to buy gold in the open market in London and this is being shipped here [New York]."[38] Although no one said it at the time, this shipment of gold marked the consolidation of a trend that greatly affected monetary policy and until mid-1937 the recovery, including the creation of millions of jobs.

CHAPTER 16

Consequences

March 1, 1935–June 1, 1937

In his dissenting speech, Justice James Clark McReynolds asserted that for a long time investors had signed contracts which protected them against a fluctuating currency: "Many men entered into contracts, perfectly legitimate, and undertook to protect themselves. The lender against depreciated currency, the borrower possibly against an appreciated one."[1] From here, McReynolds went on to declare that these contracts had played a fundamental role in transforming the United States into the strongest nation on earth; it was thanks to these contracts that long-term loans could be obtained; it was thanks to these financial instruments that large investments in infrastructure and magnificent factories were possible. "Under these obligations," the Kentuckian stated, "millions were loaned. Railroads, canals, many great enterprises were begun and their bonds sold throughout the world." He added that as a result of President Roosevelt's policies, the country was now "confronted by a dollar reduced to sixty cents, with the possibility of twenty tomorrow, ten the next day, and then one." The Court's majority, asserted McReynolds, had "a clear purpose to bring about confiscation of private rights." One of the devastating consequences of the ruling, he asserted, was that in the decades to come it would be impossible for both corporations and the government to obtain loans under the same terms as in the past. As a result, "financial chaos" was to be expected.

Senator Carter Glass, who in 1932 had been one of FDR's most enthusiastic champions, was of similar opinion, as was Senator David A. Reed, the Republican who led the opposition to the abrogation of the gold clause and the abandonment of the gold standard. Almost three decades later, in their wide-ranging *A Monetary History of the United States, 1867–1960*, Milton Friedman and Anna Schwartz argued that the abrogation of the gold clause and the ensuing rulings by the Supreme Court had a negative impact on the economy, "by discouraging business investment."[2]

Were McReynolds, Glass, Reed, Friedman, Schwartz, and others, correct in their predictions and assessments? Did the retroactive annulment of gold-linked contracts on June 5, 1933, and the Supreme Court's subsequent rulings on February 18, 1935, have a negative effect on the economy? Did financial chaos follow, and did this chaos—if it happened—discourage business investment?

These are very difficult questions. Assessing the actual consequences of this episode requires embarking in a "counterfactual" exercise where one has to investigate what would have happened if what actually *did happen* had not taken place. In the case at hand, the counterfactual exercise is particularly complex for a number of reasons: first, the data for the 1930s are not very detailed and are lacking in quality. At the time, the system of national accounts was not developed fully, nor were there systematic and homogeneous statistical series on unemployment and other measures of economic activity. Of course, this doesn't mean that evaluating the effects of the abrogation is an impossible endeavor. Throughout the years, economic historians and other scholars have constructed data that may be used to analyze whether there is, indeed, evidence that the Supreme Court decisions triggered some form of financial dislocation, and/or resulted in economic slowdown due to lower investment. In undertaking the exercise, however, one has to be aware of the quality of the data and of the fact that many detailed statistics are, simply, not available.

But more serious than the absence of fully reliable data is the fact that at the time many situations were developing simultaneously. It is, thus, difficult to disentangle the consequences and effects of one event from those of another. For example, just a few weeks after siding with the government in the gold cases, on May 27, 1935, the Supreme Court rejected by 9–0 votes three important provisions of the New Deal—that day became known as "Black Monday."[3] Moreover, during 1935 and 1936 political and economic conditions became significantly more unstable in Europe. Hitler was making further inroads in Germany, and the gold-bloc countries were facing increasing difficulties to maintain the fixed parity. These European events had an impact on capital (and gold) movements around the world, and in this way affected liquidity in the United States. At home, the NRA and the AAA were affecting the productive process and the ways in which corporations, public utilities, and trusts did business. Every one of these developments contributed, through different and intricate channels, to the evolution of investment, employment, and economic activity. It is extremely difficult—if not impossible—to determine what fraction of a particular variable's movement is due to which event, including to the abrogation of the gold clauses and the Supreme Court decisions.

In addition, any counterfactual analysis of the abrogation has to deal with two important and challenging questions: First, what was the alternative to annulling gold-linked contracts? Assuming that the devaluation of the dollar was, indeed, necessary, how could any government face the effects of a 41 percent increase in the price of gold on debtors? Were there alternatives? And if, so what were these alternatives? This inquiry immediately brings forward a second one: Was the devaluation of the dollar really "necessary" in 1933–1934? Or, on the contrary, were there policies that the United States could have implemented—and promoted internationally—that would have allowed the nation (and the rest of the world, for that matter) to get out of the Depression without abandoning, at that particular time, the gold standard?

Addressing these questions does not mean, in any way, contesting the notion that the expansion of credit, liquidity, and the stock of money that began in late February 1934, immediately after the official devaluation of the dollar, was at the center of the recovery. The contribution of expansive monetary policy to the recovery has been well established by countless scholars, from Friedman and Schwartz, to Bernanke, Roemer, and others, and will not be disputed here. In fact, I count myself among those who strongly believe that the change in the monetary stance after January 1934 was the main force behind the recovery. Having said that, the question remains of whether similarly expansive monetary policy could have been pursued at that time within the context of a (modified) gold standard, an arrangement similar to the one proposed by Jimmy Warburg just before the London Conference.

According to traditional economic theory, the violation of contracts has a number of consequences for debtors. Among other things, and under normal conditions, after reneging on promises and imposing losses on investors, debtors will have trouble accessing the capital markets and issuing new debt; their cost of capital will increase significantly, and there will be a "stigma effect" on new debt issues. In some cases, it is even expected that the debtor will be completely shut off from the debt market, at least for some time. At the level of the country, a major and generalized breach of contracts by the sovereign will typically result in a drastic reduction in the country's credit rating by international agencies, in increased uncertainty, and in a reduction in investment and, thus, in a lower growth rate. But the fact that these are the results expected for the "average" case—or even in the majority of cases—does not mean that it will happen to every debtor at every moment in time. Indeed, whether a debtor who unilaterally changes the nature of his contract faces these consequences is, in the final analysis, an empirical issue that has to be dealt with by analyzing the data carefully.

In this chapter, I analyze the ramifications of the abrogation gold clauses and of the subsequent Supreme Court rulings. I proceed slowly and in a systematic way, in order to produce a picture that is both consistent and persuasive. The first step in this analysis is a direct inquiry of whether there is historical evidence of economic dislocation and/or of financial instability in the months immediately following the Supreme Court decisions. I then move to indirect evidence and ask if, after the Supreme Court rulings, the U.S. government faced greater difficulties in placing new debt and/or rolling over its outstanding securities.

Understanding the consequences of the abrogation and surrounding policies is not only important from a historical perspective, it is also relevant to comprehend current events, and to shed light on the likely consequences of modern defaults, including debt restructurings in Greece in 2013 and Argentina in 2005. Understanding better the events of 1933–1935 is also important for understanding those episodes that will come in the future; as Carmen Reinhart and Kenneth Rogoff have argued in their treatise *This Time Is Different*, sovereign debt restructurings constitute a never-ending story, which repeats itself with an astonishing degree of circularity.

A YEAR OF ECONOMIC RECOVERY

The year 1935 was one of economic recovery. Output increased across the board, and prices inched towards their 1926 level, the goal that FDR had announced in one of his early Fireside Chats. The stock market moved upwards, and the cost of capital declined for all sorts of corporations and for the government. During the period following the Supreme Court decision, there were no signs of financial dislocation, let alone of financial "chaos."

During the weeks immediately following the gold decisions, the president was in high spirits; his program seemed to be working, the public support for the administration was solid, and the prospects for reelection looked very good. At this pace, the Depression would soon be a thing of the past, a bad nightmare that would be remember with horror, and would be told and retold to the new generations as one of the most difficult period in the nation's history. But, at the same time, the story would refer to the Roosevelt administration as a turning point, as the time when the federal government began to truly worry about little people, farmers and factory workers, union members, and the unemployed.

On Monday, May 27, 1935, the administration suffered a reality check and a serious setback. That day the Supreme Court handed down three 9–0 decisions that declared key provisions of the New Deal unconstitutional. In *Louisville Bank v. Radford*, the Court ruled that the Frazier-Lemke Act, which slowed down the repossession of farms during bankruptcy procedures, was unconstitutional. According to the unanimous opinion, the Act violated creditors' Fifth Amendment rights. In *Humphrey's Executor v. United States*, the Court ruled that the president had exceeded his power when he arbitrarily, and without cause, removed Humphrey, a member of the Federal Trade Commission, an independent agency, from his post; the fact that the commissioner opposed the administration's policies was not cause for dismissal, opined the Court. Doing so constituted an abuse of power by the Executive. In *Schechter Poultry Corp. v. United States*, the most important of the three cases, and the most devastating one for the administration, the Court ruled that certain provisions of the National Recovery Act (NRA) were unconstitutional. The opinion, written by the chief justice, was based on three arguments: first, this wide-ranging legislation aimed at avoiding price wars among firms, was not justified by a national emergency. Second, it improperly delegated too much legislative authority to the Executive Branch, a point that the Court had already made in the "hot oil" case decided in January of that year. And third, the Court pointed out that the poultry code of the NRA, involved local economic transactions and not interstate commerce; thus, the federal government had no constitutional power to regulate it.[4]

These three decisions marked the beginning of an open war between the administration and the Court, a war that escalated rapidly and reached its culmination with the president's unsuccessful attempt to stack the Court in February 1937. However, in spite of this serious judicial setback and of the ensuing animosity between two powers of the state, economic activity continued to expand during the rest of 1935 and well into 1936. It was not until the second half of 1937 that the economy would retreat into a new recession.

Figure 16.1 presents the evolution of the quarterly "real" (inflation-adjusted) Gross National Product (GNP) between 1919 and 1944. The jagged line measures actual total output in every quarter, while the smooth line captures the long-term trend in real GNP. Economic recessions are characterized by episodes where actual output falls below its long-term trend. By using quarterly data, it is possible to analyze the granularity of economic expansions and contractions, and to determine with some degree of precision at which point in time economic activity changed course. As may be seen, there are two vertical lines in the figure: the first one corresponds to the third quarter of 1933, the time when the Joint Resolution that abrogated the gold clauses was passed by Congress; the second vertical line corresponds to the second quarter of 1935, immediately after the gold decisions were handed down by the Supreme Court.[5]

In figure 16.1, it is easy to identify the 1921 recession, the Great Depression, starting in 1929, and the 1937 recession. In terms of the consequences of the Supreme Court decisions on gold, the data do not show retrogression or slowdown in the pace of economic activity after February 1935. In fact, what this figure shows is the contrary: following the Supreme Court rulings, real output in the United States expanded vigorously, until the second quarter of 1937, when as a result of a number of factors—including the implementation of contractive monetary and fiscal policies—the nation entered into a new recession. The period in between the Joint Resolution and the Court's rulings—that is, between June 1933 and February 1935—is characterized by a cyclical behavior of real GNP, with some ups and downs. However, as the figure clearly shows, the output trend was strongly positive.

Figures 16.2 through 16.4 display the behavior, for 1919–1942, of the three basic components of investment, the variable that according to Friedman and Schwartz was depressed as a result of the abrogation of the gold clauses and of the Supreme Court rulings. Figure 16.2 presents investment in machinery and equipment; figure 16.3 investment in

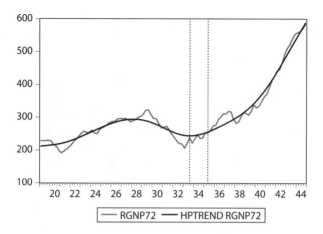

FIGURE 16.1. Real GNP, 1919–1942 (actual GNP and Dynamic Average).

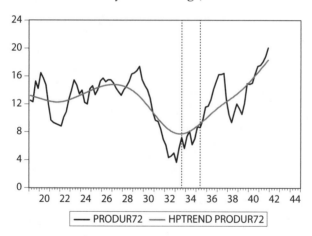

FIGURE 16.2. Real Investment in Machinery and Equipment, 1919–1942.

nonresidential structures (warehouses, factories, and the like); and figure 16.4 data on residential investment, mostly housing. As before, I have included the actual evolution of each statistical series, as well as the long-term trend. As may be seen, there is no evidence of investment retreat in the quarters immediately following the rulings. In fact, until 1937 these three series are, for almost every quarter, above the long-term trend, indicating that the economy was in an expansion mode. Notice, however, that in the third quarter of 1935, there is a small negative blip in

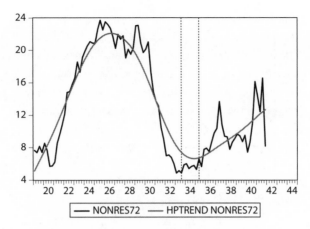

FIGURE 16.3. Real Investment in Nonresidential
Structures, 1919–1942.

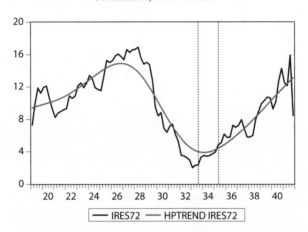

FIGURE 16.4. Real Investment in Residential
Structures, 1919–1942.

nonresidential structures (figure 16.3). This, nevertheless, is immediately corrected; there is no reason to attribute this decline in investment to the abrogation or abandonment of the gold standard. There are many other possible explanations, including the Supreme Court decisions during Black Monday in May 1935, and normal seasonal variations.

Between June 1933 and February 1935, commodity prices continued to increase, as did the general price index. Interestingly, it was in manufacturing—the sector that was supposed to get a boost from the NRA—where prices sagged somewhat. This may be seen in figure 16.5

where I present the monthly evolution of four price indexes for 1923–1942; the shaded area is for the months elapsed between the Joint Resolution and to the Supreme Court decisions. In this figure, it is also possible to see that starting in April 1935, two months after the Supreme Court handed down its decisions, most components of the wholesale price index began to move sideways. However, this relative price stability, which lasted until March 1936, does not constitute "chaos," not even a dislocation. Further, it cannot be attributed to the abrogation of the gold clauses.

FINANCIAL CHAOS?

Justice James Clark McLean predicted that as a consequence "confiscation of property rights" by the Court's ruling, the nation would sink into financial "chaos." A situation of financial disorder and tension is usually reflected in the financial markets, through lower stock prices, higher interest rates, and increased volatility. However, a detailed analysis of the most important financial variables in 1935 and 1936 does not indicate a situation of distress, let alone "chaos." Figure 16.6 contains quarterly data on the Dow Index of common stocks for 1932 through 1944. As may be seen, the data capture the recovery of share prices after the Great Depression, with its normal ups and downs. The figure also shows the market retraction in the third quarter of 1937. As may be seen, there is no

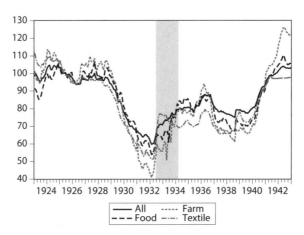

FIGURE 16.5. Wholesale Price Index and Principal
Components, 1919–1942.

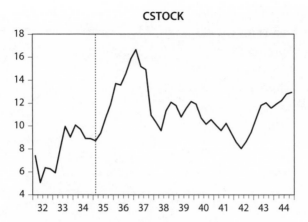

FIGURE 16.6. Dow Stock Market Index, 1932–1944.

evidence of distress or dislocation in the period immediately following the abrogation, or the Court ruling.

The bond market did not show distress during this period, either. In fact, the cost of borrowing declined across the board for corporations and for the government.[6] Figure 16.7 contains weekly data on yields on Treasuries, AAA, Aaa, and Baa corporate bonds between November 1934 and February 1936. In these figures, I have drawn a vertical line at the time the Supreme Court rulings where handed down. As may be seen, with the exception of Baa bonds, yields on all bonds continued to decline after the Supreme Court rulings. For the more speculative securities—Baa corporates—yields continued to decline for a few weeks after the decisions, and then turned slightly up. What is particularly telling is that after the Court rulings the yield differential between corporate and Treasury bonds tended to narrow, reflecting that in spite of the changes in contracts, it was not more difficult for American corporations to place debt in the market place.

Although the evidence presented above—on financial variables, prices, GNP, and investment—is strongly suggestive, it is not one hundred percent conclusive. Within the context of counterfactual analyses it is possible that if the gold clause had not been abrogated, output and investment would have recovered even faster than they did, and that the cost of borrowing would have declined even more. These outcomes are possible, but in my view, highly unlikely.

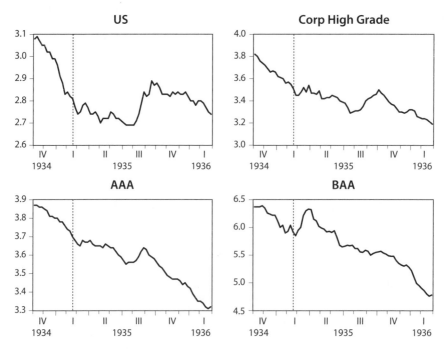

FIGURE 16.7. Yields on U.S. and Corporate Bonds. Weekly 1934–1936

THE U.S. ABROGATION AS AN "EXCUSABLE DEFAULT"

Contrary to the simple predictions of standard economic theory, after the abrogation of the gold clause and the Supreme Court rulings, the government had no difficulty rolling over its debt or issuing new securities. In a research paper with my colleagues Francis Longstaff and Alvaro Garcia, I computed the subscription ratio—or total value of bids for new offerings of government debt—of each Treasury securities auction between 1930 and 1936.[7] If the abrogation had negatively impacted the government's ability to issue debt, we would have seen that the subscription ratio decline significantly after this particular episode. Our research, however, showed that the subscription ratio for government securities was 5.23 times before the abrogation of the gold clauses, and almost 6 times after the abrogation. That is, after the abrogation, the public's interest for purchasing government paper increased, instead of declining. Interestingly, this higher demand for Treasury debt took place at the same time as the yield curve—or difference between yields of long and short bonds—became steeper. A more elaborate statistical analysis of the data using econometric techniques, confirmed these results: after the abrogation there was no increased difficulty for the government to issue new debt.

Another possible manifestation of financial distress after a debt default or restructuring episode is the stigmatization of the issuer. In particular, a number of scholars have found that most countries that default on their debts lose significant credibility, and become ostracized in the credit markets. Under these circumstances, it takes some time to regain access to the debt market and to be able to place new debt. In the case of the United States in 1933–1936, it is relatively easy to analyze whether this kind of stigma indeed developed. The reason is that, as noted, during this period the Treasury was actively trying to replace old debt that included the gold clause (and high coupons) with newer debt without the clause and with lower coupon rates. The historical evidence indicates that when offered to swap old bonds for new ones, more than 80 percent of investors decided to go ahead with such an exchange. For example, on October 16, 1933, merely four months after the abrogation, almost $2 billion of the Fourth Liberty Loan bonds were called in by the Treasury. By the deadline, 91 percent of all bonds called had been exchanged for new securities without the gold clause. But not only that: In every one of these exchanges the Treasury was able to pay a lower interest rate than the one attached to the securities that were being retired. This is a strong indication that in this particular episode there was no stigma associated to the abrogation of the gold clause in the United States in the 1930s.

Naturally, this raises the question of why this happened. Why is it that when countries such as Argentina, Russia, or Brazil default on their debts, they have a very difficult time re-accessing the debt market, and, in contrast, the United States was able to go immediately back to issuing new debt?

The most plausible explanation has to do with the theory of "excusable defaults."[8] According to this view, there are certain circumstances when the market understands that a debt restructuring is, indeed, warranted, and beneficial for (almost) everyone involved in the marketplace. A very clear example of an excusable default is given by situations of natural disasters. In general, creditors understand that after a major earthquake, for example, the debtor will have to restructure its liabilities. Under these circumstances, creditors will even be willing to lend additional funds to the debtor, in order to avoid deeper problems and more serious calamities. That is, according to this view, creditors believe that by going ahead with some restructuring (and even some forgiveness), at the end of the road they will be able to collect a higher percentage of their monies than if they had taken a very tough stance with respect to the debtor.

According to the historical evidence, it is more likely that a default will be considered "excusable" if the debtor acts in good faith, and if the restructuring is done within the context of legal institutions, including impartial and independent courts.

The devaluation of the dollar in 1933—and the concomitant abrogation of the gold clauses—fit, to a large extent, the case of an excusable default. As has been documented in the preceding chapters, by 1933 an increasingly large proportion of the population—both in the United States and abroad—came to believe that abandoning the gold standard and devaluing the currency would contribute to ending the Great Depression. More important, it was believed that these policies would result in a reduction of the burden of debts, when measured relative to the debtors' purchasing power. The fact that the court system was fully operational, and that different lawsuits moved through it according to the existing legal rules, also contributed to the notion that this was an excusable debt restructuring. Indeed, the fact that the Courts ruled in favor of the government after carefully reviewing the evidence and considering lengthy and detailed legal briefs submitted by the parties, added to the notion that this was a necessary, reasonable and justified policy measure.

This contrasts quite significantly with the situation in Argentina in 2002–2005, when investors became convinced that there was manifest bad faith on behalf of the new Argentine government. The fact that the restructuring offer was based on paying $0.23 on the dollar was considered to be a clear signal of an unnecessarily confrontational approach. In addition, the incendiary rhetoric used by the Argentine authorities—President Nestor Kirchner and his successor President Cristina Fernandez—did not help the country's case. Also, the fact that neighboring Uruguay offered to pay $0.93 on the dollar when it restructured its debt around the same time, added to the sense that Argentina was not playing by the rules of the game. The fact that the Argentine courts ruled in favor of the government was dismissed by market participants, for at least two reasons: first, there was a generalized sense that the Argentine courts were not independent. This view was, in fact, supported by a number of studies on the judiciary across different countries.[9] Second, and in contrast to the case of the United States in the 1930s, Argentina had deliberately and actively marketed its securities internationally. This meant that in order to resolve disagreements between the government and investors, it was necessary to utilize international courts or arbitration panels.

On December 31, 1974, the prohibition for private parties to hold, sell and buy gold in the United States was finally repealed. Since then a vigorous gold market has developed in the United States, and the price of bullion has gone up and down, following patterns that are difficult to decipher. For many people, gold continues to exercise a bewitching attraction. The yellow metal is still considered to be one of the safest assets on earth, and time and again investors from around the world turn to it in times of distress, fear, and uncertainty.

BROKEN PROMISES

Independently of its outcome, and of the fact that the nation benefited from it, the abrogation of the gold clauses and the subsequent devaluation of the dollar in January 1934, represented a break in a solemn promise. On November 4, 1932, four days before the election, candidate Roosevelt addressed a group of supporters at the Brooklyn Academy of Music, where he stated that "no responsible government would have sold to the country securities payable in gold if it knew that the promise—yes, the covenant—embodied in these securities was . . . dubious."[10] But that is exactly what his administration did in April 1933, when it sold $500 million of 2.875 percent Treasury notes with the gold clause. This was done after the president had announced, on April 19, that the nation was off gold, and after he had agreed to support the Thomas Amendment, the legislation that gave him authority to devalue the dollar. As many analysts and critics of the Administration—including Walter Lippmann and Justice James Clark McReynolds—argued, this was a major inconsistency, a breach in a promise that had ethical implications As noted above, it is possible that at the time the population considered the unilateral and retroactive restructuring of the debt as an "excusable default." But the fact that it was seen justified or excusable, does not negate the fact that it constituted a broken promise.

But the devaluation of the dollar (and the retroactive rewriting of contracts) is not the only time the United States went back on promises—implicit or explicit—made to its citizens and to the rest of the world. The lack of support in Congress for the League of Nations, an initiative first proposed by President Woodrow Wilson in 1918, when he delivered his Fourteen Points plan for a peace in Europe, is another example of a broken promise. Citizens in country after country expected that the United States, the nation that had emerged from the conflict as the most powerful in the world, would participate in this new institution and take a leadership position in efforts to maintain peace and avoid major conflicts. Congress's refusal to authorize the U.S. membership was not only a major disappointment, but was also seen in the rest of the world as a breach of an important and solemn promise. Most historians agree that because the United States was not a member, the League's effectiveness during the 1920s and 1930s, was moderate at best. Further, a number of analysts have speculated that if the United States had joined the Geneva organization in 1920, World War II, and the atrocities that it brought with it, might have been avoided.

Although it is too early to know, the U.S. withdrawal from the Paris Climate Accord, announced in June 2017, may be ultimately seen by the rest of the world—as well as by a large group of American citizens—as another broken promise. It is likely that, as in the case of the League of Nations, President Donald Trump's decision to jettison Paris will be considered by the majority of world citizens a unilateral decision that hurt the globe deeply.

CHAPTER 17

◇◇◇◇◇

Could It Happen Again?

During the last few years, every time I told friends, colleagues, or new acquaintances the story of the abrogation of gold clauses, they were astonished. They looked at me with incredulity, as if I was making up a fantastic tale, or pulling their leg. And then, once they realized that I was serious and that the episode actually happened merely eighty-five years ago, they asked a barrage of questions. Who was behind the idea? Did the abrogation affect everyone? Was it true that people were forced to sell their gold at below market prices? Was it really necessary to annul contracts retroactively? Who defended normal folks who owned a few gold coins? Were foreign holders of government bonds exempted? What about corporate debt? Was the devaluation effective? What were the arguments made by the Supreme Court to support the government? What were the consequences?

When listening to these conversations some people moved their heads from side to side, slowly, indicating that this was just too bizarre to be true. Others quipped that this was the kind of thing that Banana Republics would do, but definitely not the United States.

But among all the questions, the one that kept coming back again and again was this: Could this happen again?

A LOW PROBABILITY

It is almost impossible that something similar will happen again in the United States. The main reason has to do with the exchange rate regime and the monetary system. For over four decades, the country has had a market-determined exchange rate, and currency fluctuations, even very large ones, are now considered to be normal. In addition, the time when the Federal Reserve liabilities had to be (partially) backed by gold is long gone. Since 1973, the exchange rate has operated as a shock absorber, and companies, banks, and even households, protect themselves through hedging operations. This is very different from the first decades of the twentieth century, when the custom was for countries to have fixed exchange rates, and for international financial markets to operate according to the rules of the gold standard. Until the mid-1970s central banks were expected to hold gold—or other form of convertible currency—to back their monetary liabilities. Today most contracts are written in "lawful currency," and not in gold, commodities, or foreign currency. It is true that some contracts, including some government bonds, are subject to escalation clauses; TIPS, bonds issued by the Treasury, are linked to the Consumer Price Index, for example, but their total value is very small. In 1933, in contrast, the total debt subject to the gold clauses— public and private—amounted to almost 180 percent of GDP.

Equally significant, since the 1930s there have been tremendous advances in central bankers' understanding of the role, power, and limits of monetary policy. Cadres of scholars have analyzed scores of crisis episodes, and today we have a much better knowledge of how the economy works, and how changes in monetary circumstances and currency values affect economic decisions by firms and household. We cannot predict every balance of payments and exchange rate crisis, but we have good models, and we are able to alert those in charge of policy when certain indicators suggest that an economy is getting into a danger zone. Of course, our understanding of monetary economics is not perfect, but as the handling of the Great Recession by the Federal Reserve showed, we are now miles ahead of where we were in 1932–1933. If the Federal Reserve had reacted in 2008 in a way similar to 1929, the depth of the 2008–2010 recession would have been significantly greater; unemployment would have skyrocketed, and bankruptcies would have escalated significantly.

But the fact that it is extremely unlikely that an episode like the one recounted in this book will repeat itself, does not mean that we can rule out future debt restructurings in the United States. Even if the probability of a "credit event" is low, it is not zero. The most serious problem is not the documented public debt. At approximately 90 percent of Gross

Domestic Product, it is still manageable, and under a number of scenarios the debt-to-GDP ratio could even decline during the decades to come. This, however, is not the case for "contingent liabilities," or debt implicit in government promises related to entitlements. Every year the *implicit debt* that stems from promises made about future health provisions— mostly through Medicare—and future Social Security payments, increases significantly. According to some estimates, at the time of this writing the hidden (or contingent) debt of the federal government alone exceeds 400 percent of Gross Domestic Product. This is a huge imbalance, and although many economists and politicians are aware of its magnitude, there is no agreement on how to deal with in the decades to come. One possibility, of course, is that at some point in the not too distant future the U.S. government will be forced to restructure its debt, and renege on its promises. How the courts will react to this eventuality, is unclear. There is one thing, however, that we do know: in the American judicial system precedent is very important, and the gold cases analyzed in this book provide an important precedent, one that suggests that in case of necessity it may be acceptable for the government to restructure debts and change the nature of contracts retroactively.

What is particularly important is that in contrast to the late 1920s and early 1930s, the debt crisis that looms in the horizon is not related to deflation, exchange rates, or the monetary system. It has a completely different genesis: it is rooted in unsustainable promises made in the present for future delivery of services.

THE EMERGING NATIONS

The United States, of course, is not the only nation in the world. The peril of future abrogation-type episodes is much higher in other countries. In fact, when one looks at the problem from a global perspective, the question of whether it could happen again is a little puzzling. Situations that mirror what happened in the United States during 1933–1935 have occurred recently in a number of emerging countries, and it is almost certain that they will continue to arise in the future. As argued throughout this book, Argentina provides a stark example of a country that barely a few years ago—in 2001 to 2003—went through an almost identical process to the experience of the United States in 1933. But Argentina is not the only case. Similar episodes occurred, in the not too distant past, in countries as varied as Mexico, Turkey, Russia, Indonesia, and Chile.[1]

Even today, in most emerging nations, debt contracts are often written in foreign currencies—mostly in U.S. dollars, but also in euros, or other convertible monies. This is the case both for securities sold to foreign investors, as for financial instruments marketed exclusively to local parties. In fact, in many emerging countries—throughout Central America, for example—the banking system is highly "dollarized." That is, bank deposits are denominated in dollars or in other foreign money. The reason for this extensive degree of "dollarization" is that in a large number of emerging countries people do not trust the local currency. This is common in nations with a history of inflation that has systematically debased the local money. In these nations, the norm has been that transactions involving large amounts, and loans with longer maturities, are usually denominated in dollars or include some type of escalation clauses.

For firms with substantial debts in foreign currency, a large depreciation means distress, and often bankruptcy. For the official sector, a major exchange rate adjustment almost always results in substantial jumps in the government deficit and public debt. Furthermore, massive depreciations can be particular destructive for banks that have a "currency mismatch" between assets and liabilities. This is because foreign currency–denominated deposits are subject to immediate withdrawals and may generate bank runs, while loans made to local firms in dollars—or other convertible currency—are hard to recover in a short period of time. As Richard Cooper documented almost forty years ago, large devaluations in emerging nations invariably result in political upheaval, demonstrations, riots, and, in some cases, in government changes. When the political situation becomes chaotic, it is tempting for the authorities to restructure debts and rewrite contracts in a unilateral and retroactive fashion, as Argentina did in 2002.[2]

Is this likely to happen again in the emerging nations?

The answer is "yes."

When, in the future, countries default, restructure their debts, and alter contracts unilaterally, they are likely to invoke the 1935 Supreme Court decisions on the abrogation of the gold clauses as a legal precedent. The defaulting countries' authorities and lawyers will make a simple point: if the United States was able to do it legally in 1933, by using an argument of "necessity," we should also be allowed to do so now. Our "necessity," they will point out, is as serious as the United States' "necessity" in 1933. In addition, we can expect that the economic arguments used to justify a restructuring will be a modern version of those presented by the Roosevelt administration in 1935. The legal briefs will talk about compelling need, external shocks, currency misalignment, and the fact that a large depreciation is required to get the relief machinery underway. Those defending creditors and bondholders are likely to go back to the Court decision in the *Perry* case, and point out that in 1935 the majority ruled that with respect to government debt, the retroactive annulment of contracts was unconstitutional. The ruling, knowledgeable lawyers are likely to point out, was based on the extent of damages, and not on the constitutional power to borrow money, and then not pay it back to creditors.

AN ABROGATION OF THE "EURO CLAUSE"?

The emerging markets are not the weakest link in this chain. As the 2008 crisis in Iceland shows, it is possible for an advanced nation to face a gigantic external crisis with a massive devaluation and a complete collapse of the banking sector. It took almost ten years for Iceland to recover and to regain its footing. But if we look ahead, it is in the Euro Zone where, in the not too distant future, we may see situations somewhat similar to the one faced by the United States in 1933–1935. Any country that leaves the Euro Zone—be it Greece under pressure from citizens burdened by what seems like an unending adjustment process, or France led by ultranationalists—will be forced to deal with the thorny issue of contracts.

Consider the case of Greece, a nation that since 2012 has been tempted to leave the Euro Zone and reintroduce its own currency, the drachma, at a depreciated level. Those that favor this policy argue that with a currency of its own and exchange rate flexibility Greece would gain competitiveness, increase exports, and move rapidly towards recovery.

This view, however, ignores the effect of such a policy on contracts. Every contract in Greece is written in euros: labor contracts, suppliers' contracts, debt contracts (private and public), service contracts, investment contracts, and so on. After the reintroduction of the drachma, will these contracts be enforced in euros (the original currency agreed by the parties), or in the new (depreciated) currency? This issue is important, even if Greece is granted considerable debt forgiveness. In principle, the legislation that would reintroduce the drachma could also state that contracts originally written in euros would be converted into new drachmas, at a depreciated exchange rate relative to the level at which Athens joined the Euro Zone. Creditors, however, will cry foul, and will turn to the courts in an effort to receive payments according to the original contracts, in hard and convertible euros.

Greek courts are likely to side with the government—as did Argentinean courts in 2002, when the country abandoned the "convertibility" program—declare that the old contracts are void, and that the new drachma could be used to discharge debts and other obligations. But in a globalized world domestic courts usually do not have the last word. Litigation will move to international courts and arbitration tribunals. As a member of the European Union, Greece has to abide by European Union laws and regulations, and creditors will flood European courts with all sorts of claims related to the annulment of euro-denominated contracts. Greece has also signed Bilateral Investment Treaties (BIT) with thirty-nine countries, including Germany, Russia, Korea, and China. Thus, any attempt to change the currency of contracts will end up in arbitration at the International Centre for Settlement of Investment Disputes (ICSID), the World Bank's tribunal for investment disputes. In all of these legal disputes, the U.S. gold cases from 1933 to 1935 will appear as an uninvited guest, and will be used as precedents by lawyers on both sides of the arguments.

★ ★ ★

One of the key points made by the Roosevelt administration during the Supreme Court hearings was that not one of the government securities affected by the abrogation had been issued, marketed, or sold in foreign countries. This was solely a domestic matter, an economic and legal issue confined to the United States, which had to be solved exclusively by the nation's judicial system. That is, exactly, what the "nine old men" did on February 18, 1935. The decision was controversial, and it generated bitter dissent and dire prognostications. But it was resolved according to the rule of law, following procedures set up by the Constitution, and according to precedent. And because due process was observed at every turn and without exception, people and the investors from around the world came to view the episode as an "excusable default," as a situation that was justified by the magnitude of the crisis, as a needed—albeit costly—solution to one of the worst economic calamities endured by the world. With time the ruling was accepted, and as the nation moved forward and faced new challenges—wars, civil unrest, new economic turmoil, civil rights demands, and dangers of various types—the abrogation began to fade in people's memories. Today very few people know about it, and the cases that were once considered some of the most important to come in front of the Court are not taught in law schools any longer. It is time to remember this episode in the nation's history; it is time to recall that once, in the not too distant past, the United States faced such extreme conditions that it was forced to follow a difficult path, one that these days is considered to be almost unthinkable.

APPENDIX

◇◇◇◇◇

George F. Warren versus Irving Fisher's Plans for the Dollar

During 1933, George F. Warren and Irving Fisher were in the same camp, or so it seemed to most observers. They both wanted to divorce the dollar from gold, and adopt an exchange rate system that would avoid price cycles. Moreover, both economists understood that in order for their plans to be implemented, it was first necessary to eliminate the gold clause from all contracts past and future; as early as 1931 the two professors were lobbying for an elimination of the gold clause.

At the time, the public believed that their plans were almost identical, and that they had the same views regarding the inner workings of the international monetary system. That, however, was not the case. There were deep differences between their approaches, they assigned different roles to monetary policy, they believed that different channels were at work, and they came from very different traditions. Fisher was a theoretician, a mathematical economist with keen interests in statistics, while Warren was an applied agricultural economist whose concern for prices came from his field work and his closeness to farmers.

The differences between the two scholars were also reflected in the views and attitudes of their patrons. Jacob Viner, the University of Chicago professor who would become an influential adviser to the Treasury, remembered that in late 1933 he asked Henry Morgenthau Jr. if Irving Fisher was working for him. Morgenthau, who was a great supporter of George F. Warren and who had peddled his ideas to FDR, provided a categorical reply: "I've got nothing to do with Fisher and he has nothing to do with me."[1]

Although in many respects Irving Fisher's views on exchange rates were unorthodox, they were deeply rooted in received economic theory. In particular, recommendations about a "compensated dollar"—that is, a dollar liked to a basket of commodities, rather than to gold—were consistent with the "quantity theory of money," a theory first developed by the Scottish philosopher David Hume in 1752, and later adopted by University of Chicago monetarists, such as Henry Simons and Milton Friedman, as their central proposition. Indeed, Fisher had made significant contributions to the quantity theory during the 1910s. He was credited with developing the "equation of exchange"—the workhorse of the quantity theory—and was completely aware of the need to reconcile it with his theories about international finance, exchanges, and the dollar.

In 1933, Irving Fisher was sixty-six years old and had been a public figure for many years. He constantly travelled the country promoting his views on economics and social causes. His prolonged absences from the New Haven campus troubled his Yale colleagues, who with the passage of time developed a deep dislike for him. Fisher was a strong believer in Prohibition and eugenics, and an ardent supporter of the League of Nations. He wore wire rim glasses, sported a goatee, and was always immaculately dressed in three piece suits. When he spoke publicly, he did so slowly, pronouncing in a monotonous tone of voice. He was a pioneer in the use of mathematics in economics, and in 1913 he invented a card-filing system, which he sold to the Kardex Rand (later Remington Rand) Corporation for a handsome sum. During the 1910 and 1920s, he made a sizable fortune speculating in the stock market. After 1929, however, he lost most of his money. He not only failed to anticipate the stock market collapse, but he insisted that it was a temporary hiccup. At a dinner organized by the Purchasing Agents Association on October 15, 1929, he famously said that stock prices had reached "what looks like a permanently high plateau." He then took issue with the views of Roger W. Babson, a successful financier and public man who had forecasted a significant market retreat. Fisher said "I do not feel that there will soon, if ever, be a fifty or sixty-point break below present levels such as Mr. Babson has predicted." Fisher ended his speech by saying that he expected "to see the stock market a good deal higher than it is today, within a few months."[2]

Fisher's criticism of the gold standard was simple and powerful. Since gold was a commodity—in addition to a standard of value—its price fluctuated according to demand and supply conditions. New mineral discoveries led to lower prices, while an increase in its use by industry and the arts resulted in price hikes. If the value of the dollar was fixed in terms of gold, the volatility in the global market for the metal would be translated into the price level. During periods of relative gold scarcity, there would be deflation, and during periods of abundance there would be rapid inflation. The solution, he argued in several books and articles, was to allow the value of the dollar to change through time. Instead of being fixed at, say, $20.67 an ounce, the exchange rate would vary in ways that would compensate for the fluctuations in the price of gold. This would result in relatively stable prices. Fisher called his proposal the "compensated dollar," while his critics called it the "commodity dollar" or the "rubber dollar."

Irving Fisher first sketched the idea of a fluctuating dollar in his 1911 book *The Purchasing Power of Money.*[3] Two years later, in a long article in the *Quarterly Journal of Economics*, he provided the first detailed presentation of the plan. In the introductory paragraph Fisher says that the goal of the scheme was "rendering the gold standard more 'stable' by virtually increasing the weight of the gold dollar so as to compensate for losses of purchasing power."[4] Under the proposal, dollar coins would cease to circulate and would be replaced by a "virtual gold dollar" with a variable gold content. Although Fisher's discussion was based on the hypothetical case when there are positive inflationary pressures—a situation that called for "increasing the weight of the gold dollar"—the argument was perfectly symmetrical for a period of deflationary forces; this would call for *decreasing* the weight of the gold dollar (or devaluing the currency). The article had two lengthy appendixes. The first was aimed at dispelling the notion that this system would encourage speculation in gold, and the second contained an example of how the gold content of the dollar would have evolved between 1896 and 1911 under this program.

In the years that followed, Fisher worked strenuously on refining the plan, and in 1920 he published a 305-page book titled *Stabilizing the Dollar.* The subtitle illustrates clearly Fisher's policy objectives: "A plan to stabilize the general price level without fixing individual prices." Most of the technical details are confined to a number of appendixes. One of them (appendix II) is devoted to answering the criticisms that the proposal had elicited since its inception in 1911. And in appendix IV he lists a number of authors, some of them very prominent, who according to him were precursors of the compensated dollar idea. As time passed, Fisher was able to convince some members of Congress to support his plan, and in late December 1922 the House of Representatives Committee on Banking and Currency held hearings on a bill sponsored by Congressman T. Alan Goldsborough from Maryland. Although the bill never got out of Committee, Fisher was not discouraged, and he continued to work on the issue. In *The Money Illusion* (1928), and *Booms and Depressions* (1932) he devoted long passages to the plan.[5]

In *Booms and Depression* Fisher makes an important distinction between large adjustment in the price of gold, which he calls "corrections," and the repeated manipulation of the exchange rate required to maintain prices stability, which he calls "safeguard." This is a key clarification: price stability may be "safeguarded" through small and frequent changes in the price of gold—say, 1 to 2 percent per quarter—in a way that is not very different from the "crawling peg" or "managed" exchange rate regime adopted in the 1960s, 1970s, and 1980s by a number of developing countries, including Brazil, Chile, and Colombia. It also has some similarities to the "exchange rate targeting" monetary policy followed by the Monetary Authority of Singapore since the late 1990s. The key in all of these cases is that the changes in the exchange rate are small—Fisher himself thought that an upper bound for adjusting the exchange rate would be 2 percent per quarter—and frequent. A "correction," on the other hand, requires a (very) large change in the currency value; if the situation is one of deflation, this means a large devaluation. For instance, in late 1932, a straightforward application of Fisher's simulation would have indicated that a price of gold of $32.25 was needed in order to return the price level to its 1926 level; that is, the dollar would have to be devalued by 36 percent in terms of gold.

Many economists, including Brains Trust members Rex Tugwell and Adolf Berle, were leery of large devaluations. They thought that they could unleash a sequence of repeated and increasingly large "corrections," and a rapid inflationary process. There were also unknown secondary effects, including possible changes in the price of gold itself that could feed back into prices in an unpredictable fashion. During the campaign, and in spite of having endorsed the "compensated dollar" in his college textbook, Tugwell began to distance himself from Fisher. On January 14,

1933—after the election and before inauguration—Tugwell wrote in his diary:[6]

> Irving Fisher has tried to see me a number of times this Summer and Fall. Except for one occasion . . . I have managed to avoid him. However, last night he caught me fairly at dinner at the Cosmos Club and proceeded to try to pump me as to my views and impress me with his. I do not believe in outright inflation. Our policy has been shaped toward a pragmatic handling of prices.

And in his memoirs Tugwell points out the he became very concerned when he found out that Fisher had "made his way uninvited to Albany and spent some time with Roosevelt." Tugwell thought that Fisher was overbearing. He wrote that the Yale professor had "become something of a fanatic, and Roosevelt always enjoyed talking to fanatics. The impression this visit made [on FDR] was one we knew would have consequences."[7]

In Fisher's model, currency devaluation would generate an *incipient* increase in price level through higher prices of imports and (possibly) of exports. However, these increased prices would only be sustained through time, instead of petering out, if the Federal Reserve provided additional liquidity, or if the "velocity of circulation" of money—its turnover ratio—increased. In his writings, Fisher emphasized that in order for his "compensated dollar" scheme to work properly it would require the intervention—or, in his words, "the good will"—of the Federal Reserve.[8] In that regard, Fisher had a complete view of the world—or in economics jargon a "general equilibrium" perspective—with many moving parts that interacted among themselves in a complex fashion. There was a role for interest rates, expectations, monetary policy, the public debt, open market operations, relative prices, the cost of mining gold, and international trade.

George Warren had a completely different view of the matter. For him, what the Federal Reserve did was rather irrelevant, as were the quantity theory of money and its basic equation of exchange. So much so, that after explaining their basic equation, Warren and Pearson wrote that their analysis "has no relationship to the formula [for the quantity theory]. . . . No one of [our] . . . factors correspond to any factor in [the equation of exchange]."[9]

Warren's views were not due to his ignorance about standard monetary theory, or to the fact that he was little more than a crude farmer, as some of his detractors repeated again and again. Of course he knew the quantity theory in all its variations, and for a long time he had embraced it. But during the mid-1920s, as he analyzed the evolution of dozens of prices in many countries through long periods of time, he started to wonder what was exactly meant by the supply of "money." Was it currency? Credit? Gold? In a long biographical article, his loyal co-author Frank Pearson described Warren's intellectual evolution as follows: "Observing that there was a close relationship between wholesale prices of the United States and of other gold-standard countries, he reasoned that this close association must be due to a common cause; and there was only one—gold."[10]

NOTES

INTRODUCTION

1. Executive Order No. 6102. See PPFDR, Vol. 2, pp. 111–114. The first five volumes of FDR's Public Papers were published in 1938 under the direction of his long-time associate Samuel I. Rosenman. What makes this collection particularly useful is that many items have comments written by FDR after the fact. These notes clarify the intent of original orders, provide historical perspective and help understand how different initiatives were connected.

2. PPFDR, Vol. 2, pp. 61–66.

3. NYT, "President Invokes Law on Hoarders," April 6, 1933, p. 1.

4. Strictly speaking, during its first few decades the nation was under a bimetal standard, in which both silver and gold were legal tender. During those years, prices of gold and silver were fixed in dollar terms and, thus, fixed relative to each other. Silver was demonetized in 1873.

5. PPFDR, Vol. 2, pp. 137–143.

6. The Thomas Amendment gave the president three options to help increase commodity prices: devaluing the dollar, remonetizing silver at a ratio of 16 to 1 relative to gold, or to issue up to $3 billion of nonbacked currency or greenbacks. See chapter 5 for a detailed discussion of the Thomas Amendment.

7. Mitchell (1898).

8. NYT, "Roosevelt Signs Gold Clause Ban," April 6, 1933, p. 35.

9. PPFDR, Presidential Proclamation No. 2072, Vol. 3, pp. 67–76.

10. Schlesinger (1960), Vol. 3, p. 260.

11. McReynolds (1945), p. 771.

12. As will be seen in this book, there were three rulings, all of them highly complex and controversial from a legal point of view.

13. The most complete recent discussion of the drama surrounding the gold cases is in chapter 6 of Shesol's (2011) gripping book on the Court and FDR. The most detailed recent discussion of some of the legal angles of the cases is an article by Magliocca (2012).

14. Friedman and Schwartz (1963), p. 699.

CHAPTER 1. GOLD AND THE PROFESSORS

1. These data compare, for each variable, the peak and the trough throughout the cycle. The data are from the U.S. Department of Commerce (1960), and from Sachs (1934).

2. See table III in Sachs (1934) for a comparison of the 1929–1933 and 1921–1923 episodes. For a succinct history of financial crises from around the world see Kindleberger (1978); the modern reference is Reinhart and Rogoff (2009).

3. Hoover was not the first president to use the term "depression" to refer to an economic turndown. James Monroe labeled the 1819 bank panic a depression.

4. An important and the more technical question is the behavior of the wholesale price index in comparison with the GNP deflator. During 1930 and 1931, both indices moved in an identical fashion. From that point on, however, they diverged significantly. Between the third quarter of 1931 and the first quarter of 1933, the wholesale price index declined by 36 percent; during the same period, the GNP deflator declined by 18 percent. These data are from Balke and Gordon (1986), data appendix.

5. Cited in Tugwell (1968), p. 94. Lindley later wrote a classical book on the first year of the Roosevelt administration. See Lindley (1933). See also Lindley (1931).

6. *New York Herald Tribune*, "Governor Roosevelt's Candidacy," January 8, 1932.

7. NYT, "Hoover and Roosevelt," May 24, 1932.

8. PPFDR, Vol. 1, p. 625.

9. Not surprisingly, there are some divergences on the exact role played by different people in preparing each of the speeches. See Moley (1939, 1966) for details.

10. Moley (1939, 1966).

11. Tugwell (1968), pp. 73–82.

12. Tugwell, Munro, and Stryker (1925).

13. Tugwell and Hill (1934). See also Tugwell (1933).

14. Tugwell (1952), footnote 8; reproduced in Namorato (1992), p. 299.

15. Tugwell (1968), pp. 98, 165.

16. Tugwell (1968), p. 26.

17. Tugwell (1968), p. 28.

18. Rosen (1977), pp. 195–211.

19. Berle and Means (1932).

20. *Time* magazine, July 3, 1933, quoted by Tugwell (1952) in the introduction to his New Deal diaries in Namorato (1992), p. 376.

21. Moley (1939), pp. 21–22.
22. The term "high-grade research assistant" is Lindley's. See Lindley (1933), p. 23.
23. Quoted in Schlesinger (1957), p. 400.
24. Schlesinger (1957), p. 401.
25. Lindley (1933), p. 25.
26. Lindley (1933), p. 413.

CHAPTER 2. A TRAGIC DISASTER

1. Viner (1932), p. 38.
2. Similar results are obtained if the search is done for "gold standard" and "Hoover" or "Hoover and Roosevelt." The point is that the gold standard only became an issue very late in the campaign, and only as result of Hoover's attacks on Roosevelt.
3. Hoover (1952), p. 284.
4. Tugwell (1968), p. 58.
5. Delivered on May 22, 1932. PPFDR, Vol. 1, pp. 639–647, emphasis added. This speech was drafted by Ernest Lindley.
6. Moley (1939), p. 121, emphasis added.
7. Lippmann (1932), p. 309.
8. PPFDR, Vol. 1, Item 132.
9. For details on Fisher's compensated dollar, see the appendix to this book.
10. Moley (1966), p. 135.
11. PPFDR, Vol. 1, pp. 677–678.
12. PPFDR, Vol. 1, p. 678.
13. The term "Four Horsemen" had been popularized in the sports pages in 1924, in reference to Notre Dame's magnificent backfield.
14. Hoover (1952), pp. 280–283.
15. Hoover (1952), p. 284.
16. The complete speech was reproduced in the *New York Times* on November 2, 1932, pp. 12–13.
17. Berle (1973), p. 73, emphasis added.
18. In 1917 a law was passed requiring that all government debt—with the exception of very short-term bills—include a gold clause.
19. NYT, "Text of Governor's Roosevelt Speech at Brooklyn Rally," November 5, 1932, p. 10.

CHAPTER 3. THE QUEST FOR MONEY

1. NYT, "Roosevelt Cruise to End on Wednesday," February 13, 1933, p. 2.
2. NYT, "Assassin Shoots Five Times," February 16, 1933, p. 1.
3. Cable from Vincent Astor to Raymond Moley, February 16, 1933. RMP, Box 63, The Hoover Institution.
4. Schlesinger (1957), p. 450.
5. NYT, "Cash Rushed to Relieve Michigan; Banks May Reopen Within a Week," February 15, 1933, p. 1.
6. The account that follows draws on the recollections and memoirs of several people that were involved, at different levels, in this episode, including Acting Comptroller of the Currency Francis Awalt (1969), Undersecretary of the Treasury Arthur A. Ballantine (1944), Raymond Moley (1939, 1966), and President Herbert Hoover (1952). It also draws on Friedman and Schwartz (1963), Acheson (1965), and Meltzer (2003).
7. Awalt (1969), p. 355.
8. Not surprisingly, there are different and contradictory versions of this episode. President Hoover, for example, argues that Senator Couzens's intransigence, and his unwillingness to make a $1 million subordinated deposit, resulted in the failure of the Guardian Group. Hoover (1952), pp. 206–208. This, however, is not mentioned by other actors such as Raymond Moley or Francis Awalt.
9. See Moley (1966), pp. 134–135; Hoover (1952), pp. 168–169. The quote is from Ballantine (1948), p. 134.
10. Hoover (1952), p. 205. The Act was amended on September 24, 1918.
11. Hoover (1952), p. 205.
12. Hoover (1952), p. 208.
13. Hoover (1952), pp. 210–212.
14. In his recollections Awalt (1969), p. 358, referred to March 3 as the "big gold rush" day.

CHAPTER 4. A NATIONAL CALAMITY

1. NYT, "Woodin Succeeds in Many Fields," May 4, 1934, p. 18.
2. The Inaugural Address is reproduced in PPFDR, Vol. 1, pp. 11–16.
3. PPFDR, Vol. 1, p. 16.
4. Quoted in Awalt (1969), p. 361.
5. PPFDR, Vol. 2, p. 25.
6. NYT, "On Gold Standard, Woodin Declares," March 6, 1933, p. 6.

7. The dislike was mutual. FDR referred to Mills as "Little Oggie." Byrnes (1958), p. 71.
8. Moley (1939), chapter V.
9. Emergency Banking Act of the United States (1933), p. 3.
10. Emergency Banking Act of the United States (1933), p. 7.
11. Emergency Banking Act of the United States (1933), p. 9.
12. PPFDR, Vol. 2, p. 64. Interestingly, the speech was written by Arthur Ballantine, a holdover from the Hoover Administration. See footnote 17 on page 155 of Moley's 1939 memoirs. For the estimated number of listeners (and radios turned on), see Moley (1966), p. 196.
13. Moley (1939), p. 155.
14. Federal Reserve Bulletin, April 1933.
15. Lippmann (1936), p. 18.
16. PPFDR, Vol. 2, p. 115.
17. Moley (1966), pp. 223–224.

CHAPTER 5. MODERATE INFLATION IS NECESSARY AND DESIRABLE

1. LAT, "Silver Drive Ready Soon," January 23, 1933, p. 10.
2. Tugwell's diary (RGTD), entry for April 3, 1933. See Namorato (1992), p. 325.
3. NYT, "Iowa Farmers Abduct Judge from Court," April 27, 1933, p. 1.
4. NYT, "Court Martial Set for Iowa Trials," May 7, 1933, p. 3.
5. HMD, Vol. 1, May 9, 1933, p. 18.
6. PPFDR, Vol. 1, pp. 625–626.
7. These data are from various tables in "Historical Statistics of the United Sates: Colonial Times to 1957," U.S. Department of Commerce, 1960.
8. Tugwell (1968), p. 158, emphasis in the original. This view, Tugwell would recognize more than thirty years later, neglected the fact that a general price level hike would help dilute the real value of debts, whose burden had greatly increased since 1929 as a result of deflation. Tugwell (1968), pp. 158–159.
9. RMP, The Hoover Institution, Box 107.
10. PPFDR, Vol. 2, p. 75.
11. NYT, "Farm Groups Urge Deposits Guarantee," March 10, 1933, p. 3.
12. RGTD, March 31, 1933, p. 89.
13. PPFDR, Vol. 2, p. 74.
14. Tugwell's diary, entry for April 3, 1933. See Namorato (1992), pp. 90–91.
15. Tugwell's diary, entry for April 3, 1933. See Namorato (1992), p. 90.
16. Lippmann (1936), p. 21.

17. Moley (1939), p. 158.
18. Published in Lippmann's regular column on April 19, 1933, and reproduced in Lippmann (1936), p. 55.
19. Feis (1966), p. 122.
20. Moley (1939), p. 158.
21. Moley (1939), p. 159.
22. NYT, "Principal Provisions of the Inflation Measure: Expansion of Credit, Not of Currency, Sought," April 21, 1933, p. 1.
23. See Bordo and Sinha (2016) for the Fed's policy during this period.
24. NYT, "Roosevelt Directs Move," April 21, 1933, p. 1.
25. NYT, "Financial Markets: A Period of Watchful Hesitation," April 10, 1933, p. 1.
26. NYT, "Gold Standard Exchanges Up, Sterling Off," April 12, 1933, p. 29.
27. NYT, "Raids Send Dollar to Low of Years," April 14, 1933, p. 29.
28. NYT, "Gold Exports Act to Rally Dollar," April 16, 1933 p. N7.
29. Feis (1966), p. 124.
30. NYT, "Financial Markets," April 17, 1933, p. 21.

CHAPTER 6. A TRANSFER OF WEALTH
TO THE DEBTOR CLASS

1. The next day, Moley told his secretary, Celeste Jedel, the details of the meeting, and as was her custom she transcribed what she heard into her diary. See RMP, Box 1. In his memoirs Feis (1966) remembered FDR's "chuckle" and the fact that throughout the meeting Moley had a small notebook and a pen in his hands.
2. Warburg (1934), p. 95.
3. Feis (1966), p. 129.
4. Moley (1939), p. 160.
5. PPFDR, Vol. 1, p. 138, emphasis added.
6. Tugwell's diary. Note added in 1952 to the entry for April 21, 1933. See Namorato (1992), p. 338.
7. Roosevelt (1934), p. 61.
8. NYT, "Inflation Upsets Party," April 25, 1933, p. 1.
9. NYT, "Inflation Upsets Party," April 25, 1933, p. 1.
10. NYT, "Inflation Fight Is Warm," April 28, 1933, p. 1.
11. Tugwell (1968), p. 28.
12. "Mac" McDuffie served as FDR's valet from 1927 through 1939. Before joining the Roosevelt household he had been the valet to the German Consul in Atlanta, and had owned a successful barber shop. He died in Atlanta in 1946.

13. Acheson (1965), pp. 164–165; Tugwell (1968), p. 30.
14. CHT, "Woodin Offers New Bond Issue to Small Buyer," April 24, 1933, p. 21.
15. NYT, "New $500,000,000 Offering of the Treasury Draws Orders Quickly," April 25, 1933, p. 23.
16. Lippmann (1936), p. 176.
17. NYT, "President Signs Farm Bill, Making Inflation the Law," May 13, 1933, p. 1.
18. Warren (1932).
19. Warren and Pearson (1935), p. 13.

CHAPTER 7. THE GOLD CLAUSE IS GONE

1. NYT, "Gold for Contracts Is Held Imperiled," April 23, 1933, p. 25.
2. NYT, "Ignore Indenture 'Payable in Gold,'" May 2, 1933, p. 2.
3. NYT, "Gold-Bond Clause Awaits Court Test," May 7, 1933, p. XX2.
4. NYT, "Gold-Bond Clause Awaits Court Test," May 7, 1933, p. XX2.
5. The quotes from the president's second Fireside Chat in this paragraph come from PPFDR, Vol. 2, pp. 160–168. The emphases have been added.
6. The quotes from the president's second Fireside Chat in this paragraph come from PPFDR, Vol. 2, pp. 160–168. The emphases have been added.
7. PPFDR, Vol. 2, p. 168, emphasis added.
8. HMD, Vol. 1, p. 18.
9. For details, see chapters 11 through 13 of this book.
10. NYT, "Gold Clause in Foreign Bond Issue Seen Complicating Interest Payments Here," April 30, 1933, p. N7.
11. NYT, "Germans Will Stop Gold Payments Here," April 22, 1933, p. 4.
12. NYT, "Gold Ban Is Seen as a Loss to US," May 6, 1933, p. 21.
13. HMD, Vol. 1, May 9, 1933, pp. 17–19.
14. HMD, Vol. 1, May 17, 1933, p. 29. See Warren and Pearson (1932).
15. Arthur Krock, "President to Let Dollar Devalorize Itself," *New York Times*, May 9, 1933, p. 16.
16. WSJ, "Coin or Current Funds," May 26, 1933, p. 8.
17. NYT, "Bond Gold Clause Is Tested in Suit," May 23, 1933, p. 27.
18. 74 U.S. 229 (1868).
19. NYT, "Bond Gold Clause Is Voided by Court," May 25, 1933, p. 29.
20. NYT, "Gold Clause Repeal Asked by Roosevelt to Permit Payment in Legal Tender," May 27, 1933, p. 1.
21. NYT, "Gold Clause Repeal Asked by Roosevelt to Permit Payment in Legal Tender," May 27, 1933, p. 1.

22. "Cotton Jumps," *Atlanta Constitution*, May 27, 1933, p. 1.

23. NYT, "Gold Move Rushed; Committees Vote Plan as Drafted," May 28, 1933, p. 1.

24. On Sunday, May 28, 1933, the *New York Times* contained a large number of stories related to the international reaction to the proposed resolution.

25. NYT, "Switzerland to Pay in Gold," June 11, 1933, p. N8.

26. NYT, "In Washington," May 30, 1933, p. 14.

27. NYT, "Senate Repeals the Gold Clause," June 4, 1933, p. 1.

28. NYT, "Senate Repeals the Gold Clause," June 4, 1933, p. 1.

29. Henry Morgenthau's diary is replete with commentary on when to buy and sell grain for the government.

30. Indeed, this was Keynes's view as early as December 1933; see Edwards (2007b). See also the discussion in Powell (2007).

31. Irwin (2012), p. 84. See also the collection of articles written by Harvard faculty and edited by Brown (1934).

32. NYT, "From Keynes to Roosevelt: Our Recovery Plan Assayed," December 31, 1933, p. 2XX.

CHAPTER 8. A LONDON INTERLUDE

1. Leith-Ross (1968), p. 160.

2. Feis (1966), p. 126.

3. Leith-Ross (1968), pp. 160–61.

4. Dam (1983), p. 522.

5. TL, "France and the Dollar," April 21, 1933, p. 11.

6. TL, "The U.S. Gold Embargo," April 21, 1933, p. 12.

7. League of Nations (1933), No. 3, p. 8. See Roosevelt (1938), Vol. 2, p. 242.

8. Ernest Lindley (1933).

9. Hull knew, however, that these were empty words. At the last minute the president had informed him that he would not request from Congress authority to negotiate lower tariffs. TL, "Sweeping U.S. Measures," June 5, 1933, p. 15.

10. League of Nations (1933), No. 5, p. 26.

11. League of Nations (1933), No. 4, p. 12.

12. NYT, "Paris Doubts Help at London Parley," June 12, 1933, p. 2.

13. NYT, "Paris Doubts Help at London Parley," June 12, 1933, p. 2.

14. NYT, "France Insistent on Stable Money," June 12, 1933, p. 25.

15. Lindley (1933), p. 198.

16. Roosevelt (1938), Vol. 2, pp. 166–167.

17. HMD, Vol. 1, May 29, 1933, p. 37.
18. Feis (1966), p. 144.
19. Leith-Ross (1968), p. 168.
20. Leith-Ross (1968), p. 168.
21. The rumor was started after James Cox, the former Governor of Ohio, and newly appointed chair of the Monetary Committee of the Conference, uttered that a $4.00 per pound rate was appropriate.
22. PPFDR, Vol. 2, p. 245.
23. TL, "America's Two Paths," June 21, 1933, p. 14.
24. In 1932 a group of economists criticized the Fed for not undertaking counter-cyclical policy. See appendix I in Wright (1932). In mid-1933, a smaller group of Chicago economists made a more specific proposal for reforming the monetary system, which they sent to Secretary of Agriculture Henry A. Wallace. This scheme was known as the "Chicago Plan." See Tavlas (1997) for a detailed analysis.
25. Warburg (1934), p. 107. The Warburg plan had some similarities to the plan unveiled by Keynes in a series of articles in the *Times*, which he collected in the pamphlet *The Means to Prosperity*. Keynes (1933).
26. Lindley (1933), pp. 204–206.
27. Lindley (1933), p. 206.
28. Moley (1939), p 235.
29. Warburg (1934), p. 117.
30. All the quotes in this paragraph come from PPFDR, Vol. 2, pp. 264–265.
31. Hull (1948), Vol. 1, p. 262, emphasis added.
32. Hull (1948), Vol. 1, p. 263.
33. PPFDR, Vol. 2, p. 186, emphasis added.
34. NYT, "From Keynes to Roosevelt: Out Recovery Plan Assayed," December 31, 1933, p. 2XX. For a formal statistical analysis of dollar gyrations during that period, see Edwards (2017b).
35. This statement assumes that we are sitting in late June 1933; we cannot see the data that became available after that time.
36. Feis (1966), p. 182.
37. NYT, "Shifting of Influences Rumored in Washington," July 30, 1933, p. 45.
38. The Conference attracted considerable attention from contemporary analysts, including Lindley (1933) and Pasvolsky (1933). Schlesinger (1957) provides a detailed account, which draws on many of the participants' recollections. Nussbaum (1957) dedicates two pages to it. Eichengreen (1992), in the most complete treatise on the gold standard, covers it in five pages. With time, however, the gathering has faded in accounts of economic policy during the first year of the Roosevelt administration. Ahamed (2009) devotes two pages to it, as does Rauchway (2015).

CHAPTER 9. ORDER IN PLACE OF CHAOS

1. For the content of the communiqué, see the appendix to Moley's 1939 memoir.
2. PPFDR, Vol. 2, p. 186.
3. Acheson (1965), p. 174.
4. NYT, "French Bonds Soar on Exchange Here," July 8, 1933, p. 15.
5. NYT, "Commons Upholds Bond Conversion," July 22, 1933, p. 15.
6. HMD, entry for May 9, 1933.
7. As with so many episodes during this period there are conflicting accounts about the details of this meeting. Jimmy Warburg claims that it was his idea to have it and that he organized it. Henry A. Wallace makes the same claim.
8. NYT, "Roosevelt Calls Monetary Aides," August 8, 1933, p. 1; NYT, "Roosevelt Hails Increase in Prices to Average of 1914." August 10, 1933, p. 1.
9. NYT, "Roosevelt Hails Increase in Prices to Average of 1914," August 10, 1933, p. 1.
10. In his memoirs Warburg says that the idea of forming a commission was his, and that he thought about it while in transit to New York from London, after he decided to leave the sinking Conference. Warburg (1964), p. 139.
11. Warburg (1934), p. 107.
12. Keynes (1924), p. 170.
13. Keynes (1933), p. 30, emphasis added. Chapter IV contains Keynes's proposal for the World Economic Conference. This pamphlet put together (somewhat) revised versions of four articles that Keynes published in the *Times of London* in March 1933. The gold notes were a precursor of the *Bancor*, the international currency he proposed in the 1940s.
14. Acheson (1965), pp. 177–178.
15. Interestingly, this Executive Order was not included in the Public Papers of the President published in 1938. Executive Order 6260, which further regulated the hoarding and exports of gold, was published. PPFDR, Vol. 2, pp. 345–352.
16. NYT, "President Aids Miners," August 30, 1933, p. 1.
17. Salant (1990), p. 271.

CHAPTER 10. THE GOLD-BUYING PROGRAM

1. HMD, MD000, p. 96. The entry corresponds to 11/04/33.
2. NYT, "Dr. Warren Explains His Money Theory," January 21, 1934, p. SM3.

3. Warren attended the Industrial College of the University of Nebraska in Lincoln. For a very detailed biography, see Stanton (2007).

4. A preliminary version was published in November 1932 as a working paper (Memoir 142) by the Cornell Agriculture Experiment Station under the title "Wholesale Prices for 213 Years, 1720–1932." This preliminary version included an essay by Herman M. Stoker on wholesale prices in New York City.

5. NYT, "London Group Acts on Securities Here," October 3, 1933, p. 39.

6. NYT, "Europeans Defend Gold Clause," July 5, 1933, p. 2.

7. PPFDR, Vol. 2, pp. 425–427.

8. PPFDR, Vol. 2, p. 421.

9. Interestingly, this phrase, which at the time was broadly commented on in the press, was suggested by Ray Moley, who had been called in by FDR to help him draft his fourth Fireside speech. PPFDR, Vol. 2, p. 426.

10. PPFDR, Vol. 2, p. 427.

11. Acheson (1965), p. 187.

12. Leith Ross (1968), p. 172.

13. Acheson (1965), p. 189.

14. Lippmann (1936), pp. 157–162. The original columns were published in the *Herald Tribune* on October 24 and 27, 1933.

15. NYT, "First Gold Buying Puzzling to Paris," November 3, 1933, p. 8.

16. NYT, "Price Is Advanced on Domestic Gold," November 4, 1933, p. 8; NYT, "RFC Gold Buying a 'Substantial' Sum," November 7, 1933, p. 37.

17. NYT, "Fluctuations Surprise the Capital," November 10, 1933, p. 2.

18. Blum (1959), p. 121; JVP, Box 49, Folder 1.

19. NYT, "Japanese Utility Voids Gold Clause," November 29, 1933, p. 2.

20. NYT, "Brazil Ends Gold Clause," November 29, 1933, p. 2.

21. Lippmann (1936), pp. 164–165. The original column was published in the *Herald Tribune* on November 10, 1933.

22. NYT, "Senators Differ on Sprague Action," November 23, 1933, p. 14.

23. NYT, "Gold Clause Ruling Is Final in Britain," December 19, 1933, p. 38; NYT "Lord's Gold Ruling Significant Here," December 31, 1933, p. N7.

24. See NYT, December 31, 1933, p. 2XX. FDR received the letter ahead of time from Felix Frankfurter, who had seen Keynes in the UK during November.

25. Formally, the program continued through January 1934, but there was only one price change, on January 16, from $34.06 to $34.45 per ounce. As I point out below, if I extend the period considered under the program, the results are virtually identical.

26. NYT, "Decision on Gold Reported Reached," January 1, 1934, p. 4.

27. NYT, "Bill Is Sent to Congress," January 16, 1934, p. 1.

28. Section 10 (b) of the Act.

29. NYT, "Attorney General's Opinion on the Gold Bill," January 18, 1934, p. 14.

CHAPTER 11. THE PATH TO THE SUPREME COURT

1. HMD, MD001, p. 56. The manuscript is dated 1/23/34.
2. HMD, MD001, p. 79.
3. Albert Gallatin served a year longer than Morgenthau, from May 1801 to February 1814.
4. Most economic historians, however, have concluded that neither the AAA, nor the NRA, contributed to the recovery itself. In fact, a number of analysts have argued that both of these programs introduced significant distortions into the economy, and resulted in lower investment. See, for example, the essays collected in Bordo, Goldin, and White (1998).
5. The data on GNP from Balke and Gordon (1986).
6. Crabbe (1989).
7. Irwin (2012).
8. As noted by Friedman and Schwartz (1963), p. 473, since the Treasury used newly created money to pay for gold, these operations did not put any pressure on the budget.
9. Meltzer (2003), p. 465.
10. NYT, "Mix-up on Currency for Coupons Grows," January 12, 1934, p. 35.
11. NYT, "Panama Demands Gold for Our Debts," March 2, 1934, p. 3.
12. NYT, "Panama Gold Decision Interests Bondholders," March 7, 1934, p. 18.
13. NYT, "Hull Eases Minds on Panama Treaty," June 15, 1939, p. 7.
14. MacLean (1936).
15. NYT, "State Court Backs 'Gold Clause' Ban," July 4, 1934, p. 25.
16. NYT, "State Court Backs 'Gold Clause' Ban," July 4, 1934, p. 25.
17. NYT, "Gold Dollar Clause in Contract Voided," August 30, 1934, p. 31.
18. NYT, "Poland Abolishes Dollar Clause," July 8, 1934, p. 5.
19. NYT, "Gold Dollar Clause in Contract Voided," August 30, 1934, p. 31.
20. NYT, "Cummings to Represent the Government in Supreme Court," November 16, 1934, p. 37.
21. NYT, "Final Gold Ruling Is Promised Soon," November 20, 1934, p. 31.
22. NYT, "Cummings Files Gold Case Briefs," December 19, 1934, p. 37. The fact that the government was not part of the *Norman* case explains why in a number of articles and news reports from that time the number of cases is considered to be three rather than four.
23. See Friedman and Schwartz (1963) for the classical interpretation of this period. According to them the untimely death of New York Fed president Benjamin Strong contributed to the Depression. In their views, Strong was one of the few Fed officials who truly understood what was going on at the time.

24. Quoted in Moley (1966), p. 186.
25. Hoover (1952), p. 30–31.

CHAPTER 12. NINE OLD MEN AND GOLD

1. There is something of a controversy about who coined the term "nine old men" to refer to the Hughes Court. According to Leuchtenburg (1995), p. 119, the term was first uttered, in passing, by Brains Trust member Adolf A. Berle in 1933. The expression became part of common usage after a column by Drew Pearson and Robert S. Allen published in 1936 (Pearson and Allen (1936)).
2. The standard work on the Supreme Court during the time of Roosevelt is Leuchtenburg (1995). See chapter 9 for a discussion of Hughes's views on the Constitution.
3. This brief speech may be watched online at https://www.youtube.com/watch?v=NAydPcgUvAw.
4. Leuchtenburg (1995), p. 119.
5. *United States v. Carolene Products*, 304 U.S. 144 (1938), decided on April 25, 1938.
6. Leuchtenburg (1995), ch. 6.
7. Hughes (1973), pp. 300–301.
8. Knox (2002).
9. Hughes (1973), p. 300.
10. The access number of the Homer Cummings Archives (HCA) at the University of Virginia Special Collections is 9973. The pertinent boxes are 177, 197, and the folder names are "Gold cases" and "Gold cases for use of White House."
11. MacLean (1936), p. 250.
12. U.S. and RFC Brief, Missouri & Pacific Case U.S. Supreme Court, October Term 1934, Nos. 471 and 472, p. 18.
13. U.S. Brief, Perry Case U.S. Supreme Court, October Term 1934, No. 532, p. 45.
14. MacLean (1936), p. 251.
15. U.S. Brief, Perry Case U.S. Supreme Court, October Term 1934, No. 532, p. 60–70.
16. U.S. Brief, Perry Case U.S. Supreme Court, October Term 1934, No. 532, p. 70.
17. Perry Brief, Perry Case U.S. Supreme Court, October Term 1934, No. 532, pp. 11–12.
18. U.S. Brief, Perry Case U.S. Supreme Court, October Term 1934, No. 532, p. 49.
19. U.S. Brief, Perry Case U.S. Supreme Court, October Term 1934, No. 532, pp. 11–12.

20. MacLean (1936), pp. 250–251.
21. Nussbaum (1957), pp. 79–81.
22. MacLean (1936), p. 251.
23. MacLean (1936), p. 252.
24. The government also questioned the Court of Claims jurisdiction in this case.
25. *Home Bldg. & Loan Ass'n v. Blaisdell*, 290 U.S. 398 (1934).
26. Hale (1943), p. 568.
27. Mason (1956), p. 363.
28. Mason (1956), pp. 361–362.
29. A few months later the Court, also by a vote of 5 to 4, upheld a New York law fixing the price of milk. This case, *Nebbia v. New York*, 291 U.S. 502 (1934), also gave New Deal officials hope that the Court would uphold the constitutionality of the Joint Resolution that abrogated gold contracts.
30. Ratner (1935) provides a detailed discussion of the Legal Tender cases from the perspective of the 1935 gold clause cases. A key question addressed in this article is whether President Grant packed the Supreme Court. The discussion that followed partially draws on Ratner (1937).
31. MacLean (1936), p. 251.
32. HMD, Vol. 4, pp. 136–137.
33. *Panama Refining Co. v. Ryan*, 293, U.S. 399 (1935).
34. NYT, "Supreme Court Rules," January 8, 1935, p. 1.
35. NYT, "Supreme Court Rules," January 8, 1935, p. 8, emphases added.

CHAPTER 13. EMBARRASSMENT AND CONFUSION

1. CHT, "Justices Quiz Lawyers on Gold Clause," January 10, 1935, p. 1.
2. NYT, "Void Gold Clause in Bonds Argued in Supreme Court," January 9, 1935, p. 1.
3. NYT, "Void Gold Clause in Bonds Argued in Supreme Court," January 9, 1935, p. 1.
4. NYT, "Chaos over Debts Pictured if Court Backs Gold Plea," January 10, 1935, p. 1.
5. In the postscript to the Memorandum to the Attorney General, dated September 15, 1934, MacLean asked Cummings for the privilege to participate in the oral arguments in front of the Court. HCP, Box 197, "Gold cases for White House."
6. WP, "Justices Split on Gold Case, Actions Hint," January 10, 1935, p. 1.
7. NYT, "B&O Case Argued," January 9, 1935, p. 2.
8. CHT, "Justices Quiz Lawyers on Gold Clause," January 10, 1935, p. 1.

9. NYT, "Chaos over Debts Pictured if Court Backs Gold Plea," January 10, 1935, p. 1.

10. NYT, "Hughes Asks Where Power Was Found to Alter U.S. Bond," January 11, 1935, p. 1; WSJ, "Court Queries Brisk as Gold Argument Approached End," January 11, 1935, p. 1.

11. NYT, "Hughes Asks Where Power Was Found to Alter U.S. Bond," January 11, 1935, p. 1; WSJ, "Court Queries Brisk as Gold Argument Approached End," January 11, 1935, p. 1.

12. CHT, "Hughes Assails Repudiation of Gold Payment," January 11, 1935, p. 4.

13. CHT, "Justices Quiz Lawyers on Gold Clause," January 10, 1935, p. 1.

14. NYT, " 'Realities' of New Deal Tested in Supreme Court," January 13, 1935, p. E1.

15. NYT, "Nine Calm Men in the Midst of the Storm," January 20, 1935, p. SM6.

16. CHT, "Justices Quiz Lawyers on Gold Clause," January 10, 1935, p. 1.

17. CHT, "Hughes Assails Repudiation of Gold Payment," January 11, 1935, p. 4.

18. WP, "Repudiation Denied by U.S. in Gold Hearing," January 11, 1935, p. 1.

19. CHT, "Gold Payment Ruling Up to the Supreme Court," January 12, 1935, p. 1.

CHAPTER 14. THE WAITING GAME

1. LAT, "Sharp Break on Market," January 12, 1935, p. 12.

2. NYT, "Gold Issue Hits Highest since 1917," January 13, 1935, p. 2.

3. NYT, "Gold Reserves," January 13, 1935, p. E4.

4. NYT, "Along the Highways of Finance," January 13, 1935, p. N13.

5. NYT, "Treasury Steps In as Dollar Mounts on Gold Case Talk," January 16, 1935, p. 1.

6. NYT, "Reich's Stake Big in Gold Decision," February 4, 1935, p. 5.

7. NYT, "Reich's Stake Big in Gold Decisions," February 4, 1935, p. 5.

8. NYT, "Revalued Dollar Is Urged If Court Upsets Gold Acts," January 15, 1935, p. 1.

9. NYT, "In Washington," January 15, 1935, p. 18.

10. NYT, "See hint of ruling in the gold cases," January 20, 1935, p. 1.

11. NYT, "Gold Imports Sag, Blocs Moneys Ease," January 25, 1935, p. 33.

12. NYT, "Course Is Mapped on Gold Decision," February 1, 1935, p. 11.

13. NYT, "Markets Prepare for Gold Decision," February 5, 1935; NYT, "Gold Action by SEC Left to Roosevelt," February 6, 1935, p. 1.

14. NYT, "Cummings Says We Are Ready on Gold," February 8, 1935, p. 2.

15. NYT, "Supreme Court's Silence Is Truly Golden as Justices Dine on President's Gold Plates," February 8, 1935, p. 1.

16. See Shesol (2011) for a discussion on the contingency planning at the White House.
17. NYT, "Prepare to Offset a Gold Upset," January 30, 1935, p. 4.
18. NYT, "Cummings Says We Are Ready on Gold," February 8, 1935, p. 2.
19. NYT, "Course Is Mapped on Gold Decision," February 1, 1935, p. 11.
20. NYT, "Gold Bill Passed despite Gold Cases," January 31, 1935, p. 2.
21. LAT, "Gold Policy Decided by Roosevelt," February 4, 1935, p. 1.
22. NYT, "No Gold Decision Coming Tomorrow, Court Announces," February 10, 1935, p. 1.
23. NYT, "Treasury Pledges Steady Dollar," February 12, 1935, p. 1.
24. HMD, Vol. 4, p. 38.
25. HMD, Vol. 4, p. 101.
26. HMD, Vol. 4, p. 146.
27. HMD, Vol. 4, pp. 146–151.
28. The transcript of the conversation is in the Morgenthau Archives. See HMD, Vol. 5, pp. 287–290.
29. HMD, Vol. 5, p. 305.
30. HMD, Vol. 5, p. 330.
31. HMD, Vol. 5, pp. 331–334.
32. HMD, Vol. 5, p. 335.
33. HCA, Accession No. 9973, Box 197, Folder heading, "Gold cases for use of White House." The Memorandum's title is "Historical Background for a Proposed Act Dealing with Claims based on Gold Clause Certificates."
34. HMD, Vol. 5, pp. 340–341, emphasis added.
35. HCA, Accession No. 9973, Box 197, Folder heading, "Gold cases for use of White House." The draft of this legislation in the Attorney General Archives includes a routing slip from the president to the AG. The date is February 4, 1935.
36. HMD, Vol. 5, p. 235.
37. FDRPL, Master Speech File, Box 21, File 768.
38. In his February 21, 1935, column four days after the rulings, Arthur Krock informed the public that the speech had been drafted. He pointed out that he hadn't seen it, but that reliable sources confirmed its existence. NYT, "Roosevelt Speech Was Ready in Case He Lost on Gold," February 21, 1935, p. 1.

CHAPTER 15. THE DECISIONS, AT LAST

1. NYT, "Gold Clause Ruling Expected Monday," February 17, 1935, p. 1.
2. HMD, Vol. 5, p. 327.
3. NYT, "Tense Drama Grips 300 in Court Room," February 19, 1935, p. 14.

4. NYT, "Tense Drama Grips 300 in Court Room," February 19, 1935, p. 14.
5. TL, "Gold Clause Judgement," February 19, 1935, p. 14.
6. TL, "Gold Clause Judgement," February 19, 1935, p. 14.
7. NYT, "Tense Drama Grips 300 in Court Room," February 19, 1935, p. 14.
8. HMD, Vol. 5, pp. 327–328.
9. NYT, "Highlights of Decisions," February 19, 1935, p. 1.
10. NYT, "Highlights of decisions," February 19, 1935, p. 1.
11. HMD, Vol. 5, pp. 327–328.
12. NYT, "Impetus Given to Trade," February 19, 1935, p. 1.
13. TL, "The Gold Clause," February 19, 1935, p. 15.
14. HMD, Vol. 5, p. 328.
15. NYT, "Congress Is Censured," February 19, 1935. p. 1.
16. 294 U.S., p. 316.
17. Reynolds (1945).
18. See the transcript of the 1803 *Marbury v. Madison* decision. https://www
    .ourdocuments.gov/print_friendly.php?page=transcript&doc=19&title
    =Transcript+of+Marbury+v.+Madison+(1803)
19. The notion that acts of Congress that contradict the Constitution are void
    is in Hamilton's Federalist No. 78. See Epstein (2014), p. 90, for a discussion.
20. Epstein (2014), ch. 5. See Magliocca (2012) for a comparison between the legal
    philosophy behind the *Marbury* and the *Perry* opinions.
21. Holzer (1980), pp. 358–361. See also Mason (1956), pp. 389–392.
22. Mason (1956).
23. Cited by Mason (1956), p. 391.
24. NYT, "Constitution Gone, Says M'Reynolds," February 19, 1935, p. 1.
25. Schlesinger (1960), Vol. 3, p. 260.
26. Reynolds (1945).
27. JCMP, The McReynolds Papers, held at the University of Virginia Law School
    Library, contain a partial transcript provided by the *Wall Street Journal*.
28. Holzer (1980), pp. 361–381.
29. Hart (1935), pp. 1056–1057.
30. Hart (1935), p. 1096.
31. Hart (1935), footnote 23.
32. Hughes (1973), p. 308.
33. Pusey and Konefsky (1953).
34. Lippmann (1936), pp. 174–178. He attributed this phrase to Frank Kent.
35. NYT, "Grain Trade Halts after Gold Ruling," February 19, 1935, p. 33.
36. NYT, "Germans Welcome Gold Ruling Here," February 25, 1935, p. 25.
37. NYT, "Paris Views Vary on Gold Decision," February 25, 1933, p. 25.
38. NYT, "$29,206,400 Gold Received in Day," February 22, 1935, p. 33.

CHAPTER 16. CONSEQUENCES

1. All McReynolds quotes in this paragraph are from Bush (2010).
2. This assertion is presented towards the end of this massive book; no evidence is offered to support it. Friedman and Schwartz (1963), p. 699.
3. See, for example, Shesol (2011).
4. Hall (2001).
5. These data come from appendix B of Balke and Gordon (1986). The smooth, longer-term trend is obtained by applying a Hodrick-Prescott filter.
6. In the 1990s University of Chicago professor—and sometime member of the board at the Federal Reserve—Randall Kroszner wrote a paper in which he analyzed in great detail the reaction of a number of individual stocks and bonds on the day following the Supreme Court rulings. He found that the vast majority of them had a positive reaction. Kroszner (1998).
7. Edwards, Longstaff, and Garcia (2015).
8. See Grossman and Van Huyck (1986) and Edwards (2015a).
9. Chavez, Ferejohn, and Weingast (2011).
10. NYT, "Text of Governor Roosevelt Address at Brooklyn Rally," November 5, 1932, p. 10.

CHAPTER 17. COULD IT HAPPEN AGAIN?

1. Reinhart and Rogoff (2010), Edwards (2015a).
2. Cooper (1971). See also Edwards (1994). In recent years it has been recognized that protracted debt restructurings are costly to debtors and creditors. Alternative procedures for dealing with situations of international turmoil have been proposed. Among the most promising ones is the inclusion of "Collective Action Clauses" (CAC) in emerging-nations bonds. These clauses establish that if a certain percentage of bond holders—usually 75 percent—are in agreement, every bondholder will have to abide by the restructuring terms negotiated by the bondholder's committee and the debtor. In 2012 CACs were introduced, retroactively, into Greek bonds.

APPENDIX: IRVING FISHER AND THE DOLLAR

1. JVP, Princeton University, Box 49, Folder 1.
2. NYT, "Fisher Sees Stocks Permanently High," October 16, 1929.

3. The proposal is sketched in chapter 13, section 5. Fisher writes in the "Suggestions to Readers" that this chapter will appeal mostly to "currency reformers." The term "compensated dollar" doesn't appear in this book.
4. Fisher (1913), p. 213.
5. The bill was designated as H.R. 11788, 67 Congress, Second Session. Congressman Goldsborough introduced a slightly revised bill in 1924, H.R. 494, 68 Congress, First Session. Its fate was the same as the first bill. The hearings provide important information about Fisher's own thinking and on how other economists, politicians, and civic leaders reacted to the proposal.
6. Namorato (1992), p. 60.
7. Tugwell (1968), p. 98.
8. Fisher published his original 1913 paper before the creation of the Fed. Interestingly, in appendix II of *Stabilizing the Dollar*, Fisher argues that his proposal is so general that it should be supported by those that believe in the quantity theory (as himself), and also by those that reject the quantity theory (pp. 215–217). On the need to rely on "the good will" of the Federal Reserve, see the Hearings for Bill H.R. 1488, House of Representatives, Congress of the United States (1922), pp. 27–28. See also Fisher (1928), pp. 192–193. See Patinkin (1993) for a criticism of Fisher's plan that centers on the tension between the compensated dollar and the equation of exchange.
9. Warren and Pearson (1935), p. 94.
10. Pearson, Myers, and Gans (1957), p. 5601.

BIBLIOGRAPHY

◇◇◇◇◇

ARCHIVES, DIARIES, OFFICIAL PAPERS, AND MEMOIRS

PPFDR *The Public Papers and Addresses of Franklin Delano Roosevelt*, Vols. 1 and 2. New York: Random House.

FDRPL Franklin D. Roosevelt Presidential Library

GFWP George F. Warren Papers. Cornell University Special Collections.

HCA Homer Cummings Archives, University of Virginia Library.

HDW Harry Dexter White Papers, Princeton University Special Collections.

HMD The diaries of Henry Morgenthau Jr., held at the Roosevelt Presidential Library.

JCMP James Clark McReynolds Papers. University of Virginia Law School Archives.

JVP The papers of Jacob Viner, Princeton University Special Collections.

RGTD Rexford G. Tugwell Diary, in Namorato (1992)

RMP The papers of Raymond Moley, held at the Hoover Institution

NEWSPAPERS AND MAGAZINES

CHT *Chicago Daily Tribune*

LAT *Los Angeles Times*

NYT *The New York Times*

TL *The Times of London*

WP *Washington Post*

WSJ *Wall Street Journal*

BOOKS AND ARTICLES

Acheson, D. 1965. *Morning and Noon*. Boston: Houghton Mifflin.

Ahamed, L. 2009. *Lords of Finance: The Bankers Who Broke the World*. New York: Random House.

Awalt, F. G. 1969. "Recollections of the Banking Crisis in 1933." *Business History Review* 43(3), 347–371.

Balke, N., and R. J. Gordon. 1986. Data Appendix. In *The American Business Cycle*. Edited by R. J. Gordon. Chicago: The University of Chicago Press.

Ballantine, A. A. 1944. "The Corporation and the Income Tax." *Harvard Business Review* 22, 277–283.

———. 1948. "When All the Banks Closed." *Harvard Business Review* 26(2), 129–143.

Barber, W. J. 1996. *Designs within Disorder*. Cambridge: Cambridge University Press.

Berle, Jr., A. A. 1973. *Navigating the Rapids 1918–1971: From the Papers of Adolf A. Berle*. New York: Harcourt, Brace, Jovanovich.

Berle, Jr., A. A., and G. C. Means. 1932. *Modern Corporation and Private Property*. New York: Columbia University Press.

Bernanke B. 2000. *Essays on the Great Depression*. Princeton: Princeton University Press.

Bernanke, B., and H. James. 1991. "The Gold Standard, Deflation, and Financial Crisis in the Great Depression: An International Comparison." In *Financial Markets and Financial Crises*. Edited by R. Glenn Hubbard (33–68). Chicago: University of Chicago Press.

Blum, J. M. 1959. *From the Morgenthau Diaries*. Vol. 1, *Years of Crisis, 1928–1938*. Boston: Houghton Mifflin.

Bordo, M. D., E. U. Choudhri, and A. J. Schwartz. 2002. "Was Expansionary Monetary Policy Feasible during the Great Contraction?" An Examination of the Gold Standard Constraint." *Explorations in Economic History* 39(1), 1–28.

Bordo, M. D., C. Goldin, and E. N. White, eds. 1998. *The Defining Moment: The Great Depression and the American Economy in the Twentieth Century*. Chicago: University of Chicago Press.

Bordo, M. D., and F. E. Kydland. 1995. "The Gold Standard as a Rule: An Essay in Exploration." *Explorations in Economic History* 32(4), 423–464.

Bordo, M., and A. Sinha. 2016. *A Lesson from the Great Depression that the Fed Might have Learned: A Comparison of the 1932 Open Market Purchases with Quantitative Easing*. National Bureau of Economic Research Working Paper. No. w22581.

Bush, A. M. 2010. *Executive Disorder: The Subversion of the United States Supreme Court, 1914–1940*. Cornelia Wendell Bush.

Byrnes, J. F. 1958. *All in One Lifetime*. New York: Harper.

Calomiris, C. D. Wheelock. 1998. "Was the Great Depression a Watershed for American Monetary Policy?" In *The Defining Moment: The Great Depression and the American Economy in the Twentieth Century*. Edited by M. Bordo, C. Goldin, and E. N. White (23–66). Chicago: University of Chicago Press.

Cassel, G. 1923. *Money and Foreign Exchange after 1914*. London: Constable.

Chávez, R. B., J. Ferejohn, and B. Weingast, 2011. "A Theory of the Politically Independent Judiciary. In *Courts in Latin America*. Edited by G. Helmke and J. R. Figueroa (108–129). New York: Cambridge University Press.

Coe, P. J. 2002. "Financial Crisis and the Great Depression: A Regime-Switching Approach." *Journal of Money, Credit, and Banking* 34(1), 76–93.

Crabbe, L. 1989. "The International Gold Standard and US Monetary Policy from World War I to the New Deal. *Fed. Res. Bull.* 75, 423.

Dam, K. W. 1983. "From the Gold Clause Cases to the Gold Commission: A Half Century of American Monetary Law." *University of Chicago L. Rev.* 50(2), 504–532.

Edwards, S. 1994. "The Political Economy of Inflation and Stabilization in Developing Countries." *Economic Development and Cultural Change* 42(2), 235–266.

———. 2011. "Exchange-Rate Policies in Emerging Countries: Eleven Empirical Regularities from Latin America and East Asia." *Open Economies Review* 22(4), 533.

———. 2015a. "Sovereign Default, Debt Restructuring, and Recovery Rates," *Open Economies Review* 26(5), 839–867.

———. 2015b. "Academics as Economic Advisers: Gold, the 'Brains Trust,' and FDR." National Bureau of Economic Research, Working Paper 21380.

———. 2017a. "Gold, the Brains Trust and Roosevelt." *History of Political Economy* 49(1), 1–30.

———. 2017b. "Keynes and the Dollar in 1933." *Financial History Review* 24(3), 209–238.

Edwards, S., F. A. Longstaff, and A. G. Garcia Marin. 2015. "The US Debt Restructuring of 1933: Consequences and Lessons" (No. w21694). National Bureau of Economic Research.

Eggertsson, G. B. 2008. "Great Expectations and the End of the Depression." *American Economic Review* 98(4), 1476–1516.

Eichengreen, B. 1992. *Golden Fetters: The Gold Standard and the Great Depression, 1919–1939*. Oxford: Oxford University Press.

———. 2015. *Before the Plaza: The Exchange Rate Stabilization Attempts of 1925, 1933, 1936 and 1971*. University of California, Berkeley, Working Paper.

Eichengreen, B., and J. Sachs. 1985. "Exchange Rates and Economic Recovery in the 1930s." *Journal of Economic History* 45(04), 925–946.

Eichengreen, B., and M. Uzan. 1990. "The 1933 World Economic Conference as an Instance of Failed International Cooperation." Department of Economics, University of California, Berkeley, Working Paper.

Epstein, R. A. 2014. *The Classical Liberal Constitution*. Cambridge: Harvard University Press.

Federal Reserve Board. 1943. Banking and Monetary Statistics. Board of Governors of the Federal Reserve System, Washington, DC.

Grossman, H. I., and J. B. Van Huyck. 1986. "Seigniorage, Inflation, and Reputation." *Journal of Monetary Economics* 18(1), 21–31.

Feis, H. 1966. *Characters in Crisis.* Boston and Toronto: Little, Brown, and Company.

Fisher, I. 1911. *The Purchasing Power of Money.* New York. Macmillan.

———. 1913. "A Compensated Dollar." *Quarterly Journal of Economics* 27, 385–397.

———. 1920. *Stabilizing the Dollar: A Plan to Stabilize the General Price Level without Fixing Individual Prices.* New York: Macmillan.

———. 1928. *The Money Illusion.* New York: Adelphi Company.

———. 1932. *Booms and Depressions: Some First Principles.* New York: Adelphi Company.

Friedman, M., and A. J. Schwartz. 1963. *A Monetary History of the United States, 1867–1960.* Princeton: Princeton University Press.

Fusfield, D.R. 1956. *The Economic Thought of Franklin D. Roosevelt and the Origins of the New Deal.* New York: Columbia University Press.

Gregory, T. E. 1934. "Twelve Months of American Dollar Policy." *Economica* 1(2), May: 121–146.

Hale, R. L. (1943). "The Supreme Court and the Contract Clause." *Harv. L. Rev.* 57, 512.

Hall, K. L., ed. 2001. *The Oxford Guide to United States Supreme Court Decisions.* Oxford and New York: Oxford University Press.

Hausman, J. K. 2013. *New Deal Policies and Recovery from the Great Depression.* UC Berkeley, Dissertation.

Hausman, J. K., P. W. Rhode, and J. F. Wieland. 2017. Recovery from the Great Depression: The farm channel in Spring 1933 (No. w23172). National Bureau of Economic Research. Harris, S. E. 1936. *Exchange Depreciation: Its Theory and Its History, 1931–1935 with Some Consideration of Related Domestic Policies.* Cambridge: Harvard University Press.

Hart Jr., H. M. 1935. "The Gold Clause in United States Bonds." *Harvard L. Rev.* 48(7), 1057–1099.

Holzer, H. M., ed. 1980, *The Gold Clause: What It Is and How to Use It Profitably.* Lincoln NE: iUniverse.

Hoover, H. 1952. *The Memoirs of Herbert Hoover: The Great Depression.* London: Macmillan.

Hughes, C. E. 1973. *The Autobiographical Notes of Charles Evans Hughes.* Edited by David J. Danelski and Joseph S. Tulchin. Cambridge: Harvard University Press.

Hull, C., 1948. *The Memoirs of Cordell Hull*. 2 vols. London: Macmillan.

Irwin, D. A. 2012. "Gold Sterilization and the Recession of 1937–1938." *Financial History Review* 19(03), 249–267.

Kemmerer, E. W. 1944. "Gold and the Gold Standard: The Story of Gold Money, Past, Present and Future." Ludwig von Mises Institute.

Keynes, J. M. 1924. *A Tract on Monetary Reform*. London: Macmillan.

———. 1933. *The Means to Prosperity*. London: Macmillan.

Kindleberger, C. P. 1978. *Manias, Panics, and Crashes: A History of Financial Crises*. New York: Basic Books. Revised and enlarged 1989, 3rd ed. 1996.

Knox, J., 2002. *The Forgotten Memoir of John Knox: A Year in the Life of a Supreme Court Clerk in FDR's Washington*. Chicago: University of Chicago Press.

Kroszner, R. S. (1998). "On the Political Economy of Banking and Financial Regulatory Reform in Emerging Markets." CRSP Working Paper No. 472.

League of Nations. 1933. "Journal of the Monetary and Economic Conference." Various issues London.

Leith-Ross, F. 1968. *Money Talks: Fifty Years of International Finance: The Autobiography of Sir Frederick Leith-Ross*. London: Hutchinson.

Leuchtenburg, W. E., 1995. *The FDR Years: On Roosevelt and His Legacy*. New York: Columbia University Press.

Lindley, E. K. 1931. *Franklin D. Roosevelt: A Career in Progressive Democracy*. Indianapolis: The Bobbs-Merrill company.

———. 1933. *Roosevelt's Revolution, First Phase*. New York: Viking.

Lippmann, W. 1932. *Interpretations 1931–1932*. New York: Macmillan.

———. *Interpretations 1933–1935*. New York: Macmillan.

MacLean, A. D. 1936. "Outline of the Gold Clause Cases." *N.C. L. Rev.* 15, 249.

Magliocca, G. N. 2012. "The Gold Clause Cases and Constitutional Necessity." *Fla. L. Rev.* 64, 1243.

Marshall, A. 1923. *Money, Trade and Commerce*. London: Macmillan.

Mason, A. T. 1956. "Inter Arma Silent Leges: Chief Justice Stone's Views." *Harvard L. Rev.* 69(5), 806–838.

McReynolds, James C. 1945. "Corrected Dissent in the Gold Clause Cases," *Tennessee L. Rev.* 18, 768–771.

Meltzer, A. H. 2003. *A History of the Federal Reserve*. Vol. 1 Chicago: University of Chicago Press.

Mitchell, W. C. 1898. "The Value of the 'Greenbacks' during the Civil War." *Journal of Political Economy* 6(2), 139–167.

Moley, R. 1939. *After Seven Years*. New York: Harper & Bros.

———. 1966. *The First New Deal*. New York: Harcourt.

Moore, James R. 1974. "Sources of New Deal Economic Policy: The International Dimension." *Journal of American History* 61(3), 728–744.

Morgenthau Jr., H. "Farm Credit Diary." The Morgenthau Papers at the Roosevelt Presidential Library.

Mundell, R. A. 2000. "A Reconsideration of the Twentieth Century." *American Economic Review* 90(3), 327–340.

Namorato, M. C., ed. 1992. *The Diary of Rexford G. Tugwell: The New Deal, 1932–1935*. New York: Greenwood Pub Group.

Nussbaum, A. 1934. Comparative and International Aspects of American Gold Clause Abrogation. *Yale L. J.* 44(1), 53–89.

———. 1957. *A History of the Dollar*. New York: Columbia University Press.

Obstfeld, M., and A. M. Taylor. 1997. "The Great Depression as a Watershed: International Capital Mobility over the Long Run." No. w5960. National Bureau of Economic Research.

Pasvolsky, L. 1933. *Current Monetary Issues*. Washington D.C.: Brookings Institution

Patinkin, D. 1993. "Irving Fisher and His Compensated Dollar Plan." Available at SSRN 2129231, 1–34, https://papers.ssrn.com/sol3/papers.cfm?abstract_id=2129231.

Pearson, D., and R. S. Allen. 1936. "How the President Works." *Harper's Magazine* 173(2).

Powell, J., 2007. *FDR's Folly: How Roosevelt and His New Deal Prolonged the Great Depression*. New York: Crown Forum.

Pusey, M. J., and S. J. Konefsky, 1953. "Communications: Mr. Justice Hughes and the 'Court Revolution.'" *Yale L. J.* 62(2), 313–314.

Ratner, S. 1935. "Was the Supreme Court Packed by President Grant?" *Political Science Quarterly*, 343–358.

Rauchway, E. 2015. *The Money Makers*. New York: Basic Books.

Reinhart, C. M., and K. S. Rogoff. 2004. "Serial Default and the 'Paradox' of Rich-to-Poor Capital Flows." *American Economic Review* 94, 53–58.

———. 2009. *This Time Is Different: Eight Centuries of Financial Folly*. Princeton: Princeton University Press.

———. 2011. "The Forgotten History of Domestic Debt." *Economic Journal* 121, 319–350.

Rogers, J. H. 1931. *America Weighs Her Gold*. New Haven: Yale University Press.

———. 1932. "Memorandum for Governor Franklin D. Roosevelt relating to subjects discussed in conversation of November 17, 1932." James Harvey Rogers Papers (MS 421). Manuscripts and Archives, Yale University Library. Box 3, Folder 13.

Romer, C. D. 1992. "What Ended the Great Depression?" *Journal of Economic History* 52(04), 757–784.

Roosevelt, F. D. 1934. *On Our Way*. New York: The John Day Company.

———. 1938. *The Public Papers and Addresses of Franklin Delano Roosevelt*. Vols. 1 and 2. New York: Random House.

Rosen, E. A. 1972. "Roosevelt and the Brains Trust: An Historiographical Overview." *Political Science Quarterly* 87(4), 531–557.

———. 1977. *Hoover, Roosevelt, and the Brains Trust: From Depression to New Deal*. New York: Columbia University Press.

Sachs, A. 1934. "National Recovery Administration Policies and the Problem of Economic Planning." In *America's Recovery Program*. Edited by A. A. Berle et. al. (000–000). Oxford and New York: Oxford University Press.

Salant, W. S. 1990. *The Spread of Keynesian Doctrines and Practices in the United States*. No. 436. Washington, DC: Brookings Institution.

Samuelson, P., and, H. E. Kross, eds. 1969. *Documentary History of Banking and Currency in the United States*. Vol. 4. New York: Chelsea House Publishers.

Sargent, T. J. 1983. Stopping Moderate Inflations: The Methods of Poincare and Thatcher: Inflation, Debt and Indexation. Cambridge: MIT Press.

Schlesinger, A. M. 1957. *The Age of Roosevelt*. Vol. 1: *The Crisis of the Old Order, 1919–1933*. Boston: Houghton Mifflin.

———. 1960. *The Age of Roosevelt*. Vol. 3: *The Politics of Upheaval*. Boston: Houghton Mifflin.

Shesol, J. 2011. *Supreme Power: Franklin Roosevelt vs. the Supreme Court*. New York: W.W. Norton & Company.

Stanton, B. F. 2007. *George F. Warren: Farm Economist*. Ithaca, NY: Cornell University Press.

Steil, B. 2013. *The Battle of Bretton Woods: John Maynard Keynes, Harry Dexter White, and the Making of a New World Order*. Princeton: Princeton University Press.

Sternsher, B. 1964. *Rexford Tugwell and the New Deal*. New Brunswick: Rutgers University Press

Sumner, S. 2001. "Roosevelt, Warren, and the Gold-buying Program of 1933." *Research in Economic History* 20, 135–172.

———. 2015. *The Midas Paradox: Financial Markets, Government Policy Shocks, and the Great Depression*. Independent Institute, New York: Barnes and Noble.

Tavlas, G. S. 1997. "Chicago, Harvard, and the Doctrinal Foundations of Monetary Economics." *Journal of Political Economy*, Vol. 105, No. 1, 153–177.

Temin, P. 1991. *Lessons from the Great Depression*. Cambridge: MIT Press.

Temin, P., and B. A. Wigmore. 1990. "The End of One Big Deflation." *Explorations in Economic History*, 27(4), 483–502.

Tugwell, R. G. 1931. "The Theory of Occupational Obsolescence." *Political Science Quarterly* 46(2), 171–227.

———. 1933. "Design for Government." *Political Science Quarterly* 48(3), 321–332.

———. 1952, 1932–1935. *The Diary of Rexford G. Tugwell: The New Deal, 1932–1935*. Edited by M. C. Namorato. New York: Greenwood Pub Group.

———. 1968. *The Brains Trust*. New York: Viking Adult.

———. 1977. *Roosevelt's Revolution: The First Year: A Personal Perspective*. London: Macmillan.

Tugwell, R. G., ed. 1924. *The Trend of Economics*. New York: Knopf.

Tugwell, R. G., and H. C. Hill. 1934. *Our Economic Society and Its Problems*.

Tugwell, R. G., T. Munro, and R. E. Stryker. 1925. *American Economic Life and the Means of Its Improvement*. London: Macmillan.

U.S. Department of Commerce. 1960. *Historical Statistics of the United States, Colonial times to 1957*. Washington D.C.: U.S. Government Printing Office.

Viner, J. 1932. *International Aspects of the Gold Standard*. In *Gold and Monetary Stabilization*. Edited by Quincy Wright (3–42). Chicago: University of Chicago Press.

Warburg, J. P. 1934. *The Money Muddle*. New York: Knopf.

———. 1964. *The Long Road Home*. Garden City, New York: Doubleday.

Warren, G. F. "The George F. Warren Papers," Division of Rare and Manuscript Collections, Carl A. Kroch Library, Cornell University.

Warren, G. F., and F. A. Pearson. 1932. "Wholesale Prices for 135 Years." Cornell University.

———. 1935. *Gold and Prices*. New York: Wiley.

White, H. D. 1935. "Recovery Program: The International Monetary Aspect." The Harry Dexter White Papers (MC 104), Box 13, Folder 13. Princeton University Library Archives.

White House appointments diary, 1933–1934. Available at http://www.fdrlibrary.marist.edu/daybyday/daylog/.

Wigmore, B. A. 1987. "Was the Bank Holiday of 1933 Caused by a Run on the Dollar?" *Journal of Economic History* 47(03), 739–755.

Wright, Q. 1932. *Gold and Monetary Stabilization*. Chicago: University of Chicago Press.

INDEX

Page numbers in *italics* indicate figures.